D1293169

IRAN
The Illusion of Power

ROBERT GRAHAM

CROOM HELM   LONDON

© 1978 Robert Graham
Croom Helm Ltd, 2-10 St John's Road, London SW11

British Library Cataloguing in Publication Data

Graham, Robert
    Iran, the illusion of power.
    1. Iran – Economic conditions – 1945 –
    I. Title
    330.9'55'05   HC475

    ISBN 0-85664-774-8

Jacket photograph: Touna Graham
Printed in Great Britain by offset lithography by
Billing & Sons Ltd, Guildford, London and Worcester

CONTENTS

Introduction   11

Part I: The Creation of Modern Iran

1. The Coming of the Boom   15
2. The Growth of Urban Iran   22
3. Oil and the Iranian Economy   32
4. Monarchy and the Pahlavi Dynasty   53

Part II: Cycle of the Boom

5. The Big Opportunity   77
6. Limits to Oil Wealth   93
7. Successes and Failures   105

Part III: The System of Power

8. Use and Abuse of Power   129
9. Control Through Money   152
10. Influence of the Military   168
11. Problems of Culture   190

Conclusion   206

12. Appendix: Pahlavi Foundation: Known Assets
    in December 1977   214

Index   219

ACKNOWLEDGEMENTS

I am grateful to Sir Robert Stephens and Methuen & Co Ltd for permission to quote from *The Land of the Great Sophy: Iran.* My quotations from the following works are reprinted by permission of the publisher: Julian Bharier, *Economic Development in Iran: 1900-1970.* Oxford University Press (1971); Idries Shah, *The Exploits of the Incomparable Mulla Nasrudin* (illustrated by Richard Williams), Jonathan Cape (1966); Oriana Fallaci, *Interview with History*, Michael Joseph and Houghton Mifflin; Marvin Zonis, *The Political Elite of Iran*, Princeton University Press (1971).

FOR TOUNA

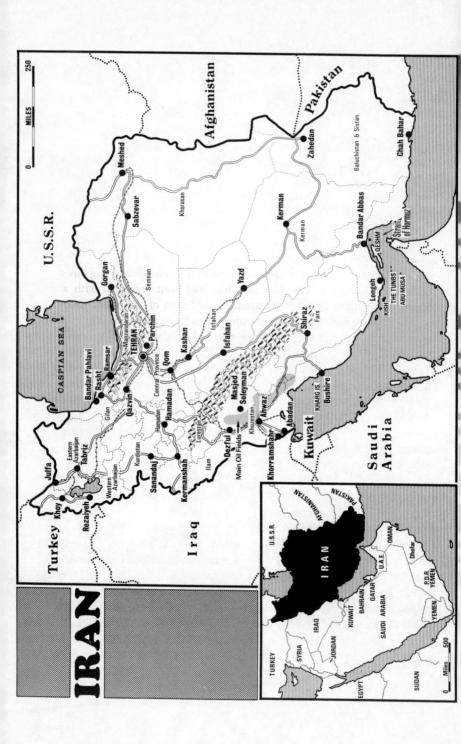

INTRODUCTION

This book is the result of spending just over two years as the *Financial Times* Middle East Correspondent based in Tehran, from June 1975 to July 1977. I arrived when the boom created by the 1973 oil price rises was at its most uncontrolled. Everyone had developed a psychosis over Iran's new-found power. One of the most lasting impressions was to see senior executives of major international companies prepared to tolerate every indignity and discomfort, including sleeping in hotel lobbies or hospitals (a Japanese even ended up one night in a mosque), and waiting for days on the favour of Iranian officials in the hope of doing business. At that stage it was clear that Iran had been presented with a unique opportunity, but the tremendous confusion of the boom made it hard to judge how well this opportunity was being exploited. Yet in a remarkably short space of time a pattern emerged which has enabled this period to be encapsulated. The capsule covers the period 1973-7. Though somewhat arbitrary, this period nevertheless follows a cycle from the sudden acquisition of increased wealth and its hectic spending through to the gradual realisation of the problems created and eventual disillusion and change of pace and style.

As far as possible I have relied upon original sources and my own contacts and observations while in Iran. I regret that Mohammed Reza Shah declined an interview. Although prepared to see people from outside, he seems reluctant to talk with local correspondents, perhaps because they know too much. Because of the nature of the régime I have been obliged to conceal frequently the identity of my sources. Except where Ministers have spoken to me or where discussion has been 'on the record', I have avoided names. Indeed it was only on the basis of unattributed background that most Iranians and foreigners connected with Iran were prepared to talk.

For background I owe an enormous debt to two authors who have helped in forming my appreciation of Iran. For an appreciation of the political apparatus of modern Iran I found Marvin Zonis' *The Political Elite of Iran* invaluable; while for an understanding of the Iranian economy I relied extensively on Julian Bharier's *Economic Development in Iran: 1900-1970*.

Although this book is largely based on material gathered while working for the *Financial Times*, the views expressed, and my approach to this material, are my own and do not reflect those of the paper. However, I am grateful to many members of the staff of the *Financial Times* who have been of great assistance during my work.

Part I

THE CREATION OF MODERN IRAN

1 THE COMING OF THE BOOM

It was a performance to match the occasion. On 23 December 1973, while the Ministers representing the Gulf members of OPEC were still in formal session, Mohammed Reza Pahlavi, Shah of Iran, called a press conference. His announcement was a staggering new increase in the price of oil. The Shah displayed his usual mannered polish but his tone had a new confidence — the confidence of a man who knew that his country's financial resources had quadrupled in just over two months. From being a developing country with moderate wealth jostling for recognition in the world arena, Iran had suddenly entered the ranks of the world's most prosperous nations with the chance to play a correspondingly larger role.

Unashamedly the Shah turned the occasion into a lecture. Typical of the message he put across was this answer to a question about the high price of oil:

We are only pricing the minimum it [oil] could be priced in comparison with other sources of energy . . . Well, some people are going to say this is going to create chaos in the industrialised world; that it is going to be a heavy burden on the poor countries . . . That is true; but as to the industrialised world they will have to tighten their belts, and they will have to work harder or eventually this help to the other countries of the world will be diminished, and this role taken up — in my opinion — by the new wealth of the oil countries.[1]

Some of his statements were more provocative:

Eventually all those children of well-to-do families who have plenty to eat at every meal, who have their own cars, and who act almost as terrorists and throw bombs here and there, will have to rethink all these privileges of the advanced world.[2]

He clearly revelled in the uncomfortable message he was conveying to the outside world. He was riding the crest of a wave and knew it.

In December 1973 there was no effective challenge to the Shah's message. A bemused industrialised world was trying to come to terms with what appeared to be a major shift in the balance of power, tilting

15

it for the first time in the direction of the producers of essential commodities, particularly oil. The seeming heedless dependence upon oil as a cheap source of energy had been emphasised by two separate but connected events — even before the December price rises in Tehran. At an earlier OPEC meeting in Kuwait in October, a 70 per cent increase in the price of crude oil had been agreed. This meeting was held against the background of the Arab-Israeli war. With fighting at its height, the Arab OPEC members decided to institute production cut-backs, as a means of generalised pressure on the West, and impose a selective oil embargo on exports to the Netherlands and the US for their pro-Israeli stance. This punitive action by the Arab oil producers led to a sudden shortage of crude in the international market, producing a desperate scramble to purchase oil at any price. Just before the Tehran meeting in December, the National Iranian Oil Company (NIOC) had carried out an auction in which oil sold at $17.34 per barrel. This was over three times higher than the increased price fixed at Kuwait two months earlier. Thus when the Tehran meeting announced a price of $11.65 per barrel as the new bench-mark price for crude sales, it almost looked as though OPEC was doing the world a favour.

The combined effect of the price rises throughout 1973 was to raise Iran's annual oil revenue from $5 billion to $19 billion. Put another way: for every barrel of oil sold, Iran received $7 instead of $1.95.[3] Never before had the oil industry seen such a quantum leap in prices and revenue. The Hudson Institute in an astute but provocative report on Iran poured cold water on the idea that such sudden new financial wealth could alter the status of Iran, ascribing this view to a 'panicky product of the industrial nations' own demoralised reaction to what has been a real, but *limited* shift in the international commodities and money markets'.[4] Though true in that the new financial muscle gave illusions of enhanced power, this nevertheless ignored the climate of the time, especially the psychological climate.

Iran, the second-largest producer within OPEC and the second-biggest exporter of crude oil in the world after Saudi Arabia, took no part in the oil embargo or the October production cut-backs. The Shah made it clear he would not countenance oil as a political weapon in this context. This position, coupled with the fact that Iran was not an Arab country, singled it out for special prominence as international attention focused on the oil producers. The soft-spoken and articulate Saudi Arabian Oil Minister, Sheikh Ahmed Zaki Yamani, appeared to be holding the world to ransom. In contrast the Shah managed to generate a more responsible and Olympian image. He cast himself as the man pushing for the correct price for 'the noble product'.[5] He was also careful to emphasise that the new price of oil was no mere windfall, rather a reflection of international demand and the cost of alternate sources of energy. This philosophy had put him in the forefront of those pressing for higher oil prices. The fact that Iran, with a population greater than the combined total of all the other Middle East oil producers, needed higher oil prices to develop its oil-dominated economy reinforced this philosophy. Thus with the biggest price increase occurring in Tehran, the Shah's views were vindicated and his personal standing as a key figure in OPEC was enhanced.

External perception of Iran was almost certainly conditioned by its ruler being a pro-Western monarch. The Shah's audience was essentially the Western world, which had a greater built-in readiness to accept the pronouncements of a pro-Western monarchy than republican or revolutionary régimes. This helped create a sense of awe towards this self-proclaimed prophet of the new order. Besides there was an uncomfortable ring of truth about the need to tighten belts, conserve energy and think ahead to the time when the oil wells would run dry.

Officials in European capitals had been knocked off balance by the sudden leap in energy import bills, and sought ways to curb energy use. Italy, for instance, 80 per cent dependent upon imported energy, banned Sunday driving as a temporary expedient — what greater challenge to the habits of modern consumer society in a country where the car had become a symbol of progress! In the US the Pentagon leaked aggressive scenarios of possible preventive take-overs of Saudi oilfields. People in industrialised societies were having to adjust to the emergence of the oil producers at a moment of recession. In this atmosphere it was remarkably easy to be impressed by the Shah confidently ordering more tanks than possessed by Britain and boasting of Iran entering the ranks of the advanced countries before the turn of the century.

The international community's view of Iran and Mohammed Reza Shah's view of his own role and that of Iran interacted and lionised each other. The interaction was a dizzy and wholly unrealistic environment in which vision and reality merged into one. It became an article of faith that within twenty years Iran would become a Great Power, the fifth Great Power. The Shah began to propagate in earnest the idea of Iran being at the threshold of the Great Civilisation — a notional state of national well-being with industrialisation achieved and a full regeneration of Iran's ancient heritage.[6]

Throughout the country there was a feeling of a transformation about to take place. The Shah's first public action after the oil price rises was to declare education free up to the 8th grade, free school milk, and, for those who wished to serve the government, free higher education. Money, it seemed, could sweep away all the problems of development; and those that remained could be tackled with the latest technology imported from abroad.

The Shah was courted by the world's leaders with a deference. Only two years previously, the Shah had been bitterly disappointed by the failure of several heads of state to honour his lavish festivities at Persepolis, celebrating 2,500 years of monarchy. President Pompidou, for instance, despatched his Prime Minister Jacques Chaban-Delmas to deputise, something the Shah never forgave.[7] Now President Giscard d'Estaing was willing to make a special visit to the Shah holidaying in the Swiss ski resort of St Moritz in the hope that French companies would receive some of the new contracts being enticingly waved by Iran. He was not the only one. Hard-pressed governments sent their Ministers to talk business with the Shah, and if successful their exploits were reported in the press with the acclaim of a major sports victory.[8] For someone who had seen his father forced to abdicate by external powers, and who himself had been installed as a puppet monarch, this was a novel and exhilarating experience.

But what does a country do when its income quadruples in less than three months — especially a developing country? There were no precedents. The basic constraint on Iran's development until then had been insufficient foreign exchange. With the foreign exchange constraint removed the possibilities seemed limitless.

In less than fifty years Iran had moved from being a poor, isolated, backward country to a position where industrialisation was taking root and a modern infrastructure being laid. Thanks to oil, the *per capita* income was high compared to the majority of its fellow developing countries. But the country's basic development needs were enormous and the population still over 50 per cent illiterate.[9] The sudden accrual of this new wealth seemed to provide the economy with just the right support to move from near-total oil dependence to self-sustaining growth. Iran's oil reserves would only last just beyond the turn of the century. Therefore there was little time to achieve 'take-off' and each year was vital.[10]

Dazzled by its new importance and spurred by the prospect of economic take-off, the Iranian response was unashamedly grandiose. The Fifth Plan, less than one year old, was set aside and in its place a new set of objectives introduced costing $69 billion: double the original estimate. The new plan, approved in August 1974 at a special conference at the Caspian resort town of Ramsar, was more a statement of intent than a concrete blueprint. It was designed to impress how great Iran was about to become. No developing country had produced such a large investment programme, and it was the first to appear in the Middle East reflecting the new spending power of the oil producers. (The Saudi development plan did not begin to become public until late October 1975.) The overriding philosophy was 'nothing venture, nothing gain.'

The obvious problems of the new Plan — the stability of future oil exports, the impact of inflation and the lack of skilled manpower and infrastructure — were brushed aside by a crest-of-the-wave confidence. 'The shortcomings you have mentioned, especially the labour shortage, might turn out more acute than you think. However, there are solutions,' the Shah told the closing session of the Ramsar conference.[11]

Moreover, his calculations were based less on economics than on politics — the politics of his own survival in a regenerated Iran. The Shah intended to use this new money to consolidate his Pahlavi dynasty in a prosperous Iran. Money would be the carrot and the stick to achieve stability.

In the 18 months that followed the Ramsar conference, Iran witnessed a period of unprecedented boom. Because the oil revenues accrued to the government, it was government expenditure that became the vehicle for disbursing and distributing this new wealth. Once the government enlarged its budget and started releasing funds, the impact was felt very quickly. In the Iranian year running from March 1974 to March 1975, the government spent the equivalent of $22 billion. This was only marginally less than the entire expenditure for the three previous years.[12] The effect of such an increase in spending was like changing from first to fourth gear in a car going downhill. Comfort and control were sacrificed to speed. Instead of the original aim of an annual growth rate of 11.4 per cent (already high by the standards of any developing economy), Iran went for 25.9 per cent.

However, the boom was short-lived. In just over two years, by mid-1976 expenditure overtook revenue and accumulated bottlenecks curbed the hectic pace of development. Official recognition of the changed circumstances took a little longer; but when it came it was a complete reversal of the arrogant self-confidence of December 1973 at the time of the Tehran OPEC meeting.

In an historic interview on 25 October 1976 with the editor of *Kayhan* (Farsi), one of the main daily newspapers, the Shah declared somewhat ruefully:

We should not allow the same vultures to gather from everywhere and tell us to do this or that with our money while we do not have enough cement, enough bricks, enough port capacity, enough roads, and enough powers of absorption. It is absolutely certain we shall not repeat the mistakes of the past. That was a short period which is over and gone.

He then added: 'The reason for this situation was that we acquired money we could not spend.'[13] The pace of Iranian development had slowed more or less to the level envisaged prior to the advent of the surplus funds.

Though brief, this two-year period was a crucial moment in the development of modern Iran. Throughout, both the style and the direction of policy were entirely the responsibility of the Shah. A sympathetic view of events would suggest that the Shah made natural and inevitable errors forced upon him by a combination of external and internal pressures. A less charitable view would be that for selfish reasons dressed up as patriotism the Shah squandered a unique opportunity. By trying to do too much too quickly he retarded the development process in Iran.

However, judgements like this cannot be made in a vacuum. To appreciate what was at stake during this extraordinary period, it is necessary to take a wider look at Iran and Iranian society.

Notes

1. *Kayhan International*, 25 December 1973.
2. Ibid. See also *Middle East Economic Survey*, 28 December 1973.
3. Bank Markazi annual report, 1973/4, p. 11.
4. Hudson Institute, Report on Iran, Paris, 1 March 1975. This was the first attempt to cut down to size the newly perceived status of an oil producer in the wake of the 1973 price rises.
5. 'Oil is a noble product which must be put to noble uses.' Shah press conference, Tehran. See *Kayhan International*, 25 December 1973.
6. *Mardom (People)* magazine, 31 December 1973.
7. Gerard de Villiers, *L'Irresistible Ascension de Mohammed Reza, Shah d'Iran* (Paris, Plon, 1975), p. 369.
8. The British government appeared gushingly grateful to the Shah when as a result of a visit to St Moritz by the Trade Secretary, Peter Walker, in January 1974, it was agreed to sell Britain 5m tons of crude oil against £110m worth of British goods.
9. International Labour Office, *Employment and Income Policies for Iran* (Geneva, International Labour Office, 1973), p. 25. According to the 1966 census 70 per cent of the population were illiterate; 15 per cent had not completed

elementary education and only 11 per cent possessed a full secondary education.

10. Unofficially Iran has proven reserves of about 70 billion barrels. NIOC officials told the author that the production ceiling could slip below 6.4 million barrels per day before 1984.

11. *Kayhan International*, 4 August 1974.

12. Bank Markazi annual report, 1975/6, p. 51. In 1974/5 expenditure was Rs1,076 billion compared to Rs1,130 billion in the three previous years (rials).

13. Shah interview with Amir Taheri, *Kayhan International*, 25 October 1976.

2 THE GROWTH OF URBAN IRAN

> Were it not for the plane trees one might overlook Tehran as
> one would a sleeping crocodile on the banks of the Nile. The
> city is of the colour and of the material of the plain. It is a city
> of mud in an oasis of plane trees.[1]

This was the opinion of a Victorian traveller, one Arthur Arnold, who
visited Tehran almost exactly a hundred years ago. Now Tehran cannot
be overlooked simply because it is such a vast sprawling urban agglomeration. Yet it remains an undistinguished city. The all-embracing bleached
brown of the Varamin Plain still merges with the city at an ill-defined
point — except now the city has spread further out and is discernible by
a murky pall of pollution.

There are no kind words to be said for modern Tehran. The architecture is unbelievably shabby, the materials look cheap and speculative,
and the finish is uniformly shoddy. Superficially, little suggests personal
or national wealth, not even vulgarity: merely that hundreds of rapa-
cious property speculators have been allowed a free reign, abusing what
is left of the natural environment. Then over the façades of marble,
brick and glass, polluted dust has produced a matt grey monotony.

A town plan exists, but buildings have spread in anarchy. The city
has developed so fast that essential utilities are either unable to cope
or under tremendous strain. The telephone system is hopelessly over-
loaded. Subscribers have increased so fast that there is no official
telephone directory. Tehran has the dubious distinction of being the
only large capital city to be without a proper sewage system. The entire
city relies upon individual wells sunk beneath each building which
absorb the liquid into the soil. The system worked well with a population of 1 million but now it is over 4 million and the sewage is pushing
up the water level in the southern part of the city so that it is only one
metre below the surface.[2] Tehran is now so large that it will take at least
30 years to install a proper system of piped sewage.

The human scale, epitomised by the covered Bazaar, has been
completely submerged. Traffic has taken over the city like an army of
ants a piece of discarded food. The road network has been obliged to
accommodate over 1 million trucks, buses and cars when it was conceived for half this flow. Traffic fumes are pouring 500,000 tons of
carbon monoxide into the city's atmosphere every year, causing a
disturbing level of pollution.[3] The public transport system is creaking

under the strain of trying to carry 2 million passengers a day. There is no train service; only buses and taxis. The municipality has 2,600 buses but a minimum of 30 per cent are out of action each day being repaired. The average waiting time for a bus, combined with travelling time, is reckoned to be four hours a day per person.[4] To cover the 86 square miles of the city, people where possible use private cars or shared taxis. On average most of the working population waste a minimum of two hours per day in traffic. Traffic congestion has become so much a way of life that Tehranis are proud of it — one suspects that it is a primitive pride over the car being a symbol of modernism. But it is a brutalising environment, which, over twenty years, has damaged the quality of life and eroded those values the Iranians considered so important — polite-ness and hospitality — and encouraged aggression and selfishness.

Though bemoaning the woes of their capital, Iranians are quick to point out that 'Tehran isn't Iran.' This is an indirect way of saying that Tehran is atypical: in the rest of Iran, and above all else in the country-side, the 'true' Iranian exists who still has a contact with the past and has a proper understanding of the order of things. Unfortunately this is a sentimental delusion.

Tehran is not typical of Iran; nevertheless it *is* modern Iran. Ever since the mid-twenties when Reza Shah began to strengthen the hand of central government, Tehran has reflected the aspirations of modern Iran. Therefore, rather than dismiss Tehran as atypical, it must be regarded as the essential product of modern centralised Iran. To a greater or lesser degree other cities in Iran are following its example, often unconscious-ly. Tehran itself is perhaps ten years — and in some instances fifty years — ahead of the rest of the country.

The Growth of Tehran

Tehran, literally 'warm place', became the capital of what was then Persia at the turn of the eighteenth century under the first of the Qajar kings, Agha Mohammed Khan. Under the Qajars Tehran remained essentially a large walled city built of mud brick, and centred round the covered Bazaar and its accompanying mosques.

In 1900, Tehran was just beginning to distinguish itself from the other major cities of the time — Isfahan, Tabriz, Shiraz — by being the first to possess some of the attributes of the industrial world. Tehran had acquired the only railway in the country — a total of eight miles of single-metre track operated by a Belgian company, primarily designed to go to and from the shrine of Shah Abdul Azim.[5] It also had a small Russian-financed tramway. It further boasted the only electric power

generating plant which doubled up as the energy supplier of a private
brick plant to which it belonged.[6] By 1910 the capital's inhabitants
could witness an automobile – it belonged to the ruler, Ahmad Shah,
but never went more than walking pace as it was accompanied by foot
servants![7]

At this time Iran's population was predominantly rural, with a high
proportion of nomads. Tribalism was strong and the nomadic tribes
accounted for almost 25 per cent of the total population.[8] One medium
estimate of the country's total population was 9.8 million.[9] Of these
some 20 per cent lived in 100 towns of over 5,000 inhabitants. Tehran
itself had no more than 200,000 inhabitants, virtually the same as
Tabriz, roughly 2 per cent of the country's total population.[10]

Even in 1919, when the present Shah was born, Tehran was still a
walled city surrounded by a dry moat. The only entrance was through
the city gates which were closed at night 'to keep out robbers and cut
throats'.[11] When Reza Shah knocked down the city walls some six years
later, this action was considered symbolic of his determination to
modernise Iran.[12]

Once Reza Shah began to exert central government control throughout the country and improve road and rail communications, including
his famous Trans-Iranian railway, the exodus to Tehran started. By
1939 Tehran had a population of 540,000.[13] The process was accelerated by the Second World War and the presence of Allied forces in Iran,
and by the gradual increment in oil revenues. People were attracted
both from other cities and from rural areas. Between 1900 and the first
census in 1956 Tehran absorbed 60 per cent of the total internal migration of 1.76 million.[14] Between 1960 and 1970 Tehran's population
increased at roughly 6 per cent a year to reach 3.2 million – this was
over double the national average. By the time of the next census in
1976 the growth rate had slowed to around 4.2 per cent a year; but in
fact people were merely settling further outside the city, especially at
Karaj, 40 kilometres away, where the population was increasing by 12
per cent a year.[15] A survey conducted in 1975 by the University of
Tehran concluded that if the population continued unchecked it would
reach 16 million in twelve years.[16]

Tehran is now the undisputed focus of political, administrative,
economic, social and cultural life. The industrial capacity of Tehran
accounts for 51 per cent of all manufactured goods produced.[17] Out
of sheer convenience the main non-oil industries, particularly the automotive sector, preferred to establish round Tehran. Thus the city's
industrial work-force represents 22 per cent of the country's total.[18]

The burgeoning bureaucracy created to govern a country of 34 million people has continued to be centred in Tehran. One-third of all government employees are based there. Over 60 per cent of the country's student population is being educated in Tehran. Roughly 50 per cent of all doctors are located in Tehran — put another way, half the country's doctors serve 11 per cent of the population.[19] Even relatively simple medical needs like X-rays often cannot be carried out in the provinces because there are no qualified personnel to operate the facilities.

Tehran is also much richer. Land, the main source of new private wealth, is considerably more expensive in the capital. With the exception of the Caspian coast, land values in Tehran average twice those of other cities. Between 1970 and 1976 the Tehran municipality issued 45 per cent of all the building permits issued for large cities.[20] Moreover the average floor space was double that of other cities. Though hard to quantify, it is almost certainly true that the average wealth of all stratas of society is substantially greater than in other cities. It is the first city to show a sizeable middle class in Iran. Middle-class wealth is reflected in car ownership and foreign travel. Approximately one in every ten persons possesses a car in Tehran; outside the capital one in ninety.[21] As many as 70 per cent of those travelling abroad, excluding those who go on religious pilgrimages, live in Tehran.[22]

Culturally, too, Tehran dominates. Although the number of cinemas in the provinces has increased considerably, 25 per cent of the country's 460 cinemas are still located in Tehran and Tehranis account for 40 per cent of the total cinema-going public.[23] Newspapers are very little read outside the capital. One estimate is that of 820,000 copies printed daily, only 20,000 are read outside the capital. Printing itself is heavily concentrated in the capital, with 72 per cent of Iran's 180 printing presses in Tehran.[24]

Thus those who live in Tehran have the chance of better access to education, health facilities, the media, jobs and money — to say nothing of access to the decision-making processes. Not surprisingly people in villages or other towns are prepared to come to Tehran in the hope of a better life, ignoring the problems of high rents, overcrowding and pollution.

The Design of Tehran

Like an archaeologist's trench, the city's growth can be traced in a series of parallel lines up the slopes of the Alborz Mountains. The Bazaar area in South Tehran represents the old centre, where behind the brick and marble facades of recent building are a mass of confused narrow lanes with mud brick houses. This still represents one-third of the capital's land area – and half the population live here. Immediately above the Bazaar and next to the Golestan Palace (a monument to Qajar decadence now used for visiting heads of state) stands Reza Shah's break with the past: Iran's first modern Ministries, styled, one suspects, after Mussolini's new administrative city on the outskirts of Rome or Atatürk's Ankara. Above these the first modern shopping area of 'Istanbul' was established by the more enterprising merchants for richer clientele – now this has become the better shopping area for the masses. On the same parallel too a new royal palace, the Marble Palace, was built surrounded by the city's most fashionable housing. The Shah has now left the Palace to the Prime Minister and moved up the hill to be followed by all but a few of the rich families, who are allowing their properties to be developed for multi-storey apartments for those aspiring to leave the Bazaar area. Further up town, above the first foreign embassies established like those of Britain and Russia (which stand in huge imperial compounds), the prestige offices of the post-war era on Shah Reza Street were established. The subsequent demand for office space has dragged the commercial area further up hill, some 2 kilometres from the Bazaar.

Further above this an entirely new commercial and administrative centre for the city is being developed on formerly barren hills. The foundation stone for this huge urban undertaking, Shahestan Pahlavi, was laid in August 1975.[25] To complete it will take a minimum of fifteen years, and it represents the final break with the Bazaar as the hub of urban life. Above Shahestan – and beyond the worst of the pollution – live Iran's rich. Mountain retreat villages, rural communities and vacant lots have been absorbed in less than fifteen years into a vast dormitory of hurriedly built villas for the new élite. Perhaps appropriately above all this, back to the mountains, are the royal palaces of Saadabad and Niavaran. Tehran has thus constructed a social pyramid that reflects geography and the political hierarchy.

The social contrasts in this pyramid are extreme and becoming more minutely stratified. Moreover, as problems of circulating within this agglomeration increase, contact between social groups diminishes. From living among the masses, the bourgeoisie is now seeking to insulate itself. The urban masses for their part have acquired a sullen resentment and envy of their superiors. The only equaliser has become a universal level of discontent: a discontent exacerbated by the city's rapid expansion and a romanticised memory of their previous life-style.

The Dual Society: Urban v. Rural

The larger cities like Ahwaz, Isfahan, Shiraz and Tabriz have already begun to show some of the same symptoms. The causes are the same — sudden influx of migrants, overloading of existing facilities, insufficient personnel for municipal administration and unchecked property speculation. These towns are attracting two types of person: those who live in surrounding villages and people after specific jobs, skilled and unskilled. Construction — the main urban industrial activity — attracts those people from the traditionally poorest groups like the Kurds, Turks, Arabs and Baluchis.[26] These people are now going to the provincial cities because they are expanding fastest: Isfahan with its enormous Aryamehr Steel complex, petrochemicals, refining industry and military ordinance factories; Shiraz, a major army and air force base and the home of an expanding electronics industry; Ahwaz, the centre of the oil industry and an important future steel-producing area; Tabriz, the centre of Iran's heavy engineering industry. The annual population growth rate in these four towns between 1966 and 1976 never fell below 3.8 per cent.[27]

The attraction, moreover, is not just towards larger cities. Iran now has 365 towns of over 5,000 inhabitants. The urban population is 46 per cent of the total and it is increasing at three times the rate of the rural population.[28]

This is an exceptionally fast switch for a traditionally rural society. The International Labour Office commented in 1973:

In the 1960s rural-urban migration transferred 400,000 job seekers to the towns from rural areas. This is a normal trend in a rapidly growing and industrialising country. However, it was perhaps more rapid than was economically necessary and socially desirable.[29]

This observation was made *before* the massive injection of funds from the 1973 oil price rises. The ILO showed equal concern over the growing gap between urban and rural incomes:

The ratio of urban to rural income per head is estimated by the Plan Organisation to have increased from 4.6:1 in 1959 to 5.6:1 in 1969. The accuracy of these figures may be questioned but the reality of the gap and the direction of the move are not widely disputed.[30]

A more recent and cruder survey estimated that an urban family spent twice as much each month as a rural family. Underneath all this is the inescapable conclusion that the modernisation of Iran has created a dual economy — a dynamic urban sector and a stagnating rural one.[31]

The contrast in life-style and living standards between town and country is as extreme as that between north and south Tehran. Rural Iranians still live in villages where 90 per cent of the houses are of mud brick. The 1976 census found there were 65,000 villages, of which only 18,000 had more than 250 inhabitants.[32] This gives Iran one of the most fragmented of rural populations anywhere in the world.

The backwardness of the countryside and the fragmentation of the rural population into small communities is an essential product of an exceptionally harsh environment. The peasants have suffered continuously from the vagaries of the elements and the despotism of governments. Over the centuries the villagers have acquired nothing but distrust for government and government officials whose interest was rarely to help and always to take money. Observing the situation in the province of Bushire a hundred years ago, Arthur Arnold remarked:

> That government [of Bushire] is free to extort all that it can get, upon condition of making a certain annual payment to Tehran. The consequence is that the entire province is kept in perpetual disorder by the demands of armed men, who plunder under the pretence of taxation, and who, by the peasantry, are scarcely preferred to robbers.[33]

Not surprisingly the peasants had little interest in making their holdings look too prosperous and, where possible, constructed their communities in the least accessible places. Iran's rugged mountainous geography encouraged them to do this.

With the exception of the Caspian coast and a few limited areas rainfall is scarce, water hard to obtain and soil poor. Thus there were very few places with sufficient resources to support large communities — usually restricting villages to groupings of 50 inhabitants, and encouraging nomadism. The 1966 census found 21,000 villages with less than fifty persons.[34] In times of good harvest the rural communities prospered; but when the harvest failed the border-line between survival and starvation was very fine. The isolation and inaccessibility which protected them from authority and robbers proved an effective barrier to obtaining extra food from a surplus area. There was virtually no interchange of agricultural goods between regions until the late twenties. During the severe famine of 1925 a major breakthrough occurred in this respect. The government decided to order 200 special trucks for famine relief to transport grain from surplus areas to those places worst affected.[35] This seemingly obvious solution, the idea of Dr Millspaugh, an American financial adviser, had never been considered before — probably because of an ingrained indifference to what happened in the remoter corners of the countryside. The general cynical attitude was that if they were poor enough to starve they were no good for tax collection.

The most telling sign of backwardness in the rural areas today is the literacy rate. In a slow uphill struggle, the Literacy Corps, formed from students doing national service, has managed to penetrate to the more isolated rural areas. In the past eleven years it has established 15,000 schools covering 25,000 villages. By 1978 almost 80 per cent of the rural population of school age should be in the programme. Yet in 1973 the ILO, examining the impact of the literacy drive, had this to say: 'Despite the remarkable achievement of the Education Corps [Literacy Corps] enrolment in primary education is only 39 percent in rural areas as against 90 percent in urban areas.'[36] Since 1973 the situation has not altered dramatically, and throughout Iran in the early seventies only 40 per cent completed primary education.[37]

This kind of poverty and backwardness does not disappear with the simple provision of funds to build roads, provide schools and install electricity, though of course money helps. It requires educated people to help, explain and convince. But at present the two worlds look at each other from opposite ends of the scale, and they are only close geographically speaking. A 'typical' peasant community can easily be located close to Tehran — a cluster of low mud brick houses with no piped water, no sanitation and no electricity; the inhabitants are too conservative to accept the formation of a government-sponsored co-operative, too wary to think again of buying a tractor because when it broke down the mechanic had already upped sticks and left for a job in town, and this restores a doubting faith in old values and old methods even when modern things are meant to be better.

The countryside then is not some quaint reminder of the past but a continuing and vivid example of the backwardness that exists behind the modernism of Iran. Little has been done to check the rural exodus, often one suspects because it was an easy way of encouraging peasants to enter the modern sector. Where action has been taken it has usually been undermined because rural incomes cannot match those of the towns. The Shah has held up the 'natural purity and politeness' of the farmer.[38] But this farmer leads a hard life, and, as the rural exodus shows, many prefer to trade in this purity and politeness for more money and more opportunity.

Notes

1. Arthur Arnold, *Through Persia by Caravan* (London, Tinsley Brothers, 1877), Vol. I, p. 204.

2. Information supplied to the author by experts from Sir Alexander Gibb, consultants (associated with Iran for many years). The situation is such that moderate rainfall or snow melting causes serious flooding in south Tehran.

3. *Tehran Journal*, 19 January 1977.

4. *Iran Almanac. Echo of Iran*, Tehran, 1977, p. 438.

5. Julian Bharier, *Economic Development in Iran: 1900-1970* (London, Oxford University Press, 1971), p. 15.

6. Ibid., p. 16.

7. Ibid., p. 195.

8. Ibid., p. 19.

9. Ibid., p. 3. Estimates went as high as 12 million and as low as 6 million. However, Bharier's estimate is the most scientific.

10. Ibid., p. 4.

11. Mohammed Reza Shah Pahlavi, *Mission for My Country* (London, Hutchinson, 1961), revised edition 1974, p. 51.

12. Ibid., p. 51.

13. *Iran Almanac*, 1976, p. 87. By then Tehran had also attracted 51 per cent of Iran's total industrial units. See Fereydoun Firouzi, 'Industrial Activity and the Economy of Iran', *Iranian Economic Review*, Vol. I (1976), p. 11.

14. Bharier, *Economic Development*, pp. 28-31. See also *Iran Almanac*, 1977, pp. 369-72.

15. Ibid. Provisional data is only available from the 1976 census, Iran's third. Karaj was found to have grown from 44,243 in 1966 to 138,774 in 1976, the fastest-growing town in Iran. The next-fastest growth was at Bandar Abbas – 34,627 to 89,103 – despite the excessive heat and humidity. (Civil servants get a special hardship allowance there.)

16. *Tehran Journal*, 22 June 1975. Some 80 per cent were born outside Tehran. The survey also highlighted the unusually high male/female imbalance: 135 males to every 100 females. This is certainly the result of influx of 'temporary' single male construction workers.

17. *Iran Almanac*, 1976, p. 87.

18. *Financial Times*, 28 July 1975.

19. *Kayhan International*, 8 March 1976. See also *Iran Almanac*, 1976, p. 360.

20. Bank Markazi annual report, 1975/6, p. 97.

21. *Financial Times*, 28 July 1975. The figure in 1975 for Tehran was 1 car per 19 persons. This has been adjusted to account for new registrations, some of which are government cars. See *Kayhan International*, 1 February 1976 and *Iran Almanac*, 1977, p. 302. About 51 per cent of new registrations are in Tehran, 40 per cent in other large towns and 9 per cent in small towns.

22. Author's guesstimate based on conversations with travel agents and airline officials.

23. *Iran Almanac*, 1977, p. 128.

24. Ibid., pp. 135-6. Assessing newspaper readership from circulation is very difficult. Newspaper circulation figures are generally inflated; but readership, especially in the smaller towns and rural areas is probably underestimated since the readership ratio per copy is high, i.e. in a provincial town like Kerman there

could be eight readers per copy or more.

25. *Financial Times*, 20 August 1975. Shahestan Pahlavi is reputedly the largest underdeveloped urban area in the world. The land had been distributed, mainly by Reza Shah, to the military and comprised some 13,000 lots, which were bought up by the municipality for $1.2 billion. There were attempts to turn the area into green space but the pressure to have an efficient administrative/commercial centre was too strong — based on author's conversation with Tehran Mayor Gholam Reza Nikpay, June 1975.

26. There are no studies on this, but this comment is based upon author's observations of labour in Tehran, other towns and in 'difficult' working areas like Bandar Abbas.

27. *Iran Almanac*, 1977, p. 372.

28. Bharier, *Economic Development*, p. 27. See also *Iran Almanac*, 1977, p. 370.

29. International Labour Office, *Employment and Income Policies for Iran* (Geneva, International Labour Office, 1973), p. 24.

30. Ibid., p. 25.

31. Firouz Vakil, 'Iran's Basic Macroeconomic Problems: A 20-Year Horizon'. This point was made politely but forcibly in the above paper presented to the Aspen Symposium at Persepolis in September 1975. (See *Iran: Past, Present and Future* (New York, Aspen Institute for Humanistic Studies, 1976), pp. 90 and 101).

32. *Iran Almanac*, 1977, p. 415. See also Bharier, *Economic Development*, p. 32. Also *Iran Economic Survey*, No. 138 (28 June 1977). This report contends there are nearer to 85,000 villages.

33. Arnold, *Through Persia*, Vol. II, p. 216.

34. ILO, *Employment and Income Policies*, p. 25.

35. Arthur Millspaugh, *The Financial and Economic Situation of Persia 1926* (New York, 1926), p. 10. Also see Bharier, *Economic Development*, p. 85. Bharier contends that the success of the Millspaugh scheme helped to raise the population growth.

36. Ibid. The Literacy Corps teaches roughly 12 per cent of all primary schoolchildren and provides 17 per cent of the primary schoolteachers.

37. Ibid., p. 69. See also *Iran Almanac*, 1977, p. 406. Of Iran's female population over 10 years old approximately 30 per cent are literate. In the rural areas the percentage is lower.

38. *Kayhan International*, 25 October 1976.

3 OIL AND THE IRANIAN ECONOMY

> Because of our huge petroleum output people commonly think
> of Iran as being primarily an oil producing country. But that is
> a mistake. For thousands of years we have been primarily an
> agricultural country, and we still are.[1]

Few foreign banks were anxious to lend money to the Shah at the turn
of the century. Their reluctance was not surprising: the risk was high
and the country had few resources to guarantee a loan. When the British-
owned Imperial Bank agreed to lend money there were only two assets
that fitted the necessary criteria of being easy to sell and easy to seize –
the customs dues of the Persian Gulf ports and the caviar-producing
Caspian fisheries.[2] Such humiliating terms may seem a far cry from the
groups of foreign bankers lobbying the Iranian government for business
since the 1973 oil price rises. But humiliating terms then were the price
imposed on a weak government and a poor country.

The behaviour of the two dominant powers, Britain and Russia, was
eloquent testimony to this state of affairs. Regarding the country in
almost exclusively strategic terms, they acted with the kind of muscle
and self-interest, particularly in the case of the British, that typified the
zenith of imperial power. Britain's chief concern was to foster a pliant
pro-British régime that would act as a 'neutral' buffer to Russian expansionism and protect the western flank of the Indian empire. The Russians for their part mistrusted the spread of British influence beyond
India and sought to have the country pro-Russian. In neither instance
was the country's economic potential considered worthy of much
attention.

Imposing mountain ranges (the Alborz to the north, the Zagros on
the western flank), high plateaus and bleak deserts created formidable
natural barriers. More important, Iran was not a convenient land route
to India. Nor were its ports in the south a convenient stopover for
Europe-India trade. (It took longer to reach the port of Bushire than
Bombay from England.) Strategic interests were the only concern, the
most important being the cable link between London and India operating since 1865.[3]

The telegraph line, operated by the Indo-European Telegraph Company, was one of several concessions granted to foreign interests either
as a result of strong external pressure or powerful financial inducements
– often a mixture of the two as the British government pressed the case

of those seeking concessions that might suit British interests. In the last years of the Qajar dynasty, its rulers were keen to mortgage or pawn whatever was available to obtain ready cash.

The most spectacular concession was one negotiated on behalf of the naturalised British subject, Baron Julius de Reuter (founder of the news agency of that name) in July 1872. Reuter acquired a seventy-year concession on exclusive rights throughout the country for tramways, mining, irrigation, water works and exploitation of the state-owned forests. In addition he gained a monopoly over the Customs plus promises of first option on any further concessions.[4] All this was for a £40,000 performance bond to be forfeited if work on a railway did not begin within fifteen months. The Shah was guaranteed 20 per cent of the railway's profits and 15 per cent on all other Reuter activities. For a country Iran's size this was probably one of the most far-reaching concessions ever granted by a ruler. Not surprisingly, it provoked bitter opposition at home that led to its speedy cancellation by the Shah, and its replacement with a lesser concession — exclusive banking and mining rights for sixty years.[5]

The mining company liquidated itself after three years' fruitless prospecting. The banking concession prospered on the other hand, in the guise of the Imperial Bank. On the whole, neither the local economy nor the foreign speculators benefited significantly, and the main impact was at the political level where the ignominious terms conceded by the rulers aroused national consciousness. In fact international interest in Iranian concessions was so low that in 1900 when an oil concession was touted around European capitals there were few takers.

It was left to an enthusiastic young Englishman, William D'Arcy, who had been fired by the success of a gold-mining venture in Australia. In May 1901 D'Arcy negotiated a sixty-year concession with exclusive exploration, production and oil-refining rights over an area of 480,000 square miles — the whole of Iran except the five northern provinces. In return for the oil concession he agreed to pay £20,000 cash plus a further £20,000 in paid-up shares of the first company organised to explore oil in Iran. On the company's net annual profits, Iran would receive further a flat royalty of 16 per cent.[6] The search for oil was exceptionally difficult and after three years D'Arcy was obliged to approach Burmah Oil for funds, having spent £200,000. Burmah agreed to step in with the necessary capital and the search continued.[7]

Just when everyone was beginning to despair of success, oil was struck north of Ahwaz near Masjed-Suleiman. It was 26 May 1908, and oil had been discovered for the first time in the Middle East.[8] The impact of this discovery was felt only slowly; and at first more by Britain than Iran. The formation of the Anglo-Persian Oil Company (APOC) in 1909 and first production in 1912 was a major factor in deciding the British Admiralty to switch from coal to oil on the eve of the First World War.[9] Also, because Winston Churchill as First Lord of the Admiralty wanted Britain to own directly at least part of the nation's oil needs, this led to the purchase of a British government stake in APOC.[10] For the time being Iran just happened to be the country where the oil was discovered, and was treated little more than an ignorant, but important, shareholder who had to be humoured from time to time.

Oil: The Backbone of the Economy

Typical of the prevailing cynicism was a letter written by Lord Curzon. Writing to the Secretary of State for India, he said: 'I advise you therefore not to think that the industrial regeneration of Persia is going to make a new start in Mr D'Arcy's hands.'[11] Although subsequent history was to prove Curzon so wrong it did take Iran a long time to benefit seriously from D'Arcy's discovery.

Initial revenues were small. Between 1911 and 1919 Iran received a mere £335,000 in royalties; and in the next ten years annual income averaged just over £1 million.[12] In 1933 a new agreement was signed which rewrote the old D'Arcy concession, reducing it in size (by almost a quarter) and altering the system of payment. Instead of being paid 16 per cent of net profits, Iran received a fixed sum of four shillings per ton of oil sold. This agreement was made to look as though it were a big step forward in Iran's favour, even flattering the sensibilities of Reza Shah by renaming APOC the Anglo-Iranian Oil Company (AIOC). But the Iranians were quickly disenchanted.[13]

Hopes of a rapid revenue increase were dashed by the depression in the 1930s and the new agreement produced direct receipts of under £2.5 million a year. In part this was compensated by the advent of the Second World War and the strategic importance of the oilfields to the Allied war effort. Iran was guaranteed a minimum annual return of £4 million.[14] But this was at the expense of national pride, because in order to safeguard the oilfields and the Eastern supply routes, Allied forces occupied Iran on 23 August 1941. Moreover it was only towards the end of the war that production and revenues began to surge ahead. By 1950, just prior to nationalisation, production was running at 31 million tons and direct revenues at £16 million – quadruple the amount of ten years back.[15]

The only previous precedent to oil nationalisation had been in Mexico in 1938. This had been a failure. Though more eventful, the Iranian experience was just as abortive. The decision to nationalise AIOC's operations in May 1951 was not a carefully planned move. Rather it was the inevitable consequence of the Prime Minister, Mohammed Mossadegh, using the nationalisation issue for internal political reasons to attack the Pahlavi dynasty.

An oil company executive in Iran at the time later observed: 'When the majles [Parliament] passed the bill nationalising oil, they simply thought it meant channelling profits — which they exaggerated — into the national coffers. No one had any real idea what nationalisation meant or entailed.'[16] Nationalisation meant operating the oilfields, running the sophisticated Abadan refinery and marketing both crude and refined products in the international market. Since expatriate personnel ran all key functions of the industry and marketing was an international cartel of the oil companies, Mossadegh was powerless once personnel were withdrawn and both AIOC and the British government decided to block the sale of Iranian oil.

In purely economic terms the net result of the abortive nationalisation attempt was disastrous. From 1951 until 1954 the Iranian oil industry virtually closed down. Iran forfeited its position as the leading producer of oil to boost their own production. Iran's first attempt at planned economic development was completely undermined; and as a result over a quarter of the funds in the Second Plan (1955-62) went towards completing projects unfinished or not initiated in the First Plan.[17] Iran was also left in a very weak bargaining position *vis-à-vis* the oil companies.

Under a new agreement signed in August 1954 Iran could only obtain a fifty/fifty division of profits, and, in return for sovereignty over certain non-essential operations like health, had to compensate AIOC very substantially for losses. Part of the agreement was the disbandment of AIOC but less in response to Iranian sensitivities than pressure from US and other international oil groups keen to obtain a share of the rich Iranian oil operation. The new company became known as the 'Consortium' comprising the seven major oil companies (the Seven Sisters) with BP holding the leading stake of 40 per cent.[18]

Unknown to Iran, the Consortium members worked out a secret agreement among themselves over the future level of production from Iranian fields. Iranian production was to be balanced against the global oil interests of the major oil companies so that any increase in production was the result of an internal agreement and Iranian revenues were entirely dependent upon the level at which the Consortium chose to produce. Details of this agreement only leaked out in 1967.[19]

The only way in which Iran could assert its independence and maximise its potential oil resources was to form a national oil company, the National Iranian Oil Company (NIOC), and with this new company, to carry out joint exploration and production agreements with the smaller and independent international oil companies. The first such deal was in 1957. Enrico Mattei, the individualistic head of Italy's state oil concern ENI, concluded an agreement whereby NIOC would get 75 per cent of the proceeds on discovery of oil. The fact that Iran could obtain such terms through negotiation – and with the foreign partner bearing all exploration costs – was a revelation. This was the first of the so-called 'new style' oil deals among the oil-producing nations, and it was to have an important catalytic effect in the creation of OPEC. Unfortunately for Iran, this and subsequent similar agreements failed to strike oil on the scale of the Consortium area.

With increased militancy within OPEC, Iran's bargaining position slowly improved in relation to the Consortium. By 1970 world demand for crude oil was beginning to place the oil producers in a seller's market. The changed circumstances were symbolised in the Tehran Agreements on 14 February 1971 between representatives of the Gulf producers and the international oil companies. It was a complex agreement that for the first time sought to compensate the producers for loss of purchasing power through inflation and dollar fluctuations. In money terms it meant a major 30 cent per barrel increase rising over a five-year period to 50 cents. Finally Iran was able to rely on oil as a principal source of revenue. Between 1970 and 1972 production increased from an average of 3.82 million barrels per day to 5.02 million barrels per day and revenues from $1.12 billion to $2.39 billion.[20]

It was now only a matter of time before Iran could carry out, albeit through negotiation, what Mossadegh had failed to do unilaterally – full control of the industry. This was achieved on 20 March 1973, in an agreement whereby the Consortium handed over all remaining operations and ownership to NIOC. The Consortium agreed to form a special contracting company, Oil Service Company of Iran (OSCO), to provide the much needed expertise to run and assist in the development of the Khuzestan Fields – an area slightly smaller than the original Consortium acreage. This contractual support was particularly important since NIOC counted on not only raising production but on investing in major secondary recovery procedures like gas injection to prolong the life of the oilfields. The Consortium agreed to contribute 40 per cent of these heavy investment costs. In return, a new interdependent relationship was established, with the Consortium guaranteed certain quantities of crude oil and refined products at a discount of 22 cents per barrel. In effect the Consortium was still being asked to act as the marketer of Iranian crude; but on the basis that this role gradually diminish as NIOC developed its own markets.

However, a combination of international market conditions, the cost of Khuzestan development and changes within OPEC's pricing structure had by the end of 1975 rendered the more important clauses of this agreement obsolete. In practice NIOC marketed much more crude than laid down in the agreement: it was over 45 per cent above quota in 1976 and 30 per cent in 1977. The Consortium for its part lifted less crude than anticipated, and according to NIOC, less than contracted. In 1975 NIOC claimed that failure by the Consortium to meet its obligations led to a shortfall in revenue of $2.7 billion.

This created considerable acrimony at the time. NIOC argued that the companies had a binding obligation to buy; they in turn claimed that market conditions had so altered as to make the agreement inoperable. In addition the companies were concerned at their investment commitments which had been rising sharply and in 1975 stood at $360 million. In October 1975 the Consortium froze all further investment payments pending renegotiation of a new agreement. These frictions led to a maturing of attitudes on both sides, assisted by NIOC's realisation that it could sell more oil than anticipated. Since April 1976 there has been general acceptance that a new contractual agreement be made on the basis of a management fee — to be paid in the form of a discount on crude bought by the companies. But the differing crude needs of the companies, especially the American majors whose stake in Aramco in Saudi Arabia had to be taken into account, complicated the conclusion of a new agreement.[21]

These latter problems with the Consortium emphasise the dominant theme that has persisted throughout Iran's possession of oil. Oil income has been a constant variable. Since 1912 income has followed a slow historic curve upwards which accelerated in the 1960s. But it has been rare indeed for the government to receive the amount of oil revenue anticipated in any one year. The disruptions were greatest in the First and Second Plans as a result of nationalisation. Latterly the variable has been on the plus side. For instance the Fourth Plan (1968-72) would have run up against serious financial difficulties had there not been the Tehran Agreement in 1971 sharply raising prices.

Moreover, as oil revenues increased and the economy became more dependent upon them, the inherent threat of lower oil revenues became potentially more damaging. For instance the Third Plan (1962-7) was 62 per cent dependent upon oil revenues; the Fourth Plan (1968-72) 63 per cent dependent.[22] By the time of the revision of the Fifth Plan (1973-8) following the 1973 oil price rises, the dependence had risen to over 80 per cent.

Despite such growing dependence, the oil industry's structural impact on the economy was strictly limited. Until the mid-1960s its impact was almost exclusively financial. Just prior to nationalisation the industry employed 50,000 men, the largest industrial payroll in the country, but under 10 per cent were salaried staff and no Iranian held a key managerial position. The oil company, AIOC, was entirely self-contained and enjoyed special import concessions.[23] The Iranian government was never kept fully in the picture and had no access to the company's books. The Iranians suspected for instance that AIOC deliberately paid low dividends to avoid having to make extra dividend payments to the government.[24] AIOC in short followed the classic pattern of a multinational. Even when the industry began to have a stronger Iranian content and became more integrated, its technology and the capital-intense nature of the operation tended to keep it in an isolated 'modern' sector.

Agriculture: the Poor Cousin

Without oil, Iran today would still be a rural economy little wealthier than Egypt. Agriculture has been, and still is, the means by which the majority of Iranians derive a livelihood but it has few attractions as a way of life. The chief handicap has been lack of water. Throughout the country rainfall averages 300mm to 350mm a year; but this is unevenly distributed with the lush subtropical Caspian coast receiving the highest and the vast arid central and eastern plateau the lowest. Insufficient water supplies have restricted the amount of land brought under cultivation, affected the type of cultivation and in many regions can mean disaster in a low-rainfall climate that is both very hot in summer and very cold in winter. Crop management is made difficult by higher summer soil temperatures, while winter frost rules out double cropping in many places.

The ancient poets who wrote about rose gardens flowing with water to the sound of nightingales gave a misleading picture. Iran for the most part is arid and unproductive. Approximately half the total land area of 164.8 million hectares (628,000 square miles) supports no cultivation of any sort. Two bleak stony deserts — the Dasht-e Lut and the Dasht-e Kavir — eat into central and south-eastern Iran, covering one-sixth of the entire country. These deserts have the reputation for being the least life-supporting in the world. The remaining land area is split: 25 per cent town, villages, roads and surface water; 13 per cent potentially cultivable and productive land; and 12 per cent forests.[25] Thus only 22 million hectares of the total land area are capable of exploitation for agricultural purposes; and of this under 8 million hectares is being cultivated.

A highly evolved system of underground channels, known as *qanats*, has been the traditional means of exploiting ground water. These channels, constructed in soft alluvial soil, and up to 50 km long, bring water from the foothills to cultivated areas relying solely on the gradient. The great advantage of the *qanat* system was that the channels could be built at times of surplus rural labour. Roughly one-third of all irrigation as late as the early 1970s relied on *qanats*. However, with the rural exodus and the increase in labour costs, *qanats* have suffered seriously because they are labour-intensive and require constant maintenance. As a result, a quarter of the *qanat* system has become inoperative through lack of repair.[26]

This traditional system also failed to retain the winter rains and melting spring snow. Only with the advent of modern dam-building in Iran (the first was completed in 1957) was water wastage reduced and supplies made available for large-scale irrigation. At present roughly 4.5 million hectares of land are capable of being irrigated; but only 70 per cent has the necessary infrastructure, and less than 30 per cent is being properly watered. However, even with irrigation Iran's problems are not solved. The poor nature of the soil means that over-irrigation can produce damaging high salinity.[27]

The convenience with which the opium crop fitted into the cycle of Iran's water supplies was one of the principal reasons why cultivation of the poppy was so important. The crop was sown in the winter and harvested in spring. Opium was also highly profitable and allowed the farmer to have a different summer crop. Up until the late 1920s when vigorous national and international measures were taken to curb opium production in Iran, Iranian farmers were producing 30 per cent of the world's production (measured in morphine content). The crop also provided as much as 15 per cent of export earnings and accounted for 10 per cent of tax revenues.[28] The crop is now grown under strict control for domestic medicinal needs. Yet an important proportion of the adult male population are still opium users. In 1976 the police arrested 14,453 persons under anti-narcotics laws and there were 170,000 registered addicts.[29]

Moves to reduce the area of opium cultivation were the first effort to alter the structure of agriculture. The only other change of note until land reform began in 1960 was the shift in the pattern of Iran's nomadic tribes. At the turn of the century Iran possessed some 2.4 million nomads, a quarter of the entire population. Within fifty years this number had dwindled to under 500,000. Their economic importance lay in their possession of 70 per cent of the country's sheep and goats — the main form of meat, and significant source of cheese and yoghurt. The wool also supplied material for the carpet-weaving industry. In short the tribes were a central element in rural Iran. Their importance was reduced once Reza Shah began to settle them in an effort to bring them under the control of the central government. The larger and more powerful groupings like the Bakhtiari, Qashgai and Turkoman were a particular target. (The Bakhtiari controlled much of Khuzestan where D'Arcy discovered oil. His initial negotiations were with the Bakhtiari whose members provided the bulk of the oil industry labour.) But if Reza Shah is blamed — in some quarters he is bitterly condemned for his strong-arm methods, like the poisoning of wells — he merely accelerated an inevitable process.

Iran was largely self-sufficient in foodstuffs up to the early 1960s and could balance the deficit by exports of cotton, fruits (peaches and limes) and nuts. However, the diet was low-calory and used little red meat. After the 1973 oil price rise food consumption shot up, creating a substantial dependence upon imports.

Despite substantial outlays on agriculture in the first two development plans after the Second World War, the results were at best moderate with production increases reflecting an expansion of cultivable land, not improved productivity. The chief obstacle to productivity was the nature of land tenure. Approximately 54 per cent of total agricultural land was cultivated by sharecroppers utterly dependent upon the landlord. The nature of the sharecropping arrangement varied: for cash crops like cotton, the landlord usually took half the production while for wheat or barley the landlord could take up to two-thirds.[30] Holdings were small and generally fragmented; and even where a single owner possessed a large land area this was still often sublet in uneconomic parcels for fixed rent or let to sharecroppers. On one estimate, 50 per cent of all land prior to land reform was owned by absentee landlords.[31]

When land reform came, little thought was given to matters of improved performance from the agricultural sector. It was a political manoeuvre by the Shah to win over the rural masses and curtail the power of the big landowners. The first law, passed in April 1960, calling for the redistribution of all private holdings in excess of 400 irrigated hectares, and 800 non-irrigated hectares, was poorly planned. It was hurried through without the compilation of a proper register of title and so provided loopholes to the landowners to retain more land.

This law was amended and on 9 January 1962 it was replaced by what became known as *the* Land Reform Law. Though still highly political in motivation the approach was more pragmatic. Holdings were not limited by size; and instead landlords could retain one village. Compensation was shrewdly fixed on the basis of taxes previously paid which meant that those who had underdeclared income in the past were caught out. Excluded from the law were 'mechanised estates', i.e. those properties employing wage labour, market gardens and tea plantations. The land went to tenant farmers and sharecroppers who were obliged to form co-operatives and repay the price of land over fifteen years. In the first phase some 16,000 villages covering 19 per cent of arable land were purchased by the government for redistribution.[32]

There then followed two more stages. In an effort to make redistribution more palatable to the landlord, five methods of settlement were offered: sale, division of land on the same basis as the old sharecropping arrangement, fixed tenancy, formation of a rural co-operative or purchase of the tenant's rights due under the law by the landlord. In many instances this new approach to reform merely formalised the existing *status quo*.[33]

The third phase, starting in 1967, was more concerned with tidying up the fragmented holdings created by the previous reforms. Smallholdings were grouped into co-operatives so that credit and direct government assistance could be used to greater effect. Yet this strategy also lacked serious planning in that there were not enough extension workers to spread around the large number of co-operatives. By 1973 the government was obliged to regroup the co-operatives into larger units, and by 1976 the early 8,450 co-operatives had been consolidated to 2,858.[34]

In spite of the political motivation for land reform, the first stage had a significant impact in the countryside. For the first time many farmers had the chance of entering the modern economy, although the measures were not comprehensive. They ignored the problems of the poorest members of the rural community — the landless labourers who comprised as much as 25 per cent of the work-force. So in many cases the divide between those with land and those without was made more stratified and pronounced.[35]

A more fundamental criticism is that land reform was initiated too late. By the time the measures were introduced and explained, the rural exodus had already gathered pace. (Two million persons had left the countryside between 1956 and 1966.) Mere ownership of title deeds, a novel concept itself among a conservative populace, was no incentive to remain on the land. Arguably the ones quitting the countryside were the most dynamic elements of rural society, leaving behind those least able to appreciate or exploit the new situation. The landlords were also able to retain in their entitlement the best lands with the best infrastructure (access to roads, electricity, etc.). Meanwhile from the peasant's point of view the change from absentee landlord as supplier of credit, seeds and fertiliser to an unfeeling bureaucracy was scarcely more rewarding.

But the real criticism of land reform was that it diverted attention away from the central issue of increased productivity. As a result of land reform over 40 per cent of title related to uneconomical holdings of 2 hectares and less.[36] By chopping a large portion of the country's potentially best arable land into inefficient smallholdings, land reform created in the new owner a luxury the country could ill afford to support. The only remedy was consolidation. Rural co-operatives apart, the government is employing three other methods of consolidation: agribusiness ventures, farm corporations and production co-operatives. In agribusiness the government buys up smallholdings and then rents a consolidated land area (usually over 5,000 hectares) to private or state-run companies. In the case of farm corporations land is consolidated by farmers exchanging their title deeds against shares in the corporation whose management is recruited and paid for by the government. In 1976 there were 85 such corporations with 32,506 shareholders.[37] Production co-operatives differ in that the farmer is permitted to retain title and these have proved more popular.

To ensure the success of land consolidation, the government embarked upon a scheme to assess the agricultural potential of the best lands. Under a Bill passed in June 1976, the best regions were divided up into a series of 'poles' (in an initial stage twenty were identified). All farms within these poles are to be combined into units of 20 hectares and more — the minimum considered viable for modern farming in Iran.[38] If the law is strictly observed, farmers who refuse to co-operate will have their land compulsorily purchased. However, before this stage is reached the government has to have completed detailed studies on these poles. In 1977 consultancy contracts had only begun to be let.

The combined effect of these measures has created a good deal of uncertainty about the direction of agriculture and government policy towards it. This has been reflected in poor growth figures. Prior to 1973 production was officially said to have an annual growth of 3 per cent and to be now running at 6 per cent: in fact a 2 per cent growth rate is more realistic.[39] Against this, consumption of foodstuffs is increasing at 12 per cent a year.[40]

Ironically the introduction of land reform coincided with the beginning of a sharp decline in agriculture's overall importance in the economy. Some claim that the Shah deliberately sacrificed agriculture in order to concentrate on building up an industrial base. In the period 1959 to 1972 agriculture received a mere 8 per cent of investment against 22 per cent for industry.[41] But this is a distortion. What happened was that, with the government's energy devoted to industrialisation, it lacked the will to follow through at a grass-roots level the unglamorous task of making land reform work. In purely money terms agriculture still received a sizeable sum.

Industry: Slow Diversification

In 1947 a group of American consultants, Morrison Knudson, were asked to submit a feasibility study on what was to be Iran's first attempt at planned development. Their advice was to concentrate on improving agriculture.[42] Sound advice perhaps; but Mohammed Reza Shah was committed to industrialisation. However there was little base to build on.

Reza Shah devoted most of his energies to opening up the country and never adopted a coherent attitude towards industry. Economics and industrialisation were inextricably bound up with political, nationalistic and strategic considerations. This was symbolised by the gargantuan project which is still held up today in Iran as one of his greatest achievements – the Trans-Iranian Railway. Connecting north and south Iran over a distance of 860 miles, the line took almost twelve years to build and was finally opened in 1938. It was a tremendous feat of engineering and human endurance, carried out under appalling conditions. Yet as Julian Bharier acidly comments: 'There is no doubt that on almost any economic criterion the railway was ill-conceived.'[43] To lay each mile of track cost £35,000. The equivalent cost of a road link would have been a maximum £525 per mile.[44] A road could have achieved the same purpose; and besides the steep gradients made it impossible for trains to carry heavy loads and the aridity combined with extreme heat made it difficult to use steam locomotives.

The industries that flourished under Reza Shah were those which foreigners towards the end of the nineteenth century had tried to introduce — matches, textiles, tobacco. Textiles were by far the most important. By 1939 there were already 40 mills (36 privately owned) satisfying half the demand for cotton yarn. In 1947 textiles accounted for 60 per cent of industrial employment and 70 per cent of installed horsepower.[45] Through the 1960s textiles retained their position as the largest industrial sector.[46]

Reza Shah's emphasis on centralisation concentrated industry round the capital. Against professional advice, he altered the siting of a proposed steel plant from Semnan to Karaj near Tehran. However, with the Allied occupation of Iran in 1941 the project collapsed, leaving in its wake 8,500 tons of unwanted equipment and Iran had to wait another 37 years before its first steel mill was operational.[47] In January 1966 agreement was finalised with the Soviet Union on the construction of a steel complex at Isfahan with an initial 600,000 ton capacity.[48] This formed part of the first major economic agreement signed between Iran and the Soviet Union but the plant was not operational until 1973. In the meantime the Shahryar Industrial Group in the private sector began operating a mill utilising scrap and imported billets in 1966.

The Soviet agreement was an historic turning-point. In addition to the steel mill, the Soviets agreed to build Iran's first machine-tool and heavy engineering plant at Arak and a gasline to carry gas to the Soviet border. Like Nasser and the Aswan Dam in 1955, the offer had come from a Communist country where Western experts had rejected the project. Iran was still at the stage where large-scale industrial ventures of this nature only held attraction as political investments and Western companies were loath to become involved. Not only were the Soviets cheaper but they also offered attractive soft credit ($260 million over twelve years). Iran's choice of the Soviets and subsequent deals with Czechs and Romanians only highlight the change in its fortunes when oil revenues increased.

The most logical industrialisation was to expand the base of the oil industry and diversify into petrochemicals: a sector where Western companies were keen to participate, especially as the world petrochemical market was on an upswing. About the time of the Soviet agreement, three joint venture petrochemical projects were signed with American companies: a fifty/fifty export-orientated venture with Allied Chemical for ammonia, urea, phosphoric acid and diammonium phosphate; an LPG (liquid petroleum gas) plant for export on a fifty/fifty basis with Amoco; and a plant to produce PVC and detergents for the domestic market on a 26/74 basis with B. F. Goodrich.[49] The development of the petrochemical and steel industries through newly formed state enterprises, or foreign joint ventures with state enterprises, accounted for almost 70 per cent of total industrial investment in the Third Plan (1963-7).[50]

During this period foreign investment, especially American, provided an important stimulus to the private sector in rubber, pharmaceuticals and construction.[51] The Fourth Plan (1968-72) envisaged greatly expanded industrial development with $1 billion earmarked for public sector projects. Meanwhile the private sector extended its activities to the automotive field, food processing, and a range of secondary industries protected by high tariff barriers and restrictive import licences. Foreign investment in local ventures was often a means of getting round tariff barriers.

The accelerated pace of industrial development was reflected in the number of large units being established in towns throughout the country. In 1956 Iran possessed a mere 694 such units. By 1961 the number had increased to 1,191. This rose to 3,661 in 1966 and took a further leap in 1972 to 5,651. This represented an annual average increase of 44 per cent between 1956 and 1972. Half these plants consisted of operations in textiles and foodstuffs, but during this period the percentage of the industrial work-force employed in these sectors dropped from 77 per cent to 57 per cent; while the share of metal industries and machinery rose from 5 per cent to 20 per cent.[52]

Overall between 1959 and 1972 industry's share in GDP rose from 13.6 per cent to almost 20 per cent. During the same period agriculture fell back sharply from 30 per cent of GDP to 16 per cent.[53]

While these figures reflect the growing impact of industry on the economy, they give little idea of the problems involved in getting this far. Unlike many poorer countries that had been left a colonial infrastructure of communications and utilities, Iran started virtually from scratch. There was no trained industrial work-force and in most instances facilities such as power, water, approach roads and telecommunications had to be specially installed. The oil industry, for instance, developed its own separate communications network (as did the military later on). Building a factory was therefore an infinitely complex process, fraught with unforeseen problems. As a result the majority of plants were late in their start up and had high cost over-runs.

Because industry, bar textiles, was so late in starting, it had a long way to catch up with consumer demand. In the late 1960s, as government expenditure increased, the gap between consumer demand and local production widened. This gap further widened in the early 1970s

even though the number of new units coming onstream was exceptionally high. The result was piecemeal industrial planning based on immediate demand, rather than building a strong industrial base for a self-
sustaining economy not dependent upon oil.

While industrial resources were stretched to the limit, it was difficult to measure efficiency. The high level of demand masked it. Alternatively, inefficiency was concealed behind monopoly or near-monopoly
and high restrictive tariff barriers. The sole official yardsticks for the
health of industry were growth and profitability. Iranian industry
entered the 1973 boom highly profitable but only in rare instances well
organised or soundly managed.

In fact it would have been difficult for industrialisation to have
started earlier. Before the Second World War the economy was too
backward and although the war and the presence of Allied forces
occupying Iran helped to generate more income, the occupation was a
disruptive influence until 1947. Third, the loss of income and the disruptions of the abortive nationalisation in 1951 delayed serious industrial development by at least eight years. Even when the Shah was in a
position to concentrate more on industry he hesitated for political
considerations. He is well aware of the inherent political dangers of
creating an industrial proletariat with a potentially powerful means of
expression, the strike. Trade unions had been banned and strikes
outlawed in 1936 by Reza Shah. Nevertheless the presence of Soviet
and British troops in Iran during the Second World War was the signal
for a series of strikes.[54] The most effective were in the textile industry,
allegedly fomented by the Tudeh (Communist) Party. In response to
labour agitation, the Shah permitted the establishment in 1944 of a
unified Trade Union of Iranian Workers. This was followed by a labour
law in 1946 and another in 1949 laying down a 48-hour week.[55]

In the wake of the overthrow of Mossadegh, labour became one of
the most politically suspect groups: not the least because of its suspected penetration by the Tudeh Party. This led to a purge of the unions,
the banning of strikes and the introduction of an officially sponsored
form of labour representation. A new labour law was introduced in
1959, later amended in 1965, with the aim of protecting worker's
rights inside the factory as the price for removing all politics from
trade unionism.[56] From then on discipline on the shop floor was reinforced by the extensive use of the SAVAK (the security police) and its
agents, coupled with the presence of armed factory guards, often
supplied on secondment from the army.

It is therefore no accident that industrialisation gathered momentum in the late 1960s after the Shah had launched Land Reform, crushed all parliamentary opposition and curbed the industrial labour force.

The New Barons

The people who emerged as entrepreneurs during this dynamic growth came from often simple origins. Traditional wealth from land tended to invest in real estate or services like banking. Economic development since 1920 had permitted a major consolidation of existing wealth, except where a family's land and assets were confiscated for political reasons. Moves by Reza Shah in 1927 and 1928 to establish proper title to urban land in the Tehran area allowed the major landholders to benefit enormously. Title had been acquired mostly by user or recognised royal gift and property delimited by fertile areas, i.e. landlords claimed to own as far as what could be watered. However, the shrewder families in 1927 delimited their land beyond what could be watered into the arid areas, so acquiring legal title to property which was not strictly theirs but which no one claimed. With the growth of the capital this land became very valuable.[57] Families like Farman Farmayan and Vosokh are said to have benefited in this way. Land Reform was also a boon to traditional wealth. It gave landlords liquidity and focused attention on urban property where values were infinitely greater. But new wealth acquired in this was not strictly entrepreneurial.

For the most part, the entrepreneurs graduated from trading operations in the Bazaar, frequently transferring from traditional commerce via a dealership or agency for one of the international companies. This usually required influence at Court and political pull; and as a result few could be called self-made men in a Western business sense. Some who achieved success through their own initiative were then drawn into the royal ambit and were used directly by the Shah to initiate specific industrial ventures.

Ahmad Khayami, who founded Irannational in 1962, which has become the biggest company in the automotive sector with one of the largest work-forces in the country, is an interesting example. Born in Meshed in 1928, he came from a traditional Bazaar trading background.

During the Second World War, I was in the export business selling dried fruits, and by the time the war finished I was bankrupt. So I established the first car wash service with a capital of Rs. 4,000. Within four years I became the representative of Mercedes Benz in my native province. I then left all my business to my brother and came north to Tehran, and 10 years after having this car service, I was able to establish Irannational in Tehran. In the first stage we used to make buses, mini-buses and trucks by the trade mark of Mercedes Benz. By the order of the Shah I then started to make cars. As soon as I started making Peykans [a version of the Hillman Hunter using ckd units from Chrysler UK], I invited my brother to join me.[58]

Leaving the general running of Irannational to his brother, Ahmad Khayami moved into chain stores. He established the Kouroush Stores, the first attempt in Iran to introduce large-scale retailing. Again this move was made at the request of the Shah.[59] Then to provide direct supplies to the stores, he set up manufacturing facilities for clothing, branched into furniture production and agribusiness. Thus within one generation there has been a change from bazaar-type trade right into the heart of the modern sector of an industrial economy and the beginnings of a vertically integrated business.

Just as remarkable is the case of Habib Sabet. Born in 1903, he went out to work at 14 as an apprentice in a bicycle shop. With savings he was able to invest in a taxi and from his earnings he bought a second-hand army truck which was the basis for Iran's first road haulage company.[60] He subsequently was able to obtain the Volkswagen and Pepsi-Cola concessions and develop ventures with General Tire and Rubber, and Squibb. His business interests now cover almost 50 companies and employ some 10,000 people. He has also become one of the single richest figures in Iranian business, demonstrating this with an exact replica reconstruction in Tehran of Marie Antoinette's Petit Trianon at a reputed cost of $15 million.[61]

There are other examples, too. The Melli Industrial Group of the Iravani family developed from one of the principal cottage industries of the bazaar — shoe-making. In a generation Melli has become the best-known brand name throughout Iran. The group is the most fully integrated of all private industrial concerns, owning its own tanneries and dyeing plants, in addition to possessing international outlets. However, the group has expanded so far beyond its origins that the hallmark, its shoes, is no longer part of the holding company's name. Melli is now involved in such diversified interests as food processing and international haulage. The biggest private group also progressed from simple bazaar activity. The Behshahr Industrial Group was formed by the Ladjevardi family in 1944 and was originally involved in the import of consumer goods, raw materials and textiles. Since then its empire has grown to cover 22 wholly owned companies and 26 partnership ventures.

A general feature of these and other new business empires is the tenacity with which they have been kept in close-knit family groups – even though the original creation of one man. It is also noticeable how the more dynamic elements in the business community have originated outside Tehran, with a high proportion from Yazd.[62] Conditions have been extraordinarily favourable for anyone with a modicum of initiative; nevertheless the adaptation from traditional trading has been remarkable. Now the new generation taking over from the parents have all had foreign education.

Conclusion

The growth of the Iranian economy has been exceptionally rapid, the major part having taken place since the mid-1950s. Industry in particular has expanded so fast, in such a short time, one forgets just how new it is: very little is more than sixteen years old. The first agreement to assemble a passenger car, the Fiat 1100, was signed in 1960. The first comprehensive attempt to survey Iran's mineral resources was initiated in 1962 with the foundation of the Geological Institute. In that year Iran's first fertiliser plant at Shiraz began to operate at near capacity. The first Iranian-assembled tractor left its Romanian-built factory in Tabriz in 1968. In 1972 the first key engineering units – machine-tool plants at Tabriz and Arak – became operational along with a small aluminium smelter. The Isfahan steel mill, the Aryamehr Complex, began proper operation in 1973. The comparative lateness with which Iran reached these industrial milestones underlines the tremendous leap Iran had to make from the poverty and backwardness of the turn of the century.

Despite the initiation of planned development in the early post-Second World War period, the emergence of strategic objectives has been a recent phenomenon. Growth until the Fourth Five Year Plan was piecemeal. This partly reflected poor organisation and lack of direction. More importantly, it resulted from an inability – not always the Iranians' fault – to mobilise resources. For instance, early efforts to rely more extensively upon oil revenues were badly upset by the Mossadegh oil nationalisation. Iran was also frustrated in maximising oil revenue by the nature of the international market and historic relationships with the oil companies. As late as 1971 Iran was still forced to rely upon advances by the Consortium against royalties as a means of additional finance.[63]

Iran's rapid economic development tended to be grafted on to old structures rather than replace them. A modern sector grew up side by side with the traditional rural economy but the two existed in relative isolation. The size of the country, disparateness and widely dispersed nature of the population, coupled with a cumbrous corrupt bureaucracy and poor communications reinforced this gap. As a result the benefits of imported technology and the spin-off from oil revenues remained, and were reinforced, around the capital and few select provincial towns. This uneven development, perhaps unavoidable, was to prove a major handicap when Iran accelerated expenditure in the wake of the 1973 oil price rises.

Like many rulers of developing countries with a large agricultural sector and an impoverished rural populace, both Reza Shah and Mohammed Reza Shah mixed politics and agricultural development so that the two considerations were completely intertwined. Agricultural development came to be treated as an issue of land ownership and the allegiance of the rural masses rather than the economic one of production. Thus when the economy began to stimulate consumer demand and living standards rose, especially from the late 1960s onwards, Iran suddenly found itself with a foodstuffs deficit. Unfortunately at a moment when structural reforms should have been introduced to tackle this deficit, there seemed so many other priorities that the agricultural sector entered the 1970s unprepared to meet a continued surge in demand.

Notes

1. Mohammed Reza Shah Pahlavi, *Mission for My Country* (London, Hutchinson, 1974 edition), p. 195.
2. Denis Wright, *The English among the Persians* (London, Heinemann, 1977), p. 106.
3. Ibid., pp. 11 and 128-36. A confidential list of British interests in 1919 put the seven major interests in order of importance. Oil was fourth – behind the Telegraph, the Imperial Bank and maritime trade in the Gulf.
4. E.B. Yaganegi, *Recent Financial History of Persia* (New York, 1934), pp. 19-33.
5. Wright, *The English*, p. 104.
6. Jahangir Amouzegar and Ali Fekrat, *Iran: Economic Development under Dualistic Conditions* (Chicago, University of Chicago, 1971), pp. 13-14. The government did not understand the important nuance of 'net profits' which therefore enabled the taxes paid to the British Treasury to be deducted from gross profits. See also Wright, *The English*, p. 108.
7. Anthony Sampson, *The Seven Sisters* (London, Hodder and Stoughton, Coronet edition, 1976), pp. 70-1.
8. Ibid.
9. Sampson, *Seven Sisters*, pp. 72-3. APOC was to prove the most valuable British oil interest until 1954.

10. Wright, *The English*, p. 10.

11. India Office Library, Hamilton Papers, Curzon to Hamilton, July 1901.

12. Amouzegar and Fekrat, *Iran*, p. 14.

13. Ibid., p. 15.

14. Julian Bharier, *Economic Development in Iran : 1900-1970* (London, Oxford University Press, 1971), p. 159.

15. Initial production was 43,000 long tons a year. In 1919 it passed the 1 million ton mark and by 1938 was 10.19 million tons. By 1950 production was 31.75 million tons.

16. Comment to the author by an executive with AIOC at the time of nationalisation.

17. Amouzegar and Fekrat, *Iran*, p. 40-3.

18. The original Consortium members were: BP (40 per cent); Shell (14 per cent); Exxon, Gulf, Socal and Texaco (each 8 per cent) and CFP (6 per cent). In 1955 each of the five US companies gave up an eighth of their holding to permit 5 per cent of the Consortium to be owned by nine US 'independents'.

19. Sampson, *Seven Sisters*, pp. 140-5 and 184-7.

20. *Iran Almanac. Echo of Iran*, Tehran, 1977, p. 258. See also Amouzegar and Fekrat, *Iran*, p. 32-5. This represented a 32 per cent increase in production and a 113 per cent increase in revenues.

21. Based on conversations by the author with various NIOC officials and Consortium members from 1975 to 1977. Also see NIOC annual reports 1973-5.

22. Amouzegar and Fekrat, *Iran*, pp. 36-8.

23. Ibid., pp. 26-7. Until the early 1930s Iran was importing most of its oil from Russia while AIOC exported Iranian oil to Europe.

24. Ibid., p. 17. Under the 1933 agreement 20 per cent of dividends in excess of £671,250 had to go to the government of Iran.

25. Bharier, *Economic Development*, p. 136.

26. *Iran Almanac*, 1977, p. 415. The *qanat* system is also to be found in Oman where it is called the *falaj* system.

27. Bharier, *Economic Development*, p. 136.

28. Ibid., p. 132.

29. *Iran Almanac*, 1977, p. 309.

30. Ismail Ajami, 'Agrarian reform, modernisation of peasants and agricultural development in Iran', paper presented to Persepolis Symposium, September 1975. Published by Aspen Institute for Humanistic Studies (New York, 1976).

31. The first major attempt at distributing Crown lands began in 1951 but this was stopped under Mossadegh, then restarted in 1960. Crown lands were acquired through gift, seizure and confiscation by Shah Reza. Purchase at market rates was rare. Religious endowments, especially the Holy Shrine at Meshed, acquired large holdings through gift. This was considered preferable to being obliged to sell at nominal rates land to the Crown. Prior to Land Reform the Crown possessed some 4 per cent of cultivable land.

32. Amouzegar and Fekrat, *Iran*, p. 116.

33. Ann Lambton, *The Persian Land Reform 1962-1966* (London, Oxford University Press, 1969). Lambton's studies on land reform are generally considered the most exhaustive and authoritative.

34. Bank Markazi annual report, 1975/6, p. 83.

35. The distribution of land to the landless labourers (the *khushneshin*) was ruled out on the grounds that this would have created even greater fragmentation.

36. *Financial Times*, 28 July 1975.

37. Bank Markazi annual report, 1975/6, p. 83.

38. *Financial Times*, 21 June 1976.

39. Comments to the author by Agriculture Minister Mansur Rohani, June 1975. The lower estimate comes from World Bank field officers and US govern-

ment field officers.

40. *Financial Times*, 28 July 1975.

41. Fereydoun Firoozi, 'Industrial activity and the economy of Iran', *Iranian Economic Review*, Tehran, No. 1 (1976), p. 4. During this period the proportion of the labour force employed in agriculture declined from 54 per cent to 41 per cent.

42. Ibid., p. 12.

43. Bharier, *Economic Development*, p. 203.

44. Ibid., p. 206.

45. Firoozi, 'Industrial activity', pp. 26-8. Because the industry expanded too fast in the early 1950s, it ran into cash-flow problems but was bailed out by government intervention.

46. Ibid.

47. Ibid.

48. Amouzegar and Fekrat, *Iran*, p. 49.

49. Ibid., p. 48.

50. Ibid.

51. Bharier, *Economic Development*, pp. 192-3. Over 50 per cent of the capital was American.

52. Firouz Tofigh, 'Development of Iran: a statistical note', paper presented to Persepolis Symposium, September 1975. Published by Aspen Institute of Humanistic studies (New York, 1976).

53. Amouzegar and Fekrat, *Iran*, p. 96.

54. Bharier, *Economic Development*, p. 36.

55. T. Jalil, *Workers of Iran: Repression and the struggle for democratic Trade Unions* (Campaign for the Restoration of Trade Union Rights in Iran (CRTUI), London, July 1976).

56. The Labour Law, Article 29 stipulates that 'syndicates, unions and confederations shall not be entitled to interfere in political affairs. They may however in cases of safeguarding their trade and economic interests express tendencies towards and co-operate with political parties.' For details of the text see T. Jalil, *Workers say No to the Shah* (CRTUI, London, April 1977), pp. 104-24.

57. Based on information supplied to the author by Moustafa Fateh, President of the Bank of Tehran.

58. Written answers to author's questions, July 1977.

59. Ibid.

60. *Newsweek*, 14 October 1974.

61. Habib Sabet now lives in semi-exile in Paris, refusing to return to Iran because of attempts to prosecute him during the anti-profiteering campaign of August 1975. However, the sons have carried on the business.

62. The Yazdis' reputation as successful businessmen is attributed to the city's position surrounded by desert, with trade the sole means of survival. Also the Zoroastrian influence in Yazd, uninhibited by the traditional Islamic rejection of usury, is said to have given Yazdis a head start.

63. Bank Markazi annual report, 1974/5, p. 157. In the three years up to 1971/2 these advances totalled $ 511 million.

4 MONARCHY AND THE PAHLAVI DYNASTY

> As one reads Iranian history, it becomes clear that most often
> the whole society was ruled as if it were the personal posses-
> sion of the king.[1]

The fundamental nature of monarchy has varied little since Cyrus the
Great proclaimed himself King of Persia in 546 BC. Continuity has been
maintained not so much by heredity as by those who have had the
strength and the will to gain power. Success conferred its own legitimacy and was the best guarantee of staying in power.

The institution survived because it was the most effective means of
wielding authority. There were moments of greatness like under Shah
Abbas in the sixteenth century; but for the most part monarchs were
rarely enlightened and generally despotic: 'A significant part of that
heritage has been a relatively centralised, authoritarian monarchy that
used agricultural surpluses to maintain its army and bureaucracy,
leaving the majority of the people powerless, illiterate and poor.'[2]

Royal lineage, therefore, was not a prerequisite for kingship; it
merely helped sustain weak monarchs. More important was to show
powers of leadership, to be *farmandeh* ('commander of the people').
Thus when in 1925 the Peacock Throne was vacated by the last of the
Qajar kings, it was within tradition that Parliament should turn to the
strongest man, Reza Khan, and ask him to become Shah. It did not
matter that he was born completely outside the establishment and had
worked his way up the ranks of the army.

The First Pahlavi

By the present Shah's own account, his father was born in Mazanderan
Province near the Caspian Sea in 1878. His parents were minor military
stock. 'Both his father and grandfather had been officers in the old
Persian army.'[3] The family house is preserved today in the village of
Alasht high in the foothills of the Mazanderan Mountains — a village
very much as it must have been then with some 200 households living
in small mud brick houses with tin or thatched roofs. The school was
built only in 1932.[4]

At the age of fourteen he joined the Russian-commanded Persian
Cossack Brigade and worked his way through the ranks, first as an
illiterate private and then, by dint of study and force of personality,
became an officer. The Cossack Brigade was the country's only fight-

ing force, some 3,000 strong. Reza Khan was an imposing figure with cold piercing eyes, who distinguished himself among his fellow officers as a man of action and high integrity with a burning patriotism. As the British prepared to withdraw their forces from the north of the country in late 1920, Reza Khan was regarded as the most outstanding soldier in the Cossacks and his promotion was accelerated as the Russian officers were dismissed for fear they might sympathise with their Bolshevik comrades.

On the eve of British withdrawal Reza Khan was put in effective charge of the Cossacks by the British commander in the area, Major-General Sir Edmund Ironside, in the knowledge that he might well use his position to depose or confront the Shah.[5] This was precisely what he did — marching on Tehran from Qazvin, and presenting the Shah with an ultimatum to change his government on 21 February 1921.

After an uneasy interregnum of four years, Sultan Ahmad Shah was deposed by parliamentary vote in October 1925, thus ending a dynasty that had the distinction of providing only one ruler that relinquished his throne through natural death during 146 years. Having graduated from being Minister of War to Prime Minister at the time of Sultan Ahmad's deposition, Reza Khan was a logical, though not inevitable, choice as Shah.

Reza Khan, much impressed by the example of Mustapha Kemal (Atatürk) who had declared a republic in Turkey toyed with the idea of republicanism. 'I am sure that my father for a time preferred the concept of a republic,' his son said later.[6] At this stage his overriding concern was how best to unify the country, establish law and order and sweep away the decadence that had characterised the final years of the Qajar dynasty. There are two plausible explanations why he opted for a monarchy. Given the traditional fear of Russia and concern over the effects of the Bolshevik revolution, the creation of a republic might well have frightened many Iranians and confused them about what he was trying to do. Second, the mullahs, the powerful clergy, would have been very suspicious of the idea of a republic. Thus at a moment when unity was critical, the creation of a republic might have provided the grounds for further strife and disunity.

Reza Khan crowned himself Reza Shah Pahlavi on 25 April 1926. His choice of the name Pahlavi was highly significant. This symbolised his desire both to associate himself with the glories of Iran's past and to give a sense of legitimacy to the dynasty. Pahlavi was the language spoken by the Parthians who ruled Persia after Alexander the Great, and is considered to be the basis of the present Persian language. Reza Shah felt himself to be a ruler of true Persian origin unlike the Qajars (of Turkic origin).[7]

The need to justify the existence and legitimacy of the Pahlavi dynasty has been a continuing theme. It was less so with Reza Shah and has been more pronounced with his son. Reza Shah, for instance, continued to sleep on the floor, refusing a royal bed; he always regarded himself as a soldier and indeed the first time he wore civilian clothes in public was when he boarded the British ship at Bandar Abbas in September 1941 that was taking him into exile. Reza Shah, though continuing the practice of a Court, was a man of simple tastes with an intuitive rather than a polished intelligence. Even in later years he was not highly literate. Marvin Zonis in *The Political Elite of Iran* comments: 'The extent to which Reza Shah was illiterate as the shahanshah is a moot point but it seems probable that he was never wholly comfortable with the skill.'[8]

His purpose was relatively simple: the regeneration of Persia and an end to foreign interference. He changed the name of the country from Persia to Iran in 1934 — Iran being by origin the same word as Aryan. (Persians were just one of the Indo-European Aryan tribes that came to settle in what is now Iran.) He was an outright nationalist. He appreciated the importance of modernisation for Iran even if he did not always understand it. He approved the sending of students abroad, encouraged the foundation of Tehran University — the first secular institute of higher learning — and abolished the full veil for women.

But he developed dynastic ambitions. These were not limited to identifying the Pahlavis with the ancient past and a regenerated Iran. He decided to marry his son, Mohammed Reza, to King Farouk of Egypt's sister, Princess Fawzia. Without his son ever having cast eyes on her the marriage went through in 1939 with the Constitution being specially altered to get round the prohibition on inheritance of the Crown through a non-Iranian parent.[9] A Pahlavi had married into real royalty and it seemed a grand alliance.

Despite some appearances of modern rule, Reza Shah was despotic and utterly ruthless. He built up his own wealth through a mixture of gifts, cheap acquisitions and expropriation, mainly in land. Zonis calculates that

> by the time of Reza Shah's abdication, more than two thousand villages passed to the control of the new monarch. Using a measure of 4.8 persons per household, some 235,800 were in the direct service of His Imperial Majesty qua landlord.[10]

In fact immediately after the abdication there was a peasant revolt in his native Mazanderan province calling for restitution of property, some of which was subsequently restored.[11]

The desire to found a durable dynasty should not obscure his achievements. He restored a sense of national dignity and laid the groundwork for a modern state by establishing a civil service and a proper army. He also broke the power of the tribal chieftains who in the past had made government authority a fiction in many provinces. He had the same powers as Atatürk in Turkey and he used them to the same ends, yet with one major difference. He did not secularise Iran, perhaps because he wished to retain the importance of the Shiia Moslem beliefs that had given Iran its special Islamic character, or because he realised that he risked provoking the opposition of the powerful mullahs. As it was, many traditional Iranians considered him contemptuous of religion since he made it known the clergy were a brake on modernisation. 'If he had not treated them [the clergy] somewhat roughly, it might have taken three or four times as long as it did to carry out his programme of modernising the country,' his son observed later.[12] This no doubt is true but his unwillingness or inability to break the reactionary force of religion was to prove a serious handicap to his son, and also a political threat.

Unlike Atatürk he did not seek to create institutions of state or to incorporate the military into a semi-constitutional status as in Turkey. He merely strengthened the power and prerogatives of the monarchy at the expense of the Constitution which the intellectuals and bazaar merchants of the reform movement had wrung from the Qajar monarchy in 1906. The Constitution, based on that of Belgium, envisaged a constitutional monarchy; but Reza Shah quickly turned it into a dictatorship, using the threat of Soviet subversion, the need for powerful rule and through the sheer force of his personality.

> Proverbially to get things done in Persia one must both reward and punish. My father relied more on punishment than he did on reward or encouragement ... Oriental psychology in these matters differs from that of the West, and my father's methods for getting things done showed no little realism in the light of our authoritarian tradition.[13]

Like many dictators he surrounded himself with undistinguished subservient men, and the circle of advisers narrowed as he grew older — 'one of the few mistakes my father made.'[14] He also failed to come to terms with the perennial problem of corruption.

In the end Reza Shah was destroyed by events bigger than himself. His country and its oilfields had become of major significance to Britain. He rarely travelled outside Iran and failed to appreciate the extent to which his pro-German sympathies antagonised the British and the Soviets at the outbreak of the Second World War. Or if he appreciated this, he failed to realise that both Britain and the Soviet Union were capable of riding roughshod over Iranian sovereignty if they felt their vital interests were at stake. The signal for this was Hitler's invasion of the Soviet Union in June 1941. Two months later Allied troops moved into Iran, forcing an ignominious abdication which led to exile, first in Mauritius then Johannesburg, where he died in July 1944. (His body was subsequently embalmed in Egypt and after the war brought back to rest in a mausoleum built near Tehran at Rey.) These errors of judgement meant that his son was placed on the throne, aged only 21, as a virtual puppet of the Allies.

Mohammed Reza Shah

Mohammed Reza Shah is altogether a more complex character than his father. He had begun life as a commoner, born a twin with his sister Ashraf, on 26 October 1919. At the time of his father's coronation he was almost seven years old. From then on as the Crown Prince, he led a protected, rarefied existence singled out to learn the rules of kingship from a gruff intimidating father. He was a sickly child and narrowly escaped dying of typhoid. This sickliness, coupled with the strong influence of an imposing father created a determined youth, eager to prove and test himself to the limit – a characteristic he continued to show in later life in his love for flying. He was of slighter build than his father and seems to have developed a complex about his size (today he wears shoes with elevated platforms and insists that all photographs be taken so as not to emphasise his smallness).

In many ways he has become the antithesis of his father. Instead of Reza Shah's tough parade-ground manner used to giving orders, there is a rather shy, soft-spoken person who has had to learn a public manner. Reza Shah had a down-to-earth view of things; his son claims to have visions.[15] Reza Shah saw himself as a patriot; his son has gone beyond this and seeks to give his rule a sense of divine mission. He finds evidence of this divine mission in his amazingly lucky escapes from at least one dangerous air crash and five known assassination attempts. Of the assassination attempts two were nearly fatal: at Tehran University on 4 February 1949, when a young man in the guise of a photographer shot him five times, and on 10 April 1965 when a group of soldiers tried to gun their way past his guards at the Marble Palace.[16]

> When you think I've been wounded by a good five bullets, one in the face, one in the shoulder, one in the head, two in the body and the last one stuck in the barrel because the trigger jammed . . . You have to believe in miracles. I've had so many air disasters, and yet I've always come out unscathed — thanks to a miracle willed by God and the prophets.[17]

Mohammed Reza Shah had the benefit of a proper education, albeit a very cosseted one with selected sons of high officials in Tehran and later with the sons of wealthy Europeans at Le Rosey in Switzerland. He was the first Iranian monarch to have a foreign education. By his own account it was an important experience, opening his eyes to a wider world. (An interesting reflection of the times was his journey to Switzerland — by boat up the Caspian to Baku, and then by rail across the Soviet Union, through Poland and Germany.[18]) Though his Swiss schooling helped to rid him of his father's provincialism, it created a cultural schizophrenia — an admiration and fascination with Western culture, technology and institutions and yet a strong, almost chauvinistic attachment to the values and traditions of Iran.

This ambivalence towards Western culture has become more pronounced with time and lies behind his assertion that a regenerated Iran will soon take its place among the world's industrial powers in the Great Civilisation. It also helps explain his desire to justify his authoritarian system of government — something his father never felt the need to do. He made a revealing statement to Oriana Fallaci in this respect:

> Believe me, when three quarters of a nation doesn't know how to read or write, you can provide for reforms only by the strictest authoritarianism — otherwise you get nowhere. If I hadn't been harsh, I wouldn't even have been able to carry out agrarian reform and my whole reform programme would have stalemated.[19]

He has also felt the need to explain the monarchy to his own people. He has come to regard the monarch's role as a combination of father figure, revolutionary innovator and patriotic leader. An indication of this philosophy appeared in 1976 when on his orders a group of academics under the Chancellor of Tehran University drew up a 7,000 word document entitled 'The Philosophy of Iran's Revolution'. Though

in many respects merely an apologia for the Shah's actions in 1963 —
the crushing of parliamentary opposition and pressing ahead with the
so-called 'White Revolution', spearheaded by Land Reform — it is a
revealing document.

> In making revolution, the leader of the nation plays the crucial role.
> A strong enlightened leader, fully comprehending existing conditions,
> nurtures and develops the idea of revolution in his mind, transfers
> the idea to the people and then moves to implement it.[20]

In other words, the nation plays a purely passive role in decision-making
and only participates once a decision has been made. The document
had this to say about the monarch as leader and father figure:

> Although there have been strong and weak monarchs, for the people,
> the idea of monarchy extends beyond the individual. Monarchy is
> seen as more than merely an executive office. The periods of Iran's
> greatness have coincided with the rule of able monarchs. The distin-
> guishing characteristic of such monarchs has been that they rose
> from the people and that they were activists, fulfilling the traditional
> role of the monarch as 'farmandeh', as commander of his people.
> Such monarchs have always enjoyed the support of the mass of the
> people, with whom they are in direct relationship. Sometimes, this
> support has been expressed through a direct reference of questions
> by the monarch back to the people, as in the national referendum
> on reform ordered by the Shahanshah in 1963. The Shah and the
> People, according to the 'Philosophy of Iran's Revolution', consti-
> tute two superforces and they have allowed 'no intermediary or
> insulator to intervene in the direct relationship between them.'
>   Together they have ensured the survival of the Iranian nation.
> The Shahanshah moreover stands above class or the interests of
> special groups in society. He is king of all the people. He is also in
> a father-son relationship to the nation. The principal of heredity is
> linked to this: to the training of the Crown Prince, the transfer of
> kingly responsibility, preservation of national unity and integrity;
> the reinforcement of national confidence and the maintenance
> of the monarchy above class and group interests. The Shahanshah is
> not just the political leader of the country. He is also in the first
> instance teacher and spiritual leader, an individual who not only
> builds his nation roads, bridges, dams and qanats but also guides the
> spirit, thought and hearts of his people.[21]

This harks back to Mussolini and Franco (for *farmandeh* substitute *Duce* or *Caudillo*). It pays no regard to the idea of constitutional monarchy as envisaged in the 1906 Constitution and seeks to justify only two institutions in the political process – the monarch and the people. Parliament does not count as the legislature; and the judiciary is ignored in this mystical union between the Shah and his people. In essence this philosophy merely formalises authoritarian rule.

Contrary to appearances, going direct to the people is not populism, though it easily could be if the Shah chose to behave this way. The present Shah is not a dazzling public speaker: his diction is dull, he is too small to be imposing and he does not seem to respond to meeting the people and 'pumping the flesh'. Cold and distant public appearances are the rule, dictated in part by the fears of his security advisers (he travels virtually everywhere by helicopter). But it also seems that this is genuinely not his personality. He comes across better in private conversations and press interviews – a medium of expression he clearly enjoys.

The pomp and formality of the Imperial Court is both a protection against the outside world and a stage set to remind that Iran has a king. (The intricacies of formality and precedence also serve to feed the self-importance of those surrounding the Shah.) The Shah seeks to achieve his mystical union with the people more by remote control. He or another member of the Royal Family is always to be found on the front pages of the press or seen on television daily. His portrait in deliberate pose as The Leader, The Father Figure or in a trinity-like trio with the Empress and the Crown Prince is found throughout the country. A particularly telling official photograph depicts the Shah as though he is waving from the top of a mountain, the nation out of sight somewhere below.

There is an obsession with associating monuments and nomenclature with monarchy. The main monument in Tehran is called the Shahyad ('remember the Shah'); the new administrative and commercial centre in Tehran is called Shahestan Pahlavi (Place of the Pahlavi Shahs). All over the country dams, boulevards, parks, towns and even ships are called after the Shah, his family or his dynasty. Meanwhile school textbooks repeat at length the lesson of loyalty to the monarchy and the achievements of the Pahlavis. The ritual exposure of the Pahlavi dynasty and the royal person can only be attributed to insecurity, vanity, or a belief that this encourages loyalty. This in part explains the elaborate celebrations at Persepolis in October 1971 commemorating 2,500 years of monarchy; and the carefully orchestrated celebrations in 1976 for the fiftieth anniversary of the Pahlavi dynasty.

To underline the role of monarchy in Iran – and in particular the part played by the Pahlavis – a loyal Parliament in March 1976 voted in a new 'monarchy calendar'. The Islamic calendar based on the Hejira year (introduced in Iran by Reza Shah) was altered in favour of a system based on the coronation of Cyrus the Great 2,535 years ago. *Kayhan* commented:

> Parliament thought it fitting that the Iranian calendar be based on such an omnipresent and intrinsic element of Iran's history. The decision itself is also a tribute to the Pahlavi dynasty in particular and to other dynasties in the same class.[22]

The change took the country by surprise and provoked considerable opposition, especially among the mullahs. The Shah's opponents persisted in using the old calendar, regarding the change as unconstitutional and a cheap means of the Shah exploiting Iran's past glories.

It is noteworthy that these moves to reinforce the institution and appeal of monarchy became more evident once Mohammed Reza Shah had acquired a male heir. From his first marriage through to his third with Farah Diba, the Shah had to wait impatiently for 21 years to obtain a male successor.[23] In fact he did not hold his coronation until 1967 partly because of this. When he did finally hold a coronation he crowned himself like his father, though this time in addition to being Shahanshah he had also acquired the title Aryamehr (Light of the Aryans).[24]

Formative Experiences

The Shah now virtually ignores the events of his reign before 1962, which heralded the beginning of Land Reform and the launching of the 'White Revolution'. This is understandable since it was only then that he felt able to do what he wanted unimpeded by opposition, external and internal. The period from his accession in 1941 up until 1963 was a difficult, testing and occasionally embarrassing era. But it cannot be forgotten for it was a period of formative experience, which is best understood in three compartments: 1941-51, the early years in which he sought to break loose from the Great Powers and restore national confidence after the Allied occupation in the Second World War; 1951-3, the trial of strength with Mossadegh over oil nationalisation that forced him to flee and be restored with American support; 1954-63, the gradual strengthening of royal authority and the ruthless establishment of internal security leading to the elimination of parliamentary opposition.

For the duration of the Second World War the Shah had to go along with the Allies. It had been made perfectly clear to him by the forced abdication of his father that so long as Hitler remained a threat and the Soviet Union needed a southern supply route, Iran would be occupied. The Shah's first real test came at the end of the war in 1945 when he sought to have Soviet and British troops withdraw from Iranian soil in what is known as the Azerbaijan crisis. British and Soviet troops were pledged to withdraw from Iran by March 1946; but as the months passed the Soviet forces withdrew only as far as Qazvin and appeared in no hurry to move. Then in November, inside the zone still occupied by Soviet troops, two autonomous republics were proclaimed — the Autonomous Republic of Azerbaijan and the Kurdish Republic of Mahabad. The threat posed by the republics and the Soviet occupation was threefold. The republics played on regional differences (the Kurdish Republic talked of incorporating parts of Turkey and Iraq) that could lead to a Balkanisation of Iran. Second, Iran faced the prospect of coming firmly within the sphere of Soviet influence as the two republics were already dependent upon the Soviet Union for protection and supplies. Finally, the republics, with their anti-monarchist tone and clear sympathy for socialism and Communism, were an encouragement to these political forces in the rest of the country, already fostered under a weak monarch during the war.

Initial Iranian moves to deal with the crisis were ineffectual. Iranian troops sent to Azerbaijan could get no further than Qazvin, where they were halted by Soviet forces. The British and Americans, so soon after their wartime alliance with the Soviet Union, seemed reluctant to confront Stalin, or were genuinely waiting to get the measure of Moscow's intentions. The matter was taken to the newly established Security Council of the United Nations; but in the end it was direct negotiations by the Iranian Prime Minister, Ahmad Qavam, regarded then as a Soviet sympathiser, that managed to persuade the Soviet forces to withdraw by dangling the promise of oil concessions in northern Iran. Soviet troops withdrew in May 1946, and before the end of the year the two republics had collapsed. Iranian forces took over Tabriz and Rezaieh, their respective headquarters, unopposed.

The Soviet action in retrospect still is not fully comprehensible. Iran was being used in the first feinting gestures of the Cold War; but in the purely Iranian context did Stalin believe that the presence of Soviet troops and the creation of two people's republics would topple a weak monarch and establish a sympathetic régime on the long underbelly of the Soviet Union? If he did, it proved a clumsy gesture that underestimated traditional Iranian distrust of Russia and led to the destruction of the Tudeh (Communist) Party — especially in Azerbaijan — which had been carefully built up during the War. The Soviets also underestimated the mood of the Iranian Parliament, which refused to ratify the agreement for oil concessions in northern Iran.

This incident reinforced the Shah's mistrust of the Soviet Union, which had already been well nurtured by his father. In 1907 the British and the Russians had concluded a treaty agreeing on a division of their spheres of control — the British taking the south and the Russians the north, with Iran getting a 'neutral' slice of territory in the centre. Soviet troops had occupied northern Iran during the First World War, and one of the first acts of the Bolshevik government in 1920 was to support the short-lived Soviet Republic of Gilan on the Caspian.

The Azerbaijan crisis was to imbue the Shah with a permanent suspicion of the Soviet Union and a mistrust of Communism in general. Reflecting in his memoirs, the Shah had this to say:

> Communism seeks to exploit not only the political, economic and social weakness of the emerging lands but also their military vulnerability. If a country fails to secure its defences, the communists play with it as a cat does with a mouse. During the Azerbaijan crisis, and again in Mossadegh's time, we Persians found ourselves in the unhappy role of the mouse. We resolved never again to be so unprotected.[25]

December 12 has become Azerbaijan day and each year a big military parade commemorates it.

Communism and Marxism have thus come to be regarded as hostile ideologies unacceptable to Iran, and their practice outlawed. The Shah himself claims that all his political prisoners are Marxists.[26] The Azerbaijan crisis put the Shah firmly in the anti-Soviet camp, aligning him with Britain and the US. Equally important, it determined the Shah that national sovereignty could only be protected by a strong army. Indeed the Azerbaijan crisis, backed up by all the indignities of occupation during the First and Second World Wars, contributed to the Shah's almost obsessive concern with Iran's security. It is this that explains in large measure his subsequent moves to create the region's most modern and largest defence forces.

The experience also conditioned the pattern of Iran's regional allian-

ces. The Shah's strong links with Israel developed in the 1950s out of
his belief that the Zionist state was an effective bastion against Communism and the rising tide of Arab nationalism which seemed aimed against
monarchies and Soviet-inspired. Mistrust of Communism led to the
gradual deterioration of relations with the Baathist government in Iraq
after the overthrow of King Feisal; and it later prompted the Shah to
support (along with Israel) moves for Kurdish autonomy in Iraq. The
despatch of an expeditionary force to Oman was motivated in part by
fears that the radical ideology of the Marxist government in South
Yemen might spread throughout the Arabian Peninsular. More recently
fears of increased Soviet influence in the Horn of Africa have led to
Iranian small arms supplies for Somalia against Ethiopia.

Iran's close ties with Pakistan, which have survived differing styles
of Pakistani leadership, have been dictated by apprehensions over
India's attitude towards the Soviet Union. This was particularly the case
in 1971 following the Soviet-Indian Treaty of Friendship which led to
powerful Iranian financial backing for Pakistan and the gift of military
hardware. Conversely, once the Shah became reassured of India's independence *vis-à-vis* the Soviet Union, relations improved. By the same
token, the end of the Nasser era in Egypt and President Sadat's expul-
sion of his Soviet military advisers in 1972 led to increasingly close
ties between Iran and Egypt.

The Challenge from Mossadegh

The Azerbaijan crisis was primarily a challenge to the sovereignty of
Iran. The 1951-3 period when Mohammed Mossadegh became Prime
Minister was a direct challenge to the Shah's authority as monarch —
and he came very close to losing.

The extent of the Shah's powers had been an issue during the
Azerbaijan crisis. The Prime Minister, Ahmad Qavam, had been delegated much of the diplomatic leg-work and on occasions became enormously frustrated at the ambiguous nature of where his power ended and
that of the Shah began.[27] His view and that of Parliament was a constitutional one, intimately linked with the lengthy struggle to obtain a
constitutional monarchy under the last of the Qajars. It was a simmer-
ing conflict that sooner or later was bound to create a confrontation,
especially with a monarch who was anxious to assert himself.

Mossadegh became Prime Minister on 28 April 1951, at the age of
70, having held a variety of posts, including the portfolio of Foreign
Affairs and the Finance Ministry under Reza Shah (who incidentally
imprisoned him once and threatened exile on another occasion).

Without doubt Mossadegh was the country's most seasoned politician. He had been denied the premiership until then, in good measure due to his ill-concealed contempt for the Pahlavi dynasty, whom he regarded as social upstarts and unconstitutional. (His opinion was not unconnected with his mother being related to the deposed Qajar dynasty.[28])

He had made himself into a national hero by playing skilfully on the Iranian hatred of the foreigners, symbolised by AIOC, which was exploiting Iran's vital oil resources. Well before coming to office he had made a platform out of oil nationalisation. Even if this was against the Shah's better judgement it was a policy he was in no position to oppose. Mossadegh knew this and stipulated nationalisation of AIOC as a precondition of accepting office. Once in office this was his first move, but it soon became clear that he was as much concerned to humiliate the Pahlavis as nationalise the oil industry.

For the next eighteen months Mossadegh ruled Iran, gradually eroding the Shah's authority and isolating him from political contact. He forced the Shah's twin sister, Princess Ashraf, into exile in the belief (almost certainly correct) that she had great influence over the Shah and was a more determined and scheming person. Mossadegh set in motion a careful scrutiny of how the Pahlavi family had built up a vast fortune in less than a generation. The distribution of Crown Lands was halted because Mossadegh argued that the Shah had no right to obtain kudos from the distribution of possessions illegally acquired. Moreover, he sought to weed out pro-Shah elements within the armed forces, realising that once stripped of the armed forces' loyalty the Shah was impotent.

The erosion of royal authority culminated on 16 August 1953 when the Shah abortively sought to replace Mossadegh. Mossadegh promptly announced that the Shah had attempted to overthrow him. The Shah, who for months had geared himself up to the prospect of fleeing the country, now did precisely this — first to Baghdad and then on to Rome. The next day the statues of the Shah were pulled down in Tehran. Yet in an extraordinary change of fortune the tide was turned against Mossadegh within three days. A combination of support from outside, in the form of the CIA, loyal troops within the armed forces and paid mobs recruited in the Bazaar re-established control in Tehran — successfully capitalising on the mood of doubt and confusion that developed in the wake of the Shah's flight. From being an exiled king morosely buying presents in Rome boutiques to console his wife, the Shah was able to return to a 'heartwarming, tumultuous welcome'.[29]

Mossadegh was arrested and put on public trial in November charged

with treason. Although his Foreign Minister, Hussein Fatemi, was tried
for the same offence and executed, Mossadegh was given three years'
imprisonment. He then was allowed to live in his country house near
Tehran in what amounted to house arrest until his death in 1967. A
full account of this turbulent period is still not possible, but some
judgement has to be made of Mossadegh.[30]

From the start Mossadegh made one important miscalculation. He
believed that the Americans, who had no stake in the Anglo-Iranian
Oil Company, would support nationalisation. This belief was based on
American resentment of Britain's role in the region and the influence
flowing from British involvement in AIOC. His misreading of the scene
was not entirely his own fault as the American Ambassador in Tehran,
Henry Grady, encouraged this view.[31] In the event the Americans
sided with the British, at first merely to ensure that nationalisation did
not work. Then, as they feared the Soviet Union might exploit the situation and the outlawed Tudeh Party gain ground in Iran, they considered the more drastic solution of overthrowing Mossadegh. This was
preferred to direct military intervention, although at one stage British
paratroops were on standby in Cyprus.

The opposition of Britain and the US to Mossadegh was crucial, but
the role of the CIA in all this can be exaggerated. The fact that America
chose to withhold aid and deny loans when all oil revenue was halted
proved a vital destabilising factor, which created a propitious climate
for subversion. Subversion was primarily orchestrated by the CIA, and
the man responsible, Kermit Roosevelt, has never disguised the agency's
role. However the Shah has preferred to portray Mossadegh's overthrow
as a spontaneous expression of pro-Shah loyalty.[32]

In retrospect there are striking similarities between American behaviour over Mossadegh and the toppling of President Allende in Chile.
Both were men embarked on paths considered too dangerous to tolerate. Apart from blocking aid, the Americans acted as co-ordinator,
financier and counter-propagandist. The reports that appeared in the
press at the time played up three themes — the infiltration of Communist elements, Mossadegh's growing dependence upon Tudeh support
and the grotesque gestures and appearance of Mossadegh, who was
invariably ridiculed for his tearful outbursts or his press conferences in
pyjamas. As to whether he played into the hands of the Tudeh Party,
most of the evidence produced so far has been one-sided, with a vested
interest in proving that he was a figurehead whom the Communists
would dump once he had served his purpose.

Having miscalculated the American position, Mossadegh compounded his difficulties by failing to see the problems of selling oil in a cartel market. By the same token he underestimated the economic consequences of the loss of oil revenue. Thus the euphoria of nationalisation favoured him so long as nationalisation was seen to be working. As time dragged by without the expected results, people became impatient, and the conservative elements, who for nationalistic reasons had applauded the move, were turned against him by propaganda that he was encouraging the Communists. Indeed as conservative support waned, so he had to lean more on the socialist- and Communist-minded. It was also a natural, though dangerous, bargaining move to threaten the British and Americans with a closer Soviet alliance – his only area of diplomatic manoeuvre.

Mossadegh lost out not merely because his moves were poorly planned. He underestimated the strength of the opposition, and he did not have sufficient support within the armed forces. The crucial issue was confirmation of the traditional adage that an Iranian ruler survives as long as he is successful. So long as Mossadegh was on top the Shah could command little support; but as Mossadegh's position weakened, the Iranians once again began to hedge their bets.

Consolidation of Power

Despite all his mistakes and the greater strength of his opponents, Mossadegh nearly held the field. For Mohammed Reza Shah it was a traumatic experience that had a lasting effect on his view of government. From now on he was determined that the Prime Minister be a servant of the Crown, and that defence of the Crown be the single most important consideration.

Those who served him well during this period were handsomely rewarded and still hold key positions. General Nematollah Nassiri, latterly head of SAVAK, the Iranian security services, was the man designated to deliver the fateful message dismissing Mossadegh on 16 August 1953. Mohammed Khatemi, the pilot of the aircraft that flew the Shah out of Iran, rose to become Commander-in-Chief of the Air Force, married the Shah's half-sister, Princess Fatima, and was a central figure in the armed forces establishment until his death in an accident in 1975.[33] Those who offered financial assistance were subsequently well placed to obtain monopolies or contracts. Amir Hushang Davalou, an aristocratic figure related to the Qajars, was in France in 1953 but put his funds at the Shah's disposal. His reward was the concession to export caviar to Europe. Sir Shapoor Reporter (knighted for his services to Britain) acquired a major entrée to the business world, having helped coordinate intelligence activities. Those who hedged their bets were not forgiven, like the Iranian Ambassador in Baghdad who tried to get the Shah arrested, or the chargé d'affaires in Rome who refused to let the Shah have his own car keys.[34]

With the Shah's successful reinstatement the Americans supplanted the British, fashioning a new role as protector and guarantor. Within a month of Mossadegh's fall Eisenhower had approved $45 million in emergency economic aid, even though the nationalisation issue had not yet been settled. Between 1949 and 1952 America had provided a total of $33 million in grants and loans; but between 1953 and 1957 a total of $500 million was extended, of which one-quarter was earmarked for the military.[35]

America had already acquired a small foothold in 1943 when asked to reorganise the gendarmerie, turning it into a full paramilitary force. But the trust earned from helping the Shah over Mossadegh paved the way for deeper involvement. The instruments were economic and military aid and assistance in reorganising the security services. American aid and technical assistance established the security agency SAVAK (coined from its Iranian name Sazeman-e Ettala'at va Amniyate Khasvar) in 1957.[36] This organisation was also assisted by the Israeli intelligence service, Mosad. The Shah had already turned to the Israelis for the provision of his personal security after deciding outsiders were more efficient and trustworthy.[37]

SAVAK was to become a key instrument in the Shah's acquisition of absolute power. Just as Mossadegh eroded the Shah's power in 1951, so the Shah now set about consolidating his own position, at the expense of the political parties and Parliament. Political parties were banned and replaced by two puppet parties, the Melliyun (Nationalist) and the Mardom (People's) parties, headed by loyal lieutenants of the Shah. Press censorship became tight. All this was backed up by a ruthless suppression of suspected opponents, especially those with links to the National Front Party of Mossadegh or the Tudeh Party.[38] The armed forces were thoroughly purged of suspect members. Some 600 Tudeh members were said to have infiltrated and had even got as far as being accepted into the élite Imperial Guard.[39] The Shah also made sure that a careful watch was kept on the clergy, and moved to suppress any power that the Bazaar might wield. He was trusting few people and relied upon a contracting circle of loyal associates.

The political parties finally expired after a brief rally between 1960 and 1963. When encouraged in the belief that the Kennedy administration supported greater liberalisation, former followers of Mossadegh sought to prevent the Shah assuming absolute power. Under pressure from the Americans, the Shah appointed a former Mossadegh Finance Minister, Dr Ali Amini, as Prime Minister. Since the Shah was known to dislike the man intensely this was interpreted as a sign of weakness. The National Front took heart and began to reorganise. The party quickly proved that the name of Mossadegh was still an emotive rally for all shades of opposition.

A confrontation with authority was inevitable – the National Front had been accused of inciting Tehran University students that provoked an exceptionally bloody army raid.[40] More seriously, it was calling for a return to constitutional government and demanded a boycott of a national referendum called by the Shah to approve Land Reform. The Shah at one stage considered having the National Front co-opted into the Cabinet as a means of controlling them. When this idea failed he went on the offensive.

National Front members were rounded up and the referendum went ahead to a predictable success – 5.5 million in favour of Land Reform out of 6.1 million eligible voters. There was now only one real source of opposition: the clergy, whose spearhead was a fiery mullah and theologian, Ayatollah (a special title accorded only to the most respected mullahs) Khomeini. He opposed Land Reform, arguing that it was against Islam, and likewise opposed enfranchisement of women. It was a reactionary position, but he expressed it with passion and he attracted a large following, especially among the urban poor suspicious of the Shah's efforts to modernise and bitter at their exclusion from the benefits of oil money.

In 1963, immediately after moharram (the holiest period in the Shiite year), Khomeini was arrested in Qom, provoking the worst riots of the century which raged throughout the country's major cities for three days. In response the Shah countenanced a bloody law and order operation by the army which resulted in serious loss of life – perhaps over 1,000 killed or seriously wounded.[41] This ferocity cowed the opposition as the message was now clear: the army would be used to back up the régime whenever necessary. The Shah's gamble had paid off: the suppression of the riots curbed the mullahs and their faithful supporters, who could draw in elements who were not necessarily religious, but who could use religion as a front for political protest.

There now followed a period of disaffected calm which was to set the pattern for the coming years: a docile rubber-stamp Parliament, the appointment of technocrat Ministers and the increased use of SAVAK for political repression. The only remaining protest was desultory opposition from within the universities which, despite closures and arrests, continued to flare up. The mullahs also continued to protest but in lower key and they were easily arrested. Faced with tough and heavy-handed repression, a number of the educated élite preferred exile abroad.

Subsequently, an underground guerrilla movement emerged, mainly carrying out acts of sabotage and attacks on SAVAK or SAVAK-associated personnel. The guerrilla movement attracted members from both the extreme right and the extreme left, relying for its main strength upon disaffected students. They were denounced as 'Islamic Marxists' by the authorities who invented a common ideological brand. However, this blurred the distinction between those who espoused Marxist revolutionary views (and who had had training in China, Eastern Europe, Cuba or latterly in hostile Arab countries) and a more home-grown right-wing fanaticism. But their actions were never more than irritants and their operational strength at any one time was no greater than 300.

Opposition from within the system ceased to present any serious challenge as well. Amini was the last Prime Minister with any authority of his own – and he lasted under two years. He had sought to control the Shah's heavy spending on the military and initiated a tough anti-corruption campaign. Yet the removal of the National Front from politics and the suppression of all opposition eliminated Amini's power base and the Shah was able to ditch him in early 1963. A similar fate befell his radically minded Agriculture Minister, Hassan Arsanjani. His fault was to have been too good at his job and too popular among the peasants on whose behalf he was carrying out Land Reform.[42] Others who troubled the Shah were eliminated in various ways – some civilised, others brutal. General Zahedi, who had played a critical role in the overthrow of Mossadegh and who succeeded him as a 'loyal' Prime Minister in 1953, was subsequently obliged to retire to Geneva – he had become too powerful. General Pakravan, the donnish second head of SAVAK, was pensioned off as Ambassador to Pakistan for allegedly being too accommodating to the Shah's opponents.

The fate of the first head of SAVAK, General Bahktiar, was more dramatic. Bahktiar apparently took no part in the overthrow of Mossadegh; but his competence attracted the Shah and he was of the same clan as Soraya Esfandiari, the Shah's second wife. Having built SAVAK into a very powerful organisation, Bahktiar was dismissed in 1961 – the Shah forestalling the man from having ambitions of his own. A year later he was 'invited' to leave Iran for Europe. He then went into exile, associating himself more and more with the opposition, even collaborating with the Baathist government in Baghdad to attack the Shah. He died in what was officially reported as a hunting accident some twenty miles inside the Iraqi frontier in August 1970. The Shah subsequently admitted that he had been eliminated by SAVAK.[43]

This background makes something of a mockery of the 'White Revolution' or the 'Shah-People Revolution' that began in 1962. The White Revolution merely marked the end of a Western-style parliamentary democracy and the beginning of absolute monarchy. For the Shah the revolution was symbolised by the overwhelming support given to his six-point referendum held on 26 January 1963. The points were: (i) the abolition of the landlord-serf relationship; (ii) nationalisation of the forests; (iii) sale of government factories to pay for Land Reform; (iv) amendment of the election law, including the enfranchisement of women; (v) approval of workers sharing company profits; (vi) establishment of a literacy corps to facilitate compulsory education.[44]

There is no doubt that these reforms were needed. The Shah's argument is that without a referendum these reforms would have been obstructed in Parliament. However, this ignores two essential points. First, the reforms, populist in tone, were in response to a deteriorating political situation where the Shah needed to attract popular support. A characteristic of his reign has been the ability to respond to pressure before it gets too strong (like the distribution of Crown lands or in 1975 the launching of workers' profit-sharing schemes — first approved in the referendum). Second, the opposition to reforms in Parliament was less against the policies and much more against the Shah's attempts to gain absolute power.

The importance attached by the Shah to the referendum result and his propagandist promotion of the idea that a 'revolution' had taken place reveals an interesting ambivalence. At the level of power politics, the Shah accepts that strong authoritarian rule is essential. 'To get things done you need power, and to keep power you shouldn't have to ask permission or advice from anyone,' he is on record as saying.[45] Yet emotionally there is an apparently genuine belief in a special bond between Shah and people. Practically, he knows he must exclude the people, emotionally he wants to include them. This ambivalence permits him to ignore how others view the political process in Iran.

Two years before the White Revolution he had this to say about dictatorships:

Communist dictators resemble Fascist ones in that they both enjoy holding elections. They hope to give the ordinary working man the

idea that he has a voice in the Government of his country. But the
Communist rulers allow only one political party; anybody who tries
to start another, or who speaks against the ruling party, is likely to
be liquidated. In the elections (if you can call them by that name),
the voter has no choice, for the only candidates listed are those of
the ruling party. Purely as a matter of form, the citizen is urged or
ordered to go and vote; the authorities then triumphantly announce
that, let us say 99.9 per cent of the votes cast were for the ruling
party. I wonder how many intelligent people are fooled by that
sort of thing.[46]

In fact the Shah was giving a preview of his own style of government.
He even established a single party system in March 1975 — the Rastakhiz (Resurgence) Party — apparently tired of orchestrating two loyal
parties and concerned lest one party be used as an opposition base.[47]
The one difference between Iran and the situation he described was
that throughout the 1960s oil was generating a great deal of ready cash
which was used to bend or buy friend and foe. The mystical union of
Shah and people owes much to the material benefits of the oilfields.

Notes

1. Amin Alimard and Cyrus Elahi, 'Modernisation and Changing leadership in
Iran', paper delivered to Persepolis Symposium, September 1975. Published as
Iran: Past, Present and Future (New York, Aspen Institute for Humanistic Studies,
1976), p. 217.
2. Ibid., p. 218. For a penetrating early view of government and the role of
kings, see Nizam ul-Milk, *Siyasat Nama (The Book of Government or Rules for
Kings)*, translated by Hubert Drake (London, Routledge and Kegan Paul, 1960).
3. Mohammed Reza Shah Pahlavi, *Mission for My Country* (London, Hutchinson, 1974 edition), p. 35.
4. *Kayhan International*, 27 March 1976.
5. Denis Wright, *The English amongst the Persians* (London, Heinemann,
1977), pp. 181-3. This contains previously unpublished material from the Ironside diaries. Ironside's version contradicts slightly Mohammed Reza Shah's version
which claims his father 'engineered the dismissal of the Russians'. Mohammed
Reza Shah Pahlavi, *Mission*, p. 38.
6. Ibid., p. 39.
7. Ibid., p. 35.
8. Marvin Zonis, *The Political Elite of Iran* (Princeton, N.J., Princeton University Press, 1971), p. 124. Reza Shah's lack of education should not be taken out of
context. At the time of his birth less than 10 per cent of the country's population
were literate due to the absence of schools.
9. Zonis describes the marriage as the Shah's 'first great service to the monarchy, his country and legitimacy of his father's rule' (ibid., p. 20). Fawziia left the
Shah in 1947 and was granted a divorce in 1948. She never liked Tehran and was

apparently unhappy with the Shah, though they produced a daughter, Princess Shahnaz. Princess Ashraf, the Shah's twin sister, also married an Egyptian, Ahmad Chafik, but as her second husband.

10. Ibid., p. 55.

11. Ibid., p. 56.

12. Mohammed Reza Shah, *Mission*, p. 47.

13. Ibid., p. 49.

14. Ibid., p. 322.

15. Ibid., pp. 54-5.

16. The three other known attempts were: on 19 May 1967 a commando group attacked the royal car but the Shah was not riding in it; on 4 June 1967 an Iranian student tried to use a car laden with explosives as an assassination device while the Shah was visiting West Berlin; in April 1973 a plot was uncovered to assassinate the Shah and kidnap the Empress. Two persons were subsequently executed for this plot.

17. Oriana Fallaci, *Interview with History*, translated by John Shepley (Boston, Houghton Mifflin, 1977), p. 269. This interview is the most revealing of his character of all the many granted to journalists during his reign.

18. Mohammed Reza Shah Pahlavi, *Mission*, p. 55.

19. Fallaci, *Interview*, p. 273.

20. *Kayhan International*, 11 November 1976.

21. Ibid.

22. *Kayhan International*, 15 March 1976.

23. The Shah married Soraya Esfandiari in 1951 and divorced her in 1958 after a childless but apparently happy marriage. He told Fallaci of the break-up: 'for a certain period of time, it was one of the greatest sorrows of my life. But reason prevailed very soon, and I asked myself the following question: what must I do for my country? And the answer was find another spouse with whom to share my destiny and from whom to ask for an heir to the throne:' Fallaci, *Interview*, pp. 269-70.

24. The title 'Shahanshah' derives from the fact that the ancient Persian monarchs had sovereignty over four kings — Afghanistan, Georgia, Kurdistan and Arabistan (now Khuzestan but still called Arabistan in many Arab textbooks).

25. Mohammed Reza Shah, *Mission*, p. 296.

26. Interview with BBC reproduced in *Kayhan International*, 18 December 1976. 'Two things are not allowed in this country. One is communism which is outlawed. The second is insulting the person of the King who has been revered by our people for such a long time . . . First of all there are not more than 3,300 political prisoners and it happens to be that all of them are Marxists.'

27. The Shah comments in his memoirs: 'One day he [Qavam] told me that he wished I would either make all decisions or give him a completely free hand. It was obvious he wanted the latter.' *Mission*, p. 116.

28. 'Mossadegh had relatives of Qajar blood, and he himself bitterly resented my father's coming to power. His policy was clearly to do everything possible to discredit the Pahlavi dynasty and to advance slowly, a millimetre a day, towards exterminating it,' the Shah notes. *Mission*, p. 97.

29. Ibid., p. 105.

30. Zonis, *The Political Elite*, p. 70.

31. Anthony Sampson, *The Seven Sisters* (London, Hodder and Stoughton, Coronet edition, 1976), p. 132.

32. Gerard de Villiers, *L'Irresistible Ascension de Mohammed Reza, Shah d'Iran* (Paris, Plon, 1975), pp. 221-50. This is a racy account but includes material based on an interview with Kermit Roosevelt. Also see Andrew Tully, *Central Intelligence Agency* (London, Arthur Barker, 1962), pp. 91-101.

33. General Khatemi took over command of the Imperial Iranian Air Force in

1958. He was an outstanding athlete and a magnetic figure in the services. He was killed in a water ski-gliding accident on the Dez Dam in September 1975. While alive he was generally regarded as the man who would hold the armed forces loyal if anything were to happen to the Shah, the Air Force being crucial in this respect.

34. Mohammed Reza Shah Pahlavi, *Mission*, p. 105.

35. Zonis, *The Political Elite*, pp. 108-9.

36. Established one year later was the Imperial Iranian Inspectorate intended as a special watchdog body for the Shah with responsibility for also surveying SAVAK.

37. Assistance from Israeli intelligence has never been confirmed either in Iran or Israel, but the author is satisfied by the veracity of this assertion after checking in both Tehran and Tel Aviv. Since the end of the Kurdish revolt in 1975 Israeli intelligence has been less in evidence in Iran.

38. Zonis, *The Political Elite*, p. 43.

39. Mohammed Reza Shah Pahlavi, *Mission*, p. 105.

40. Zonis, *The Political Elite*, pp. 72-3.

41. Assadollah Alam, the then Prime Minister, said 86 people were killed. In a later interview he gave his views of what happened. See Margaret Laing, *The Shah* (London, Sidgwick and Jackson, 1977), pp. 168-9. The author has been told by ex-National Front members that the total of seriously wounded and killed was over 1,500. The estimate has been scaled down against anticipated exaggeration.

42. Zonis, *The Political Elite*, pp. 54-61.

43. De Villiers, *L'Irresistible Ascension*, p. 322.

44. *Iran Almanac*, 1977, p. 387.

45. Fallaci, *Interview*, p. 266.

46. Mohammed Reza Shah Pahlavi, *Mission*, p. 162. Later in the same chapter the Shah says: 'If I were a dictator rather than a constitutional monarch, then I might be tempted to sponsor a single dominant party such as Hitler organised or such as you find today in Communist countries' (p. 173).

47. In an interview with West German TV published in *Kayhan International*, 18 September 1975, the Shah said: 'The old system [multi-party] was no longer efficient, since whichever party was in power would claim all the benefits of progress and minority parties were 100 per cent the losers, despite the fact that they were totally loyal. With the new system minority politicians have been given a chance to participate and cooperate with the Government.'

PART II
CYCLE OF THE BOOM

5 THE BIG OPPORTUNITY

It is the earnest hope of all Iranians, guided by their great leader His Imperial Majesty the Shahanshah Aryamehr and inspired by his wise commands, that this Plan will prove to be the spearhead of one of the country's most brilliant and significant transformations, and that its implementation will bring greater prosperity to the nation and its people, and guide Iran more rapidly to the period of the Great Civilisation.[1]

In January 1974 the Plan and Budget Organisation (PBO) began examining the effect of the new price of oil which had quadrupled during the course of the previous year. From the start the planners were under tremendous pressure. Their instructions were to draw up in as short a time as possible a blueprint of what to do with the oil money. The existing Plan, the Fifth Five Year Plan, due to run from March 1973 to March 1978, had been operating for less than a year. To begin making substantial alterations so early was bound to be disruptive, especially as there were already signs of an overheated economy; but the planners knew the Shah wanted a large upwards revision of expenditure and national goals to reflect Iran's dramatically altered position.

It was an unsatisfactory brief, to say the least. But it was made a little easier to execute by the fact that the PBO had already begun at the end of the previous year to consider raising the level of investment under the existing Plan. By July 1974, the PBO had prepared a framework for the revision of the Plan based on three alternative scenarios. The alternatives centred round public sector investment – the main motor for disbursing oil revenue. The scenarios were as follows: a 'modest' (31 per cent) increase in public sector investment from Rs1,548 billion* to Rs2,028 billion; a medium (98 per cent) increase to Rs3,064 billion and a high (141 per cent) increase to Rs3,730 billion.[2]

At the same time the Ministries had been asked to submit their own individual estimates of their proposed new expenditure. These submissions, coupled with the alternative scenarios of the Plan, were presented at a special session of senior officials and Ministers, presided over by the Prime Minister, Amir Abbas Hoveida, at the mountain resort of Gajareh near Tehran. This was a workshop session during which the blueprint was redrawn. Then there followed a more formal meeting from 1 to 3 August at Ramsar on the Caspian, presided over by the

*Iranian rials.

Shah, which approved the revised target of the Plan.

None of these crucial meetings was public except speeches by the Shah, and the local press neither sought, nor was allowed, to gauge how this restricted debate was conducted. The Iranian public was simply presented with the end result and attendant rhetoric like the chapter opening. The result was the doubling of expenditure to Rs4,698 billion ($69 billion) and acceptance of a public sector investment target of Rs3,118 billion ($45 billion) just above the PBO's medium scenario.

Versions of what happened during these meetings are fragmentary. According to Abdol Majid Majidi, Director-General of the PBO at the time, he was fully aware of the dangers of opting for high growth and seeking to spend so much money so quickly. He pointed out the problems inherent in the shortage of skilled manpower, the likely shortfall in electricity supplies, the inadequacy of construction materials and the bottlenecks in the ports.[3] He also maintained that this view was shared by the other Ministry most directly concerned with the economy, the Ministry of Finance (which had been reorganised in June 1974), and the Central Bank. The Finance Minister, Hushang Ansari, said he was fully aware of the problems of high growth but nevertheless approved a 'maximalist' approach.[4] However, pointing out the dangers of trying to spend too much too quickly was one thing, actually opposing such action was another. At Gajareh only certain officials of the PBO were willing to argue against the general mood that favoured spending as much as possible. Indeed according to one report, Majidi did not seek to defend very vigorously the views of people in his own Ministry.[5]

By the time of the Ramsar meeting there were really only three actors – the Shah, the Prime Minister Amir Abbas Hoveida, and Majidi. The decision on what to do was to be the Shah's: Hoveida was there like an obedient doctor to give the Shah the political pulse of the country, Majidi was the Harvard-trained technocrat with the statistics and the projections. The Shah through the alchemy of his leadership would turn this into national objectives in the march towards the Great Civilisation.

Back in December 1973, the Shah still sounded relatively cautious, at least compared to his subsequent tone. He had announced that the Plan would be enlarged 'maybe by one third'. But he had given the impression that this was the upper limit because of the inflationary effects greater expenditure would have.[6] Yet by the time of the first meeting at Gajareh, he had abandoned earlier caution. His opening remarks to the Ramsar conference set the tone:

Those present at Persepolis where the original Plan was shaped can remember that I personally advocated higher goals, more difficult targets ... I did so because in my own mind the future course of events entailing the Plan's revision had already been clearly designed.[7]

The Shah and Hoveida showed a certain contempt for the cautious views of the economists who could not see beyond problems to a broader vision of an industrialised Iran. The Shah was also dismissive of those who did not share his vision of Iran's future as the world's fifth industrial power by the turn of the century. Against conventional wisdom the Shah had opted for what was considered a very ambitious investment target of $10.88 billion in the Fourth Plan (1968-72) and had been vindicated — largely as a result of the increased oil revenues arising from the 1971 Tehran Agreement, an agreement which the Shah himself had been instrumental in shaping.

It was this same sense of vindication that overcame any doubts about the possibility of achieving the new targets. As it was, the Shah had been impatient about the investment level in the original Plan of $36 billion.[8] The main constraint had been the shortage of foreign exchange, and the consequent need to rely upon foreign borrowing. For oil revenues had been projected at a mere $22 billion over the five-year period, covering 60 per cent of total expenditure. Now oil revenues were anticipated at $98 billion, covering 79 per cent of expenditure (see Table 2). Thus it was beguiling to assume that with the foreign exchange constraint removed, the other constraints — especially manpower shortages and poor infrastructure — were not serious.

The sole success of the PBO at Gajareh and Ramsar was to prevent the adoption of a high-growth scenario. This had not been easy. At one stage the total submissions from Ministries and government agencies for public sector investment amounted to Rs4,096 billion ($60 billion)! A senior official later commented:

Only a small proportion of the people discussing the revised Plan appreciated the enormity of the challenge it presented us. For most it meant an open cheque, and for those who did grasp the significance of revising the Plan I think they allowed themselves to be often overruled by their ideas of self-aggrandisement — regarding a large extra increase in their ministry's budget as mainly a reflection of their own importance, ignoring the problems that such an increase in expenditure would cause.[9]

Those that had doubts in the end stood silent out of fear, or in the belief that the realities of the situation would impose their own logic on the new Plan. The Shah genuinely seems to have believed that the problems underlined by Majidi could be solved and were subordinate to the lofty objective of accelerating the occasion of a self-sustaining economy, independent of oil. He told the assembled dignitaries at Ramsar: 'The Great Civilisation we promise you is not a utopia either. We will reach it much sooner than we thought. We said we will reach the gates in 12 years; but in some fields we have already crossed its frontiers.'[10]

Main Objectives

The new Plan unveiled after Ramsar was a breathless example of what was going to become of the new Iran. In essence it borrowed what was convenient or eye-catching from a twenty-year macro-schema which the PBO had been working on at the time of the 1973 oil price rises. It was an impatient attempt to concertina the time scale to economic take-off. The real change was not one of substance but form: more money to be spent on bigger projects in a shorter time; better imported technology; more foreign experts and a host of marginal items that had seemed a luxury in the old Plan – especially in the military field. To the ordinary Iranian, it showed that more money was being spent on education, low-cost housing, food subsidies, health and jobs; to the infant bourgeoisie it offered better salaries in government and new possibilities to the private sector to benefit from the huge government injections of cash into the economy; to the armed forces it opened an accelerated vista of regional power through new weapons purchases; and to the outside world it was proof that Iran was on the move.

Taken individually, the objectives of each Ministry were not necessarily far-fetched or unreasonable. When put together, it became apparent that there were enough projects to cover not just the Fifth Plan but also the Sixth Plan that would follow in the five years after 1978.

The crude increases in investment over the original Plan can be seen in Table 1.

On the basis of this investment the annual average growth rate envisaged in the old Plan of 11.4 per cent was expected to rise to 25.9 per cent. An International Monetary Fund team visiting Iran in late 1974 described the three priority sectors:

Firstly considering Iran's comparative advantage, the petroleum and petrochemical sectors have been assigned high priority. Secondly, it

Table 1: Total Fixed Investment 1973-8 (billion dollars)

	Original	Revised	Share of Revised Budget %	Increase on Original Budget %
Industry and mines	8.18	12.53	18.0	53
Agriculture/natural resources	2.67	4.58	6.6	72
Transport and communications	2.79	7.29	10.5	161
Housing	5.96	13.70	19.7	130
Oil and gas	6.83	11.72	16.8	72
Others	10.41	19.77	28.4	90
Total	36.84	69.59	100.0	

Conversion based on $1 = Rs 67.50.
Source: compiled from Bank Markazi annual report, 1974/5, p. 34.

is clear that considerable investments are required to overcome the anticipated bottlenecks in ports, the transportation system, the power section and in the supply of construction materials. Thirdly, the agricultural sector has been selected for special emphasis since industrial expansion requires greater agricultural inputs and expanded production of foodstuffs will be needed to meet increased demand for food engendered by rising incomes and high income elasticities.[11]

There was also an important social aspect to the revised Plan: it represented the first comprehensive attempt to lay the groundwork for a form of welfare state — free schooling, free school meals, food subsidies, and infant schemes for social insurance and public health. This was also to be matched by a major effort to provide popular housing.

The main financial features of the Plan were the importance of oil as a source of revenue, the small anticipated use of foreign loans, substantial investment abroad of surplus income, and accelerated repayment of foreign debts (see Table 2).

It is interesting to note how the plan document itself enumerates its objectives:

 (i) raise the quality of life for all social groups;
 (ii) maintain rapid, balanced and sustained economic growth, together with minimum price increases;

Table 2: Projected Overall Finances 1973-8 (billion dollars)

A. Receipts	
1. Oil and gas	98.2
2. Direct taxes	8.1
3. Indirect taxes	9.1
4. Other receipts*	3.7
5. Foreign loans	2.2
6. Sale of bonds	0.7
Total	122.0
B. Payments from General Revenue	
1. Current expenditures	50.2
(a) general affairs	(6.7)
(b) defence	(29.2)
(c) social affairs	(11.1)
(d) economic affairs	(3.2)
2. Fixed capital formation	42.2
3. Repayment of principal of foreign loans	6.0
4. Other payments	13.4
5. Investment abroad	11.0
Total	122.8

*Includes $2 billion revenue from public sector investment in, and loans to, other countries.
Source: Plan and Budget Organisation, *Revised Plan 1973-78*, p. 41.

(iii) increase the income of various groups, particularly low-income groups;

(iv) expand social, economic, political and cultural justice with particular emphasis on the equitable distribution of services among all social groups;

(v) improve the quality and increase the supply of active manpower in order to raise productivity and eliminate development bottlenecks;

(vi) preserve and improve the environment, with particular attention to the quality of life in large cities;

(vii) develop science and technology and promote creativity;

(viii) establish competitiveness in the production and export of goods;

(ix) utilise foreign exchange reserves to the full so as to remedy domestic shortages and check inflationary pressures, and for foreign investment and the creation of sources of national wealth to replace depleting oil resources;

(x) maintain and revive the nation's valuable cultural heritage.[12]

The Boom Accelerates

At the end of the Ramsar meeting, few realised they had just agreed to a 'hyper-boom'. Even as the Shah pushed through this doubling of proposed expenditure, all the evidence pointed to dangerous overheating in the economy.

Oil revenues in the Iranian year 1973-4 (March to March) had raised *per capita* income from $501 to $821. This brought *per capita* income close to the $850 target which had been projected for 1978 in the original Plan.[13] Every sector of the economy, with the exception of agriculture, evidenced dynamic growth. The industrial and mining sector during 1973-4 had raised output by 18 per cent. Increased industrial activity was reflected by an 81 per cent jump in iron and steel imports (responsible for 15 per cent of the non-military import bill). Industrial use of electricity increased 48 per cent. The number of new companies registered in large cities increased by 46 per cent to 2,208 and total capitalisation rose almost threefold to Rs52.8 billion.[14]

Yet over all there was a widening gap between supply and demand.[15] The Central Bank noted in its annual report, which was released in July 1974 (i.e. before Ramsar):

Shortages in building materials, the low rate of agricultural growth (as compared to other sectors) and scarcity of imported raw materials, combined with the infrastructure bottlenecks, created limitations in the supply of commodities and broadened the gap between aggregate supply and aggregate demand.[16]

Although tactfully expressed, the Bank's report was a clear signal of the problems ahead but the Central Bank itself had no authority and was merely part of the empire that Ansari sought to control from the Finance Ministry. Ansari, like the Shah, was committed to high growth and lofty targets. With exceptional management the Iranian authorities might have achieved a good part of their objectives. Instead they were swept along in a careless euphoria. Symptomatic of this carelessness was the sloppy production of the Plan document itself: the Iranian original approved by Parliament contained a large quantity of mathematical errors and literal mistakes.[17] Virtually everyone in authority had become dazzled by the power of new oil wealth, with oil revenues now coming in at $1.5 billion per month.

The immediate economic impact of the oil revenues was in current expenditure rather than new investment. The Plan expected current expenditure to account for 45 per cent of total outlays but in practice it absorbed 63 per cent, not least because the published defence allocations were placed under current expenditure, and defence was earmarked for 23 per cent of total spending.[18]

Table 3: Actual Revenues and Expenditures 1973/4, 1974/5
(billion dollars)

	1973/4	1974/5	Change (per cent)
Revenues	6.8	20.6	+202
1. Oil and gas	4.6	17.8*	+286
2. Other	2.2	2.8	+ 21
Expenditures	7.1	16.9	+138
1. Current	4.7	10.8	+129
(defence)	(1.9)	(5.5)	(+189)
2. Capital	2.4	5.1	+112
3. Advance payments		1.0	
Deficit/surplus	−0.3	+3.7	

Conversion based on $1 = Rs 67.50.
*This represents only eleven oil instalments from the Consortium since the twelfth had been held over following a dispute.
Source: Compiled from Bank Markazi annual report, 1974/5, p. 14.

The importance of current expenditure in global disbursements can be seen in Table 3. This table also illustrates the extraordinary change in Iran's financial position during the course of one year. More significantly, it demonstrates the ease with which Iran was able to absorb the increased revenue. The quantum jump in defence spending meant that defence expenditure in 1974-5 almost kept pace with the increase in total revenues. The government also embarked on a hurried programme of welfare measures and a whole new range of subsidies on services, commodities and foodstuffs. In 1974-5 over $1.8 billion was spent on the purchase of such foodstuffs as wheat, meat and sugar, and their subsequent subsidised sale.[19] The rise in current expenditure also reflected the switch from credit to cash payments, and the settling of important outstanding domestic obligations.[20]

However, the high level of current expenditure was also due to a slackening of budgetary discipline — perhaps an inevitable reaction from an administration that had been financially stretched throughout the previous 24 years of planned development. During the period of the Plan current expenditures were to average 18 per cent over budget.[21] This meant that from an early stage funds earmarked for capital investment were diverted into the day-to-day running of the government.

From the outset it was recognised that the new Plan would trigger powerful inflation which would in turn affect the cost of domestic investment. The IMF mission which visited Iran in late 1974 was particularly concerned by this problem. In its report it noted the Iranian response:

> The Government is willing to pay this price [higher investment costs] in order to make use of the opportunity for accelerated development which has been provided by the increase in oil revenues. The authorities believe that sufficient domestic productive capacity should be established in certain major areas and the longer the expansion of these basic industrial sectors is postponed the more costly their development will become.[22]

Iranian officials, like other OPEC members, blamed imported inflation for their own rapid rise in costs. In 1974/5 the average cost of imports from the industrialised countries rose by 28 per cent.[23] The consumer was reportedly paying only 11.9 per cent, with the government covering the rest through subsidies and lower import taxes. That imported goods became more expensive — in some instances substantially more so — was incontestable. The industrialised countries were merely passing on the cost of the oil price rises, and one suspects using the quantum price leap as an excuse to hide previously unjustifiable cost escalations. Contractors, particularly in the military sphere, were quoting 'one price for Iran and the Gulf, another for the rest of our clients'.[24] Yet despite imported inflation the real cause lay in the frenetic release of extra funds.

The IMF mission advised authorities to reduce the planned level of the government's net domestic expenditure to avoid serious inflation, but this advice was ignored.[25] The boom, which had already begun before the Plan revision, had gathered momentum which was difficult to stop. Besides, none of the Shah's Ministers was willing to advise a cut-back in planned expenditure less than six months after Ramsar.

Money supply increased by 61 per cent as domestic expenditure continued to rise and the banks were allowed to continue a liberal credit policy. Such an increase, between March 1974 and March 1975, was unprecedented; yet almost 37 per cent of the entire increase occurred in the final month of the Iranian year (20 February to 20 March).[26] Almost 40 per cent of the increase in loans by the commercial banks to the private sector took place in the last quarter, at a time when the Central Bank was exercising minimal credit control over the commercial banks. Some attempt to reduce credit expansion to the private sector had little effect because other measures like the reduction of import registration deposits and import registration fees caused a substantial fall in the demand for credit in what was a previously significant area. Meanwhile the government removed all credit limits on the specialised banks as they were promoting investment in industry and agriculture. In 1974/5 the specialised banks granted almost $1 billion worth of loans, a 60 per cent increase; and in line with this their capital increased 44 per cent. The commercial banks, also under-capitalised for such an increase in their scale of operations, were obliged to raise their capital 100 per cent.[27]

Table 4: Money Supply and Banking System Assets (billion rials)

	1973/4	1974/5	Per Cent 1973/4	Change 1974/5
1. Foreign assets of banking system	167.9	544.2	77.9	224.1
(foreign exchange)	(154.2)	(528.9)	(90.6)	(243.0)
2. Loans/credits to private sector	489.1	698.3	35.0	42.8
3. Public sector liabilities to banking system	298.4	445.9	34.8	49.4
4. Public sector deposits with banking system	209.9	364.3	58.9	73.6
Money supply	207.7	327.2	27.7	61.4
Quasi-money	313.1	502.9	30.1	60.6

Source: Bank Markazi annual report, 1974/5, pp. 15 and 148.

Out of Control

By early 1975 the Iranian economy was almost out of control. During the first quarter of the new Iranian year (mid-March to mid-June) government spending was up 208 per cent on the same period the previous year. Over 40 per cent of the total planned credit allocation of the commercial banks had been used up. Some banks had already exhausted their entire allocation for the year and were turning to the international market for short-term funds. Money supply was still increasing at 60 per cent per annum. Meanwhile imports, running at $1.2 billion a month, were almost 100 per cent up on the same period in 1974.[28] Already the second main principle of the revised Plan had been abandoned: 'maintain rapid, balanced and sustained economic growth, together with minimum price increases'. Less and less was being achieved at greater and greater cost.

The development of the ports illustrates the point. The boom in expenditure stimulated imports and put even greater pressure on the already strained port infrastructure: in 1974 the volume of imports increased 39 per cent.

Port handling equipment was insufficient and poorly maintained. Maintenance in the southern ports with their high humidity and scorching summer temperatures was difficult and machinery was constantly breaking down. Because of the inclement climate it was difficult to find regular labour to operate a continuous shift system in the four hottest summer months (July and August temperatures at Khorramshahr, Bushire, Bandar Shahpur and Bandar Abbas go over 45 degrees). The southern ports handled over 80 per cent of all maritime imports with insufficient berthing space and very limited warehousing. All this was compounded by an elephantine bureaucracy which could require up to 28 signatures to clear goods from customs. Import licences were frequently the responsibility of more than one Ministry. A banker, for instance, spent over four months trying to clear a canoe from customs because the Ministry of War insisted on knowing what form of armament it carried and the nature of its radar system – even though the Commerce Ministry had given prior approval.

At Khorramshahr, the principal port, over 200 ships were waiting to unload their cargoes by mid-1975: ships were having to wait 160 days and more before entering harbour. At one point more than 1 million tons of goods were being kept in ships' holds awaiting the opportunity to unload. It was a chaotic situation, only subsequently rivalled by the port of Jeddah in Saudi Arabia. Once the offloading of goods was speeded up, many goods lay around unwarehoused. At Khorramshahr 12,000 tons were being unloaded per day but only 9,000 tons were being removed per day. At the most congested point, in September/October 1975, there were over 1 million tons of goods piled up on the jetties and around the port.

Goods were cleared slowly for two main reasons. First, almost 50 per cent of the imports were government purchases, and Ministries took sometimes up to six months – and more – to clear them. Second, there were not enough trucks. A special emergency government purchase of 2,000 trucks and 6,000 trailers proved no remedy in itself. The trucks needed drivers and 2,000 more Iranian drivers were not available. As a further emergency measure it was decided to 'import' 800 South Korean and Pakistani truck drivers, but they were brought in hurriedly, without proper arrangements for accommodation or familiarisation with local conditions. They quickly became disenchanted, especially when they discovered that Iranian drivers were being paid higher wages. By July 1975 most of these drivers had left after less than six months. Finally, the government was forced to consider what it should have done in the first place – a crash course for Iranian drivers. This only filled the gap slowly, and a large number of unused trucks rotted in the hostile climate. Even in 1977 it was still possible to see rows of trucks, neatly parked at Bandar Abbas, that had been awaiting drivers for three years.

The delays in the ports were immediately transferred to the construction sites and other projects. There was a built-in delay of six months on the start up of virtually every project, added to which much of the goods suffered in poor handling, causing further delay. The cost is difficult to quantify. The only readily identifiable costs were demurrage charges for keeping ships waiting at anchor. In 1974/5 these cost Iran over $1 billion, almost 5 per cent of total foreign exchange earnings. There were also disguised costs. Importers resorted to the quicker but more expensive form of international truck transportation, through Turkey, and air freight. The customs officials profited from the situation, pocketing large sums of money against often empty assurances of priority clearance. Delays in the ports almost certainly cost Iran much more than its imported inflation.[29]

Another key factor affecting development costs was the increase in the price of land. Once money began to circulate, property values were the first to rise, attracting the Iranian entrepreneur. Land values changed, not even by the month, but by the week. The rises were most dramatic in Tehran; but it was a country-wide phenomenon. An industrialist wishing to buy land in Tabriz in 1974 had to pay Rs45,000 per square metre ($660) – land which could have been bought in 1971 for Rs5,000 per square metre. With the development of mining in Kerman, land in the centre of the town rose from Rs2,000 per square metre in 1959 to Rs15,000 in 1974. In Rasht on the Caspian, where industry began to be located after restrictions on expansion round Tehran, land prices rose from a mere Rs20 per square metre in 1969 to Rs2,000 by 1974.[30]

As much as 47 per cent of the cost of housing was absorbed in land costs. In industrial development the proportion was not so substantial but it was nevertheless high. Land purchase was often a complex and lengthy affair. The Italian consortium, Italcontractors, building a new commercial port near Bandar Abbas, arrived with a preliminary work-force in December 1975. They were prevented from starting work by armed gendarmerie because there was a dispute about purchase of the land. The government was still negotiating the purchase price of what only two years before had been worthless land. Work on the site was delayed until May 1976, and this was one of the most *essential* infra-structure projects in the country.[31]

A side-effect of the spiralling cost of land was higher rents, and consequent demands for higher wages by the urban work-force, since housing had become the major element in living costs: up to 60 per cent of pay. It was soon recognised that the only way of ensuring a stable level of wage increases was to ensure adequate housing, particu-larly for the lower-paid. However, with the cost of land so high and a premium on quick profits, speculators opted for the upper end of the market, which aggravated the situation.

Wages rose in 1974/5 at an average of 30 per cent in the 21 major industries, according to official estimates.[32] This undoubtedly under-stated the trend. Substantial wage increases were officially encouraged as part of the Shah's policy of ensuring that wealth be more fairly dis-tributed. The Ministry of Labour insisted that industrial workers were paid a minimum of an extra month's pay, going as high as 60 days' extra pay. The previous repressive attitude towards industrial action was softened because the Shah now had the means of producing loyalty from labour with money, not force. In 1974/5 strikes, work stoppages or go-slows generally centred round bargaining for improved end-of-year bonuses. The Ministry of Labour apparently on the Shah's orders only rarely took the management's side in such disputes. This was a tremendous spur to wage demands but there was no determined effort to tie higher pay to higher productivity.

Official support for increased wage demands was reflected in the not untypical experience of a factory near Tehran where there was a dis-pute over a profit-sharing bonus.

We came in at noon on a Wednesday and they [the workers] had all stopped work. They were standing or sitting by their machines. We realised it was a strike or sit in. Thinking strikes were illegal we called in the SAVAK. They didn't appear until about four in the afternoon. And when they came they didn't seem to take much notice of the workers who were on strike. The next day we called in a lawyer who was an expert on labour relations and he didn't have much success either with the workers' representative. Then on Saturday — after the weekend break — they were still not working so we went with the workers' representative to the Ministry of Labour. It was strange, because the Ministry of Labour never once referred to them being on strike. We argued but in the end it was clear to us we had to give way — a 40 per cent increase in bonus payments. Profit sharing is just part of the cost of labour.[33]

More important still was the labour shortage. Ordinary labourers' income rose relatively slowly but skilled workers like welders, carpenters, machine-operators, mechanics, pipe-fitters or technically or professionally trained personnel could dictate terms. Scarce labour was poached and government workers often left for the higher-paid private sector. While an unskilled construction labourer was earning $5.50 per day, a pipe-fitter could take home $440-60 per month. A good bilingual secretary was being paid almost $1,200 per month; an engineer just qualified (especially if the education had been abroad) could command over $2,000 per month excluding perks; while a graduate manager aged thirty could demand over $4,500 per month.[34]

The Shah was to comment over a year later, after salaries and wages had continued their upwards spiral, that an engineer could earn almost $7,000 per month, 'several times higher than the salary of an engineer in Europe'.[35] Foreign and local contractors by mid-1975 discovered that it was cheaper to employ expatriates than Iranians, especially in projects in remote parts of the country. Kraftwerke Union, building two nuclear power stations at Bushire, offered official pay rates to Iranian labour but got few takers, and instead imported Turks and Yugoslavs. The high pay for skilled work, plus the various perks, made it difficult to assess the real overall wage increase. In 1974/5 it was almost certainly close to 40 per cent and probably higher. This meant an important increase in disposable income for Iranians; but the benefit was eroded by the cost of living.

Employment of foreigners was also an important inflationary factor. By mid-1975 there were some 35,000 foreigners living in Tehran alone — mostly Europeans acting as technicians, managers, advisers or foreign company representatives, including a sizeable portion connected with defence and defence-related contracts. They were willing to pay almost any price for scarce accommodation, subsidised by companies hopeful of high profits from Iran. The country was held to ransom by its shortage of skilled manpower. It was expensive to attract expatriate skills to work in a harsh environment and in the defence field some American technicians were costing up to $150,000 a year to work in Iran.[36] It cost Iran an average $9,000 per month for American defence personnel in 1975 and by then there were some 20,000 defence and defence-related personnel. In many instances the 'software' side of defence contracts — personnel, advisory and technical back-up, training of Iranians — was more than half the cost of the whole contract.

Official figures were produced for inflation. But they were doctored to produce a publicly acceptable norm.[37] Published prices tended to reflect what they ought to have been, rather than what they were. The indices paid no attention to the tremendous shortages which forced individuals, companies and even government agencies to buy at black-market prices. For instance the four-door saloon Peykan car assembled in Iran was selling for 35 per cent above its list price because production was unable to meet demand. Yet even allowing for official reticence on inflation, the figures showed an accelerating trend. From March to August 1975 the consumer price index rose at an annual average of 28 per cent.[38] The real rate was probably nearer 35 to 38 per cent.

Notes

1. Plan and Budget Organisation (PBO), *Iran's Fifth Development Plan 1973-78*, revised version, May 1975, v.

2. Information supplied to the author by PBO.

3. Comment to the author by Abdol Majid Majidi, 16 July 1977.

4. Comment to the author by Hushang Ansari, 4 May 1977. Ansari was insistent that those at the top were fully aware of the problems they faced.

5. Based on information supplied to the author by a senior official present at Garjareh.

6. In the Shah's press conference of 23 December, he had said, 'We are going to enlarge it [the Plan] a lot — maybe by one third; but no more than that because we risk the creation of terrible inflation.' See *Kayhan International*, 25 December 1973.

7. *Kayhan International*, 2 August 1974. The local press played up references by the Shah to end corruption. This was considered to be one of the keynotes.

8. The original Plan had total fixed investment of $32 billion. This dollar figure altered when the dollar/rial parity altered.

9. Comment to the author by an official present at Ramsar.

10. *Kayhan International*, 4 August 1974. The Shah also said it would be 'an unforgivable' sin to waste this 'unique opportunity'.

11. International Monetary Fund, staff report on Iran, January 1975, p. 4.

12. PBO, revised Plan, pp. 6-7.
13. Bank Markazi annual report, 1973/4, p. 14.
14. Ibid., p. 205.
15. In 1973/4 the official index of wages in 21 major industries showed an annual average increase of 27 per cent. This almost certainly understated the trend.
16. Bank Markazi annual report, 1973/4, p. 62.
17. Comment to the author by Roger Cooper, translator of the PBO's revised Plan.
18. This percentage excluded military construction which was placed under 'other Government buildings'. See PBO, revised Plan, p. 388.
19. Bank Markazi annual report, 1973/4, pp. 35-9.
20. Repayment of domestic obligations totalled Rs35.1 billion.
21. Capital expenditure for instance was $7.47 billion in 1975/6; $9.94 billion in 1976/7; $13.89 billion (projected) in 1977/8 while current expenditure during the same period was respectively $13.75 billion; $17.46 billion and $18.36 billion (projected) — equivalent to 64 per cent, 63 per cent and 56 per cent of the General Budget (PBO figures supplied to author).
22. IMF report, p. 4.
23. Bank Markazi annual report, 1974/5, p. 74.
24. Based on information supplied to the author by numerous foreign contractors.
25. IMF report, pp. 6-8. The mission felt that any increase in money supply above 40 per cent would accentuate 'the upward pressure on prices'.
26. Bank Markazi annual report, 1974/5, p. 48.
27. Ibid., pp. 47-52. Commercial banks' capital increased from Rs28 billion to Rs56 billion.
28. *Financial Times*, 27 August 1975.
29. Based on information supplied to the author by the Ports and Shipping Organisation; shipping companies and Conference Lines. See also *Kayhan International*, 19 November 1975; *Tehran Journal*, 23 November 1975 and 18 July 1976; and *International Herald Tribune*, 13 March 1976.
30. Translated from an article in *Rastakhiz*, 11 August 1976.
31. Based on information supplied to the author by Italcontractors.
32. Bank Markazi annual report, 1974/5, p. 183.
33. Comments to the author by an expatriate plant manager. The incident occurred in March 1976.
34. Information gathered by the author in Tehran during late 1975.
35. Interview by the Shah with Associated Press, December 1976.
36. Ibid.
37. Based on comments by an expatriate economist who assisted in the preparation of a new price index in 1976. Iranian economists also express great suspicion at all official figures. In this context Julian Bharier in *Economic Development of Iran: 1900-1970* (London, Oxford University Press, 1971) stresses the unreliability of Iranian statistics.
38. Bank Markazi annual report, 1974/5, p. 74.

6 LIMITS TO OIL WEALTH

Question: Critics say Iran moved at a pace so rapid it was economically unsound.
Answer: Why? Because we will have a 17 percent growth rate this year? Is this bad? Last year we had a 42 percent growth rate, but a 20 to 22 percent inflation rate. This year we will have zero inflation. Is this what bothers the critics?[1]

Question: ... Looking back to 1975 do you confirm the view that your country's development projects were somewhat too ambitious?
Answer: Perhaps. Perhaps it is so. Definitely.[2]

The contrast between the Shah's bullish first response in February 1976 and the more pensive answer in the second interview in December reflects the transformation that occurred in Iran during 1976.

The warning signals that Iran was overspending had come much earlier; but the response had been muted. In July 1975 for instance the Finance Ministry authorised foreign borrowing by government agencies.[3] Only seven months previously this had been thought unnecessary before 1978.[4] At the same time the instructions were sent to all Ministries to observe 'the utmost care and economy'; to be followed by an order to submit monthly accounts to the PBO for scrutiny.[5] But like many orders in a faction-riven bureaucracy, this was half-observed, diluted, or the figures distorted to give the impression that orders were being obeyed.

Belatedly the Central Bank (Bank Markazi) reacted, invoking classic instruments of monetary control. In August 1975 the ratio of obligatory deposits on short-term borrowing abroad was raised from 15 per cent to 30 per cent – a measure designed to deter the banks from getting round their credit ceilings by borrowing abroad. Simultaneously the minimum reserve requirements were raised, and the import deposit guarantee (reduced only the previous year) was also raised. Though limited, these measures helped to bring the expansion of money supply down to a more manageable annual growth of 36 per cent by the end of 1975.[6]

The Shah's reaction was essentially political and was concerned to forestall any resentment among the poorer sections of the community who felt oil wealth was passing them by or was making life more difficult. First, he reactivated a languishing scheme of compulsory divesti-

93

ture by manufacturing companies of 49 per cent of their shares to their employees and the public. Second, he instituted a sweeping curb on prices by rolling back the prices of some 16,000 items to January 1974 levels. Profiteering was outlawed in a well publicised campaign which led to the arrest of 7,750 persons in the first two weeks of operation.[7]

These measures were instituted in July but began to take hold in August. They were hastily introduced palliatives which diverted attention from the real issues: the social objectives of the revised Plan were being undermined by an accelerating urban/rural and rich/poor gap; while the economic objectives were being undermined by inadequate infrastructure, lack of skilled labour and an alarming increase in costs and overall wastage. The lack of forethought for the wider economic consequences of these countermeasures merely underlined their political motivation.

Political Gestures

The share divestiture scheme was an industrial replica of what happened with land reform thirteen years before. Both were aimed at giving underprivileged groups the semblance of more of the national cake. Both were hurriedly introduced and subsequently revised. Share participation was made the thirteenth principle of the Shah-People Revolution and anti-profiteering the fourteenth on 8 August 1975. Earlier, 320 companies had been listed as eligible for the scheme, whereby shares should first be offered to the employees and then to the wider public.[8] The companies were broken up into three groups, a first batch of 106, to be followed by a further 108 and then the remainder – all of whom were expected to have completed their 49 per cent divestiture by October 1978.

It was reckoned that some 1 million industrial workers would benefit, plus a further 2.7 million in agriculture. To facilitate the purchase a special government-financed credit institute with a Rs1 billion ($15 million) capital was established. This institute could provide up to Rs100,000 credit to employees at 4 per cent over ten years, to be repaid by dividend or capital gain on sale. On the assumption that not all shares would be taken up, an investment company was also formed (National Investment Company of Iran, NICI) with a $150 million capital subscribed by the banks and insurance companies.[9]

This sounded fine in theory, and undoubtedly had an important psychological impact among industrial workers. But, like Land Reform, it excluded those who were least privileged. In the case of Land Reform it was the landless labourer; and in industry it was the workers in the small company who accounted for over 70 per cent of the industrial labour force. Also the scheme did not relate to control of industry, it was merely concerned with providing a sense of participation and greater financial gain. The move was not anti-business nor anti-capital (banks were excluded), nevertheless the industrialists reacted with alarm, fearing that this was the beginning of state intervention: a fear perhaps exaggerated by the previous cotton-wool treatment industrialists enjoyed. There was also a widespread fear that the share price evaluation by the government would be artificially low.

In many respects these fears proved groundless. The government timetable was impossibly ambitious. It also became clear fairly quickly that 320 companies could not be found to fit the original set of criteria for the scheme. By July 1977 only 151 companies had distributed 20 per cent of their scheduled 49 per cent. Certain changes were made to appease the industrialists, the most important of which was the raising from 6 per cent to 14 per cent the proportion divested that could be paid in cash by the government. By July 1977 72,235 industrial workers and 125,745 farmers had benefited from the scheme – a much smaller number than anticipated in 1975.[10]

However, the fears of the business community had an important impact on investment, which fell off sharply at the end of September 1975. Fearing closer monitoring by government and higher taxes, the instinctive reaction was to transfer profits and liquid cash abroad: a move facilitated by the relaxation of previously rigid exchange controls in December 1974. The flight of capital was in one sense aided by the share divestiture scheme, which turned industrial assets into cash in a country with a strictly limited capital market. A number of foreign companies affected by the scheme, especially those with American equity, reacted unfavourably. The share participation scheme was one of the chief reasons which led General Motors to seriously contemplate pulling out of Iran or withdrawing its name from its Iranian car assembly operation. GM, in fact, is said to have agreed to stay on in September 1975 only after specific guarantees from the Shah over privileged treatment and high-level White House consultations following a threat by the Shah to cancel the $2 billion F-14 contract with Grumman.[11] The scheme prompted B. F. Goodrich, one of the first US companies to enter a joint venture in Iran, to sell up its 58 per cent stake in 1976.

However, the share participation scheme was not alone responsible for damaging business confidence. The anti-profiteering campaign and the 'price war' also played an important part. This campaign was a crude effort to brand the entrepreneur and the tradesman as the chief culprit of higher prices. Among those arrested were two of Iran's more successful businessmen, Habib Elghanian and Mohammed Wahabzadeh. Elghanian had built up a large plastics business with extensive retail outlets; while Wahabzadeh was mainly concerned with cars, being sole agent for BMW. A summons was also served *in absentia* on Habib Sabet.

High profits were being made and some unscrupulous merchants were taking advantage. Yet profiteering was a symptom, not a cause. The cause lay in the inability of production, or imports, to meet demand. The campaign was also highly selective, and it was significant that the most vigorous action was taken in those areas where the aspiring middle class had been most affected — for instance the rising costs of buying and maintaining a car. Wahabzadeh was accused of selling BMW cars for Rs1.08 million instead of Rs800,000.[12]

Imposing draconian price controls in a severely overheated economy was inevitably disruptive and ultimately counter-productive. Matters were not helped by the bands of ill-informed inspectors, frequently students, sent out to check prices and decide sometimes with complete arbitrariness the correct price for a product. The price war was the first political test of the newly formed single party, Rastakhiz; and on at least one occasion youths in the name of the party and the municipality sacked a Tehran supermarket, said to be overcharging, in a manner reminiscent of the Red Guards during the Cultural Revolution in China. The party subsequently admitted that its involvement in the prices campaign was a mistake — or rather that it would not be repeated.

As a whole the price campaign was a failure. Official indices went down for six months but black-market prices for essential commodities rose sharply. The shortages were not relieved, and if anything became more pronounced. Importers decided in many instances that if controls were to be placed on profit margins of products it was more economic not to import at all: the same applied to local manufacture. Elghanian's plastics operation, arguably the most efficient in Iran and marketing the most sophisticated range of products, closed down, never to reopen. Sabet, aged 72, stayed in Paris, refusing to return to run his empire and sought to put his capital elsewhere.

The anti-profiteering campaign and price controls also had a damaging effect on the ports. Because goods had been 'under-invoiced' the government fixed the price and profit margin on the price declared. This meant that importers were being made to sell at below cost price. Although a clever ruse by the government to encourage the importers to be more honest, it backfired. Rather than declare the real price or accept the fixed price, many importers preferred to just leave their goods unclaimed. As much as 40 per cent of all goods lying on the quays at Khorramshahr was unclaimed in 1975. By the time the customs came to auction them the goods were frequently too badly damaged to be worth buying, so continuing to clutter the port.[13]

More importantly, an important opportunity to overhaul the country's distribution network was wasted. Reducing the middle man's profits did not solve the key question of getting goods quickly and efficiently into the market. The technocrats in the Ministry of Commerce would have liked to have seen this happen but the political will was lacking.

The obstructive tactics of the merchants, mainly the traditional merchants of the Bazaar, proved too strong; and the Shah was neither ready nor willing to risk a confrontation. Indeed to mollify the merchants, Commerce Minister Fereidoun Mahdavi was removed on 7 February 1976. He had been the main champion of reorganising distribution — including the creation of a model market like London's Covent Garden (a scheme which was shelved with his demise).[14] Some considered it significant that the bigger names prosecuted in the anti-profiteering or prices campaigns were often outsiders — members of the Bahai sect, like Sabet, or Jews, like Elghanian.

Oil as a Variable

The dampener on the boom came not from inside Iran but outside. Oil sales failed to meet expectation and revenues fell. By December 1975 oil production was running 20 per cent below the same period the previous year. For the year as a whole the average daily production was almost 12 per cent down.[15]

Throughout the summer sales had been slack. A surge of buying just prior to the biannual OPEC meeting in Vienna in September 1975 proved a temporary phenomenon. Continued world recession and a mild European winter kept international demand sluggish. Iran was especially affected because of the nature of its crude oil: a 'light' crude of high quality with a low sulphur content; and a 'heavy' crude with a higher sulphur content suitable for fuel oil.[16] The heavy crude was most similar to that of Kuwait, while the light competed with the high-volume crude of Saudi Arabia. Normally Iran exported a ratio of 52/48 light/heavy. However, the mild winter severely affected demand for fuel oil, and through the complex OPEC pricing system that differentiated various types of crude, Iranian heavy oil became uncompetitive, especially when both Kuwait and Saudi Arabia reduced the price of their heavy crude and Iran refused to follow suit.

The drop in revenue was keenly felt because it came in the last quarter of the Iranian year when Ministries traditionally spent the larger part of their budgets. The government resorted to a simple, but effective, expedient: payments to contractors were abruptly halted. By March 1976 as much as $3 billion was owed to contractors by government departments.[17]

The new budget had to be recalculated and appeared six weeks late at the end of February. As a result of a 14 per cent drop in oil purchases by the Consortium, officials estimated a revenue shortfall of $2.7 billion. The budget for 1976/7 showed a deficit of $2.4 billion, with substantial resort to international borrowing.[18] It was as much a surprise to the Iranians as the international community that the situation should change so quickly.

In broader terms these developments, which had such a traumatic effect on the Iranian economy, reflected two important trends: the increased inter-dependence of the oil producers and the consumers; and the changing nature of OPEC leadership. With the 1973 price rises the producers sought to rectify in one move the historic price anomalies of the oil industry. But having done this, price became very sensitive to market forces. For instance, Iran would have sold more crude almost certainly if the price of heavy crude had been adjusted in line with Kuwait and Saudi Arabia in the winter of 1975. Later NIOC found that to expand sales it had to offer substantial discounts.[19]

The price sensitivity of oil was reflected in the relatively modest increases approved by OPEC: at Vienna in September 1975 10 per cent; at Bali in May 1976 a price freeze; at Doha in December 1976 the OPEC majority accepted 10 per cent with Saudi Arabia and the UAE opting for 5 per cent; at Stockholm in July 1977 Saudi Arabia agreed to realign its prices; and at Caracas in December 1977 a freeze for 1978 was agreed. In other words the 1973 price rises were — for the foreseeable future — a once-and-for-all leap, to be followed by regular but modest increases.

This trend was reflected in Iran's vital foreign exchange receipts from oil and gas. After an increase of 200 per cent in 1974/5, the increase dropped in the following year to 2 per cent (see Table 5). In the two years from March 1975 to March 1977 receipts grew at an average of just under 5 per cent. Yet during the same period total expenditure increased three times as fast.[20] While the 1973 price increases were so substantial that outlay could not match revenue, the succeeding increases were so small that the reverse was true.

Table 5: Balance of Payments (billion dollars)

1. Current Account	1973/4	1974/5	1975/6	1976/7
Current Receipts	6,232	20,922	21,971	24,385
A. Revenue from OSCO	4,490	16,216	17,296	16,726
Revenue from others	182	862	700	622
Purchase of foreign exchange from NIOC	186	1,445	874	3,140
Purchase of foreign exchange from others	215	149	183	159
B. Gas sales to USSR	87	131	202	183
C. Export of goods	548	563	448	462
D. Services				
Private sector	326	598	966	1,929
Public sector	198	958	1,302	1,164
Current Payments	5,879	12,393	19,025	20,038
A. Import of goods	4,966	10,633	15,924	15,715
B. Gold (non-monetary)	3	11	122	260
C. Services				
Private sector	372	803	1,429	2,550
Public sector	310	614	1,251	1,219
Interest paid	228	332	299	294
Balance	+353	+8,529	+2,946	+4,347
2. Capital Account				
A. Inflow of official long-term loans	1,296	257	300	560
B. Inflow of private loans and capital	209	445	661	400
C. Repatriation of official capital				518
D. Repayment of debts	−541	−1,313	−729	−710
E. Foreign aid, loans and investments	−1	−2,388	−2,941	−1,771
F. Other payments	−48	−221	−912	−838
Errors/omissions	109	−199	−298	−464
Overall balance	1,024	5,076	991	2,025

Source: Bank Markazi.

Moreover Iran was severely affected by the two-tier price structure that evolved at Doha in December 1976. In January 1977 sales slumped 30 per cent, obliging the government for the second year running to rewrite the budget at the last minute.[21] Over $3.5 billion was pruned from expenditure and the revenues for the coming year were recalculated anticipating a 10 per cent drop in over-all oil sales, and a reduced growth target of 13 per cent.[22]

Since oil had been expected to underwrite 78 per cent of the revised Plan, the impact of such fluctuations in international demand was dramatic. Iran had returned to the unstable conditions of the 1950s when the size of the oil revenue had never been certain. The PBO Minister, Abdol Majid Majidi, acidly commented at the time of rewriting of the 1977/8 budget: 'The drop in oil exports indicates that the Government is now confronted with fluctuating income from this source.'[23]

Market conditions were not the only key issue. Of equal significance was the political stance of Saudi Arabia within OPEC. In 1973 Iran had been at the zenith of its influence within OPEC; but this dominance was dependent on Saudi and Iranian interests coinciding. Once the historic price rise had been achieved, Saudi Arabia had diametrically opposite interests to Iran. With a production potential twice Iran's yet a population ten times as small, Saudi Arabia did not need maximised revenue. Indeed high oil price rises were viewed with positive alarm in Riyadh. The opposing interests of OPEC's two biggest producers were exposed at Vienna in September 1975. Iran sided with the hawks within OPEC and initially supported a 21 per cent rise proposed by Iraq. Although this move was subsequently explained as a tactic to achieve a 15 to 16 per cent rise, it completely misjudged Saudi intentions.[24] The Saudi Oil Minister, Sheikh Ahmad Zaki Yamani, refused to go above 10 per cent, backing this up with the threat of raising production and selling at the Saudi price. The rest of OPEC acceded.

There was similar confrontation right through to the Stockholm meeting of OPEC in July 1977. Saudi Arabia was always able to impose either a price freeze or moderate rises. During this period, the Shah, who dictated oil policy, continually underestimated the Saudi position and their capacity to enforce it. The Shah seemed unable to accept changed political circumstances — witness his refusal to lower the price of Iranian heavy crude until three months after the Saudis in February 1976.[25] Within NIOC there was opposition to the Shah's general policy of trying to lead the international market on prices. A more pragmatic approach was favoured but this only appeared at Stockholm and at Caracas in December 1977.

The strength of the Saudi position is twofold. With enormous accumulated surplus and a small population it can cope with fluctuations in world demand, no matter how sharp. Second, the sheer size of Saudi productive capacity means that OPEC cannot afford to ignore a threat of raised production and a flood of cheap crude. To a significant degree

Iran had become dependent upon Saudi Arabia for the level of its oil revenues. Unprecedented personal attacks on Sheikh Yamani after the Doha meeting published in the officially controlled Iranian press only served to underline this sense of frustration.[26]

Full Circle

Although the changed oil scene affected revenues, there was a general reluctance at the top to alter objectives in early 1976. The Shah was still unwilling to admit that things had gone wrong. The 1976 budget sought to increase total expenditure by 27 per cent to $44.7 billion. The Shah was determined to press ahead with military spending. Instead of paying in cash or against credit, he now sought to barter crude oil. In April 1976 three-cornered discussions were initiated with oil companies and arms suppliers. Two deals were proposed: (1) the purchase of up to 300 F-16s from McDonnell Douglas and 4 Spruance Class destroyers from Lytton Industries to be acquired via the sale of 300,000 barrels per day of crude by NIOC to be marketed to two American oil companies, Ashland and New England Petroleum; (2) the purchase of tracked Rapier missiles worth £400 million from British Aircraft Corporation (BAC) via the sale of 16,000 barrels per day of crude to be marketed by Shell.[27]

Subsequently barter was used outside the military sector and there was scarcely a large contract for which payment was not considered on this basis. The Iranian tactic was to keep barter as an option available when convenient.[28] Since such deals were highly complicated to arrange, foreign suppliers were generally reluctant to accept them. The first barter contract was with BAC, concluded on 18 November 1976.[29] The basic problem for the Iranians was that some form of discount had to be included in the sale of the crude and the deals were very time-consuming, especially where more than one supplier was concerned in a single contract.

The emphasis on barter served to underline a growing sense of unease among the technocrats over the way the revised Plan had developed. In July 1976 a critical report from the PBO circulated to Ministries and government agencies. It pointed out bluntly that agriculture was being ignored, that production and labour costs had risen so fast in the past three years as to jeopardise the future of Iranian non-oil exports, and that the bottlenecks had been ineffectually tackled. The conclusion was slower growth and tighter control on government spending. This document was never published.[30]

Although the public were kept ignorant some of the more marginal

Table 6: Budget Receipts and Expenditure (billion dollars)

		1975/6	1976/7	1977/8*
1.	General Budget			
	(a) Taxes	3.84	4.39	5.89
	(b) Oil/gas	17.68	19.98	19.47
	(c) Domestic loans	–	–	2.12
	(d) Foreign loans	0.08	1.14	1.41
	(e) Special revenue	3.14	0.64	0.95
	(f) Other	0.91	0.98	1.18
	Sub-total	25.6	27.2	31.02
2.	Total state receipts (including state enterprise borrowing)	32.76	44.73	49.17
3.	Total expenditure (including state enterprises)	32.76	44.73	49.17
4.	Gross deficit	–	2.05	1.74

*Projected.
Rs70.5 = $1.
Source: Plan and Budget Organisation.

projects began to be shelved. Talks on the construction of a new naval base at Chah Bahar on the Indian Ocean were dropped. This was the first indication that the Shah was being obliged to cut back. Ministries scrutinised their budgets and optional extras were pruned. For instance orders for up to 24 extra French turbo-trains were cancelled. The turbo-train was to provide fast inter-city transport; but on the Tehran-Meshed run the poor track reduced maximum speed by 40 per cent. The trains, a splendid symbol of modernism, were ill suited to the hot dry climate and frequently broke down, so requiring expensive expatriate technical back-up.

It was not until October 1976 that the Shah chose publicly to de-nounce the euphoria that had been generated by the 1973 oil price rises. The editor of *Kayhan*, Amir Taheri, expected a routine birthday inter-view. Instead it turned into a lengthy auto-critique of the past three years. Iranians had been living in a fool's paradise unaware that there was a definite and relatively short timescale for the duration of oil money. Oil alone had been responsible for the subsidies, the low taxes, the initiation of welfare, the sudden leap in living standards. Unless people were prepared to work harder, produce more and pay higher taxes there would be nothing to replace oil, he said.[31]

'We have not demanded self sacrifice from people: rather we have covered them in soft cotton wool. Things will now change. Everyone should work harder and be prepared for sacrifices in the service of the nation's progress,' he said grimly. This was almost exactly the opposite of what he had told the nation at Ramsar in August 1974. Compare what he said then: 'We do not expect Iranians to tighten their belts, eat less and labour away for the promised heaven which is put off by a year every day. We try to offer the nation the welfare and care we have promised – today.'[32]

Within two weeks of this interview, the Shah announced the creation of an Imperial Commission to investigate wastage. The Commission was composed of government representatives but more importantly members of the Shah's own special watchdog investigative body – the Imperial Inspectorate – and the security services, SAVAK.[33] It was the first real attempt to find out what was going on in the economy; and it was to report direct to the Shah, not the Ministries. In keeping with the new mood, profligate spending disappeared and was replaced by parsimony. The 1976/7 budget was underspent. It was now policy to finish what had been begun and leave major initiatives to the Sixth Plan, no matter if they had been expressed objectives of the revised Plan.

Notes

1. Shah interview with *Newsweek*, 1 March 1976. In the same interview he is asked 'Is the boom over?' His reply: 'Not at all.'
2. Shah interview with *Der Spiegel*, published in *Kayhan International*, 8 December 1976.
3. Comment to the author by Hushang Ansari, Minister of Finance, July 1975.
4. *Financial Times*, 17 December 1974.
5. *Kayhan International*, 8 July 1975.
6. Bank Markazi annual report, 1975/6, p. 15.
7. *Kayhan International*, 8 August 1975.
8. The criteria for selecting the 320 companies were the following: registered capital of Rs100 million or over; or fixed assets exceeding Rs200 million; or turn-over exceeding Rs250 million. The combined capital of the first 106 companies was the equivalent of $707 million.
9. *Financial Times*, 28 July 1975.
10. *Financial Times*, 25 July 1977.
11. Based on information supplied to the author by GM Iran general manager, Lew Wilkins.
12. *Tehran Journal*, 18 August 1975.
13. *Tehran Journal*, 23 July 1976.
14. Fereidoun Mahdavi also seems to have been blamed for the excesses of the

Rastakhiz Party during the prices campaign.

15. Average daily production was 5.3 million barrels per day against 6.02 million barrels per day in 1974.

16. Iranian light crude oil is classified as 34 degrees API; and Iranian heavy crude is 31 degrees API.

17. This was an unofficial figure accepted by the Bank Markazi and used in the US Embassy Tehran's semi-annual trends in May 1976. The situation was eased when the government released new funds from the budget.

18. The foreign borrowing envisaged was by state enterprises. During the year the government was obliged to raise the ceiling for these enterprises on domestic borrowing from $227 million to $1.04 billion and on foreign borrowing from S481 million to $1.7 billion.

19. NIOC was offering discounts in the form of extended credit. The normal payment period for NIOC clients was 60 to 90 days but in some cases this was now extended to 180 days.

20. Bank Markazi annual report, 1975/6, p. 51.

21. At the time it seemed the Iranian government had overreacted. Justifying the Iranian position, Dr Jamshid Amouzegar, Minister in Charge of OPEC told the author on 28 April 1977: 'The position taken by the representative of Saudi Arabia was such that I thought they are tying it [the price] to a political solution in the region.'

22. *Financial Times*, 22 February 1977.

23. *Kayhan International*, 12 January 1977.

24. Based on information supplied to the author by Dr Amouzegar, 13 October 1975. It was not Amouzegar's view that Iran had misjudged the Saudis. (Amouzegar and Yamani enjoy a mutually antagonistic relationship.)

25. Iranian heavy crude was reduced by 9.5 cents to $11.40 per barrel. After the Bali meeting of OPEC in May 1976, Iran agreed with other Gulf producers to make a further 7 cents per barrel cut.

26. The Saudi decision was not Yamani's but he was used as a whipping-boy not to over-embarrass relations. Saudi hesitancy about raising production to beyond 11 million barrels per day was in part due to a desire not to exacerbate the situation.

27. Based on information supplied to the author by General Toufanian, Vice-Minister of War, 9 August 1976.

28. Based on information supplied to the author by Finance Minister Hushang Ansari, 4 May 1977. Ansari was in charge of co-ordinating the barter deals.

29. The oil was sold to BAC who then by an agreement with Shell had it marketed for a fee.

30. Based on a copy of the document shown to the author.

31. *Kayhan International*, 26 October 1976.

32. *Kayhan International*, 2-3 August 1974.

33. *Iran Almanac. Echo of Iran*, Tehran, 1977, p. 114.

7 SUCCESSES AND FAILURES

> This period of transition began when a great deal of money came our way precisely at a time when we did not have the means of spending it.[1]

The official justification for trying to accomplish so much so quickly was that the maximum could only be achieved by aiming high and stretching the nation's ambition. The problem lay in not establishing priorities to channel the nation's energy.

At the outset of the revised Plan there was no fixed system of priorities but every government agency assumed it had priority, so that when raw materials, manpower — and subsequently funds — became scarce there was a scramble for these resources far more disruptive than any of the individual extravaganzas. Marginal projects died or were shelved: it mattered little that the revised Plan's commitment to buying three Concordes was forgotten.[2] However, it did matter that there was no specific priority on the completion of essential infrastructure projects and the training of manpower *before* setting out to build 810,000 urban housing units or direct reduction steel plants.

It has been suggested that the absence of clear priorities was presentational and that in practice the Shah and his Ministers knew very well what they wanted.[3] This may be, although a detailed look at the implementation of the revised Plan raises serious doubts.

Impossible Targets

Housing

The government was pledged to make a major new effort in housing. It was seen as an essential part of the transformation of Iran and a significant element in satisfying socio-economic aspirations aroused by the country's increased wealth. Accordingly government credits to housing were raised 129 per cent and accounted for 17 per cent of total allocations for Social Affairs.[4] In terms of new units, the Plan proposed 810,000 in urban areas and a further 240,000 in rural areas; the bulk to be built by the private sector.[5]

This target was based on a 1972 survey showing the urban areas to be at least 1.1 million units short. However, wanting to meet the shortage and being able to do so were two separate things. Throughout the Fourth Plan (1968/9-1972/3) a total of 290,000 units were built and at

105

no time had the rate of annual construction topped 100,000 — despite a major building boom. Even the original Fifth Plan target of 630,000 units was considered 'reasonably ambitious'.[6]

A large-scale housing programme was only possible if the government prohibited construction in other sectors. Already the government had been obliged to impose a temporary ban on construction permits — first in Tehran and then other cities — from April 1973 through to January 1974 to alleviate a very severe shortage of construction materials. The ban had been lifted not because the shortage had eased but as a result of pressure from builders and property speculators who were being squeezed by the banks.[7] But despite cries from the private sector there was no doubt that government projects came first, especially if military. The Bank Markazi, reviewing the year ending March 1974, reported one month before the Ramsar meeting: 'The implementation of certain Government construction projects of high priority necessitated the transfer of a greater part of construction activities to the Government sector.'[8] This was a polite way of saying that the private sector had to rely on its wits and the black market. By the last year of the revised Plan, in 1977, housing starts in the private sector were under 90,000 in urban areas.

Cement

The revised Plan blandly stated that 'annual production of cement mills will increase from 3.6 million tons to about 20 million tons in the final year of the Fifth Plan.'[9] A regular and adequate supply of cement, either locally produced or imported, was essential to the success of Plan targets. Cement production had increased from only 2.3 million tons in 1968/9 to 3.4 million tons in 1973/4; and in the first year of the original Plan production increased a mere 4 per cent although demand was increasing at over 15 per cent.[10]

To fulfil the new production target would have meant increasing production for the remaining four years of the Plan by an annual average of 113 per cent. The Ministry of Industry eventually revised the figure for local production to 9 million tons by 1978: the 20 million ton target would be for the Sixth Plan.[11] In fact cement production in the first two full years' operation of the revised Plan increased only 25 per cent to 5.1 million tons, while consumption rose to 6.4 million tons. Meanwhile the cement shortage was playing havoc with construction costs and schedules. The government issued permits to contractors which theoretically enabled them to obtain the required quantity of cement at the official price. In practice, these guaranteed quantities were impossible to obtain except for military projects. As a result the black-market price soared. Against an official price of Rs200 per 50 kilo bag, contractors were paying up to Rs1,000 in 1977.[12]

Steel and Oil

In many other sectors the revised Plan targets were unrealistically high, ignoring completely the experience of the previous few years and making impossible demands upon the nation's physical resources. For instance, the Plan talked of expanding steel production at the Aryamehr steel complex to 1.9 million tons and establishing 'direct reduction steel mills with a capacity of about 10m tons'.[13]

A steel industry was fundamental to industrialisation and Iran was beginning to consume large quantities of steel. However, the steel target, with a production schedule of 15 million tons by 1982/3, ignored the experience of the infant steel industry in Iran. The construction of the Aryamehr complex at Isfahan, the country's first integrated steel works, had started in 1967. Production did not begin until 1973 and production problems were still preventing it from reaching its 600,000 ton capacity until the end of 1976. The direct reduction process was much more technically advanced, and delicate. Besides, it involved not merely the provision of gas but required proper co-ordination of ore supplies since Iran's own resources were inadequate. By mid-1977 it was reckoned that a total of 6.7 million tons could be produced via direct reduction by 1982/3, if all went well. Yet only one direct reduction unit with a 300,000 ton capacity at Ahwaz was ready during the Fifth Plan, and start-up of this was held up by almost six months because the connection of the necessary utilities, including gas, had fallen far behind schedule.[14]

Many of the targets, in retrospect, were more a statement of intent than a realistic objective. This even applied to the crucial oil sector where Iran wanted to expand productive capacity and extend the life of existing oilfields. The Plan talked of raising production capacity by 43 per cent to 7.3 million barrels per day.[15] This centred on developing and improving the Khuzestan fields that account for almost 90 per cent of Iranian production. Since primary recovery in these fields would only be possible for another seven or eight years, it was considered vital to introduce secondary recovery via gas injection.

In the event the Plan took much longer — not surprisingly, as this was the most complex system of secondary recovery ever developed. The main problem was the shortage of skilled manpower. By 1977 NIOC reckoned the project was over two years behind schedule and it switched to its own schema outside the Plan and allocated $4.5 billion, roughly 55 per cent of total NIOC investment. Meanwhile it had been tacitly recognised that the production ceiling could not exceed 6.7 million barrels per day and that the Plan target would have depleted reserves and limited the ultimate amount of crude recoverable.[16]

Infrastructure and Manpower Shortages

The authorities also underestimated the time lags inevitable in any major project. A year – sometimes two – could pass between outline agreement, final contract signature and the initiation of work. The construction of the largest petrochemical venture in the Plan, an olefins and aromatics complex at Bandar Shahpur in southern Iran, was held up for two years by discussions about finance and the market. During the delay the cost escalated from $600 million to $1.8 billion. Originally due onstream in 1978, work began only in early 1977 and was not scheduled for completion until 1980.[17]

Many targets were also highly unrealistic in terms of the country's infrastructure. The revised Plan document recognised the problems involved. Referring to transport and communications facilities it said much was

> below the minimum requirements ... at present many industrial, agricultural and tourism projects representing heavy investment by both the private and the public sectors are on the verge of completion and commissioning, while the communications facilities required for them to be fully utilised are inadequate.[18]

Roads were too small and poorly maintained; power lines were not ready nor the generating capacity installed; more serious, port capacity was wholly inadequate.

The original Fifth Plan anticipated almost trebling port handling capacity from 3.8 million tons to 9.7 million tons. The revised Fifth Plan trebled capacity again to 29 million tons: nearly ten times the 1973 capacity. The main new port with a 15 million ton capacity was to be built at Bandar Abbas in difficult terrain in southern Iran with only a very limited existing infrastructure. It clearly could not be relied on to be operational in 1978 when work began only in May 1976.[19]

In most projects there were also formidable manpower problems. The original Plan was particularly concerned to reduce unemployment and underemployment and it was feared that the anticipated investment would not create sufficient jobs. Under the revised Plan the situation was completely reversed. Investment was expected to create 2.1 million new jobs with 40 per cent in the industrial and mining sector. The local labour market was only capable of supplying some 1.3 million persons and it was recognised that there would be a shortfall of 721,000, of which almost 80 per cent would be skilled and semi-skilled industrial workers, and skilled construction workers.[20]

Even if this shortfall was to some extent notional it meant that an enormous effort had to be made in vocational training. Imported foreign labour was not desirable even although some 90,000 foreign personnel would be needed, including almost 30,000 already working in the country.[21] The major shortages were therefore in the areas least likely to be filled by a nation still over 60 per cent illiterate. Moreover, due to the construction boom, manpower shortages were already evident in the first year of the Plan. By early 1974 unemployment had dropped to 1.1 per cent of the active population from almost 8 per cent at the beginning of the Plan.[22]

Real and Marginal Need

The problem with establishing priorities in 1973 was that Iran had so much money that it was difficult to choose between the essential and the marginal.

The experience of the hospitals' programme is revealing in this respect. A scheme to build 6,000 hospital beds with international assistance was conceived as the central element in a vastly expanded hospitals programme to create 20,000 extra beds by 1978.[23] In early 1974 three international consortia were selected by the Ministry of Health from some 40 bidders. The consortia appeared to have been chosen deliberately on the basis of nationality — part of a conscious policy of dividing well defined shares of new contracts among Iran's main trading partners. The consortia were an American group headed by American Medicorp, a British group led by Cementation and a French group headed by Sedim. Each consortium was asked to draw up plans for just over 2,000 beds in five hospitals — Iran wanted the very best, cost no object.[24]

The companies warned that this brief might lead to cost overruns on the original estimate of Rs3 million ($44,000) per bed. The Ministry of Health intimated that this did not matter. However, when the proposals were presented, the Ministry was shocked at the three quotations: Cementation offered a bed cost of Rs20.3 million; American Medicorp Rs9.8 million and Sedim Rs8.7 million. The plans were rejected as being too expensive. In the course of just over a year, two further sets of estimates were rejected, and each time the project was reduced so that finally 6,000 beds were to be squeezed into three hospitals instead of five. The scaling down corresponded almost exactly with the drying up of Iran's surplus oil income.

With three sets of proposals rejected, the consortia were confused — the more so by the Ministry of Health and the Ministry of Social Welfare competing to control the project. Finally the Iranian authorities realised that the project made little practical sense: they were ordering large and expensive hospitals, each with a different system of administration and a different approach to standards and medical needs. In February 1976 allegations appeared in the Iranian press claiming the consortia had been seeking to defraud the government. The contracts were cancelled. Although never proved, the allegations appeared a convenient means of wriggling out of what had come to be an embarrassingly expensive and impractical deal that ignored the opportunity to standardise. Under the original agreement the companies were entitled to $2 million in the event of cancellation. This was never paid. Subsequently Medicorp was engaged as a consultant to design a new hospital system but none of the original 6,000 beds was even started.[25] This was a serious blow to the over-all public health programme and merely encouraged an increase in profitable private clinics and hospitals, mostly in Tehran, that catered only to upper-income groups.

The hospitals' project was just one victim of Iran's changed financial circumstances. Others died for lack of will, even though they were important. The automotive industry was earmarked as one of the key industrial sectors. Irannational, the largest car and truck producer, talked of producing some 400,000 saloon cars by 1980.[26] More attention, however, was given to the idea of this volume target than developing a local industry to support such production. In March 1975 the British engineering concern Guest Keen and Nettlefolds (GKN) agreed on a £20 million joint venture plant to manufacture and assemble components for the motor industry. The plant was intended to make clutches, propellor shafts, universal joints and axles, in addition to establishing a forge.[27] This was conceived as an important step towards creating indigenous production, since these were all essential components for a motor industry. However, after 18 months GKN dropped out of the project, having failed to find a suitable local partner, and the authorities made little effort to resuscitate the project. As a result Iran lost at least three years in moving towards vital indigenous production and by 1977 the local manufacture content, in the case of Irannational, was less than 55 per cent, a 5 per cent increase on 1973.

There were other schemes which died a more welcome death, like the transformation of Tehran into a major world financial centre. At the close of an Irano-British investment conference at Persepolis in November 1973, the then British Trade Minister, Peter Walker, canvassed the idea enthusiastically: 'There is surely no doubt that Tehran could become and will become one of the great financial centres of the world.'[28]

For the next two years this idea was actively promoted by a large group of international banks represented in Iran. The Iranians themselves saw a financial centre as yet another reflection of the country's new international importance but had little idea of what it entailed. The international banking community had precise ideas: a financial centre in Tehran was a polite way of saying that the surplus oil income would be employed by the international banks on the international market with little regard to Iran's own needs for development finance.

The concept was wholly unrealistic. The Iranians believed that a financial centre could be created quickly. Yet none of the necessary structures existed. Iranian banking practice and regulations were already overwhelmed by the expansion of business since 1973. More than half the staff had had under five years' experience in banking.[29] Telecommunications were poor and telex facilities were impossible to obtain quickly. Local banking procedure was so cumbrous that a loan, which took two hours to arrange abroad, needed a minimum of three days in Tehran.

A proper capital market would have required a major overhaul of the communications system, revision of banking practice and regulations, a crash programme of training, and very careful control. The only alternative was to hand the operation over to foreigners, which was unacceptable. In early 1976 the scheme began to be forgotten and by 1977 no mention of it was made at all.[30]

The new financial situation affected not only development projects but also projects in the military sphere, notably the proposed naval base on the Indian Ocean at Chah Bahar. The base was conceived as part of Iran's expanding regional military role and essential for policing the Indian Ocean. Construction required not only a port but a township and air base in one of the least accessible parts of Iran. Nevertheless in November 1975 a contract was drawn up for a British group, Costain, and American company, Brown and Root, to build the base at a total cost of $2.5 billion. Work was seriously interrupted in January 1976 by the arrest of twelve of the most senior officers in the Navy, including its Commander-in-Chief, Rear Admiral Ramzi

Abbas Ata'i, on charges of corruption.

Ata'i was found guilty of embezzlement; but details of the charges were never released. However, it was known that military investigators had examined the Chah Bahar contracts.[31] This investigation led to a fundamental reappraisal of the project. An expatriate involved at the time commented: 'I think they [the inspectors] received quite a surprise. Chah Bahar was going to be built so lavishly that they had more or less allowed for fountains with golden dolphins.'[32] New plans were duly prepared on a more modest basis. However, the escalation of costs was such that the pared down plan cost virtually the same as the original project. The Navy was still determined to press ahead with the project; but when oil revenues fell back in January 1977 Chah Bahar was shelved, not to be finalised until March 1978. Perhaps this was just as well, since if it had been completed by the original 1980 schedule, there would have been no destroyers to berth, due to delays in learning how to use them.

Investment Abroad

In pursuit of a grander international stature, the Shah determined on a major programme of foreign investment and assistance in 1974. The surplus income might be a temporary phenomenon but it would allow him to purchase prestige and influence. On this basis $2.38 billion was disbursed in 1974/5 on foreign loans, grants and investments – more than twice the amount that Iran spent in the first two development plans from 1949 to 1962.[33] Of this sum $887 million went to the IMF and the World Bank, and $283 million was handed out in soft loans to developing countries. Meanwhile $728 million was either loaned to, or placed on deposit in, Britain, Denmark and France, and a further $136 million went on investments. Having disbursed all this and having accelerated repayment of external debt, there was still an over-all payments surplus in 1974/5 of almost $5 billion.[34] The authorities perhaps could be forgiven for feeling the surpluses would continue a bit longer (see Table 5).

Yet some of these commitments, so eagerly undertaken, were to prove an embarrassment in less than eighteen months. The case of a $1.2 billion loan to Britain symbolised this turn-round. The loan was negotiated in July 1974 on the basis of three tranches being paid at market rates to a British local authority over a three-year period. The first $400 million tranche was paid on time to the National Water Council. However, the second tranche had to be split into two separate payments of $200 million each by special arrangement in June and September 1976.

This was because Iran could not afford to release so much foreign exchange at one time.

By the time the final tranche was due, Iran did not want to pay. By mutual agreement the British government waived the final tranche, while Iran agreed to use the money to proceed with a number of British arms deals which had been delayed through lack of funds. Both governments felt it too embarrassing to admit to details of the deal.[35] Commitments to place $1 billion with the Banque de France met similar problems. These were the first major loans by an oil producer to industrialised countries. In retrospect, they would probably have never been conceded if the Shah had foreseen the rapid reduction of surplus income. But in the last resort the motivation for the loans was not economic; they were rather the first attempt to use oil surpluses as an arm of foreign policy, and in this the Shah succeeded, binding Britain and France closer to Iran.

The Shah was lobbied by many top executives of European and American companies who held out the offer of shares, technology and access to markets in return for cash injections. Very few of these offers materialised. For instance, serious discussions were initiated with General Electric to purchase a 25 per cent stake in the company's plastics division — one of the largest plastics producers in America; the rationale being that GE would have a guaranteed long-term supply of feedstock and in return provide the National Iranian Oil Company with an important new outlet. Negotiations broke down on a price for the feedstock and GE wearied of dealing with the Shah, the mercurial Ansari in the Finance Ministry, NIOC and its then affiliate the National Petrochemical Company.[36] Grumman and Union Carbide also had discussions on share participation which never developed, but Iran came close to buying a 13 per cent stake in Pan Am. Iran was to provide a $245 million ten-year loan in return for 13 per cent of voting stock plus a further $55 million cash purchase of 55 per cent of the Intercontinental Hotel chain. This was to be a rescue package to ease the company's financial position in early 1975. But the complexity of the airline's debt structure and problems over voting rights finally broke up the deal in July 1975.[37]

Until the Pan Am proposal fell through, foreign investment had been carried out or considered on an *ad hoc* basis with the influence of the Shah's own prejudices clearly visible. The first purchase in September 1974 had been a 25.04 per cent stake in the steel subsidiary of the West German group Krupp — Krupp Huttenwerke. Krupp had been closely associated with Reza Shah, added to which the Shah admired

German industry, needed to balance American and British influence in Iran, and was fascinated by gaining a foothold in one of Europe's oldest industrial establishments. He also had established a strong personal rapport with Krupp president Berthold Beitz. At the time the Shah sought to buy into Krupp proper, but then the nature of the foundation that contained the family trust made this impossible, so he paid DM300 million for Huttenwerke, the group's chief loss-maker.[38] He went on to buy into two Krupp Brazilian subsidiaries for DM250 million and in October 1976 acquired a 25.01 per cent share in the foundation that controlled Krupp, reportedly for DM550 million.[39] Yet if this showed an element of consistency (and persistence) the purchase of a 25 per cent stake in Deutsche Babcock Wilcox in January 1975 was more chance – a ready-made package presented to the Shah by a British company which wished to sell a stake in its German subsidiary.[40]

Other discussions were held with well known international companies. Interestingly, those which appealed most to the Shah nearly always involved companies that were family-controlled or run by a powerful figure. This was the case with Krupp, as well as with Fiat and Occidental – two sets of discussions that failed to materialise. A proposed sale of 30 per cent of Occidental's equity collapsed over voting rights difficulties,[41] while Fiat turned down the Shah's overture allegedly because an Iranian stake was politically unacceptable.[42]

There was a great deal of unnecessary fuss about Iran's foreign investment programme. Neither side thought the initial arrangements through with any thoroughness. In general, the initial agreement was made by the Shah or his Finance Minister Hushang Ansari, and the details were left to lower officials. Deals were publicly proclaimed even before the technicians had a chance to investigate. Discussions with Arnold Hammer of Occidental were initiated without NIOC being consulted; yet NIOC was to be the Iranian partner and the source of technical data on petroleum. Foreign investment was kept firmly within the grasp of Ansari at the Finance Ministry – in conjunction with an investment office in Washington run by his brother, Cyrus.[43] The system was based upon personalities and in the end Iran was probably fortunate that so few investments came off. Even if they had, Iran would have been pressed to find the right personnel to monitor the performance of the investments.

The ventures which made the most sense to Iran were oil or oil-related, widening the scope of Iran's 'downstream market'. Even before 1973 Iran had shares in refineries in Durban, South Africa and

Madras, India. Another refinery venture in South Korea was initiated in 1976. Iran also sought to buy into BP, finally achieving a small stake when in July 1977 it acquired 700,000 shares, the maximum allotment, when the British government disposed of 17 per cent of its share in BP.[44] Inconclusive discussions were also initiated with the Italian state oil company, ENI, in 1974 on a stake in refining and distribution operations. This foundered because the Iranians felt they were being offered the most unprofitable operations.

It also made more sense to invest in ventures which gave access to much-needed raw materials, like an agreement in April 1975 with India whereby Iran undertook to invest $630 million in the development of iron-ore mines at Kudremukh which would supply ore to the Iranian steel industry. Other projects like the financing of textiles and cement in Pakistan or fertilisers in Egypt were more marginal but could be justified in terms of foreign policy.

Agriculture and the Boom

In mid-1971 the Iranian government invited a team from the International Labour Office (ILO) in Geneva to organise a comprehensive employment study for Iran. This study was submitted in June 1972. Although overtaken in many respects by the 1973 oil price increases, the study nevertheless offered a set of priorities and objectives which made interesting comparisons with the evolution of the revised Plan.

Summarising its main recommendations, the ILO mission stated:

the development of agriculture, which has and will for a long time continue to have the largest share of the economically active population, has an effect both on the provision of basic food requirements of an increasing population and on anticipated employment levels; more equitable distribution of income is a prerequisite for the expansion of domestic markets on which industrial expansion will largely depend; education and training are the essential means by which the supply of skills is matched by demand.[45]

The report did not seek to talk Iran out of accelerated industrialisation; instead it stressed that without more attention to agriculture and the creation of balanced rural development there would be no base for future industry since rural incomes would not be high enough to buy the goods.

The specific recommendations included the following points:

(1) the implementation of an urgent family planning programme;
(2) a major effort to improve and enlarge irrigation, facilitate access to agricultural credit and subsidise agricultural inputs;
(3) extend rural services to improve living standards and curb the large-scale exodus to the towns;
(4) create balanced industrial employment that did not tip the scales too much in favour of capital-intensive projects;
(5) build up industrial estates in small towns;
(6) avoid using prefabricated techniques and heavy construction equipment except where demonstrably necessary in housing;
(7) emphasise low-cost housing in the construction programme;
(8) provide special incentives to attract qualified personnel to small towns and rural areas;
(9) decentralise as much as possible all decision-making.[46]

The ILO's chief concern was to prevent the urban/rural gap widening and to point out the dangers of industrialisation, even though this was where the new jobs would be created.

Family planning was stressed because of the scarcity of water and the limitations this placed on Iran's long-term ability to feed itself. The population in the early seventies was growing at just under 3 per cent a year and threatened to double within twenty years. The revised Plan paid attention to family planning, aiming at a reduction in the birth rate to 1.5 per cent a year by 1994. In practice family planning assumed a low priority because the authorities believed that industry and the service sector could absorb increased manpower. There was also a widespread belief that surplus oil revenue would provide the necessary funds to purchase foodstuffs abroad and so offset the shortfall in agricultural production. This was evidenced by the resort to government subsidies for imported foodstuffs beginning in 1974.

Subsidies reduced the amount the consumer paid for basic commodities; but the reduced price, coupled with higher incomes, stimulated demand. This put further pressure on domestic agricultural production and imports and helped create a thriving black market. Shortages of essential foodstuffs in the shops were frequent. Increased demand was particularly evident in the consumption of red meat. In 1960 *per capita* consumption of red meat was 28 kilos: by 1975 it had reached 47 kilos per head per year. Demand was increasing at over 12 per cent a year, yet local production was only rising by 9 per cent a year. To prevent growing dependence upon imports, the government started importing large quantities of high-quality livestock from the US and Europe by air freight for breeding purposes (making it among the costliest live-stock in the world). These foreign breeds were on the whole unsuited to the Iranian climate and required much higher amounts of animal feed — and of better quality — than local strains. So not only was the government paying dearly to obtain more locally produced red meat, it was paying twice by subsidising the produce to the consumer. Only in late 1976 was this policy slowed down.[47]

The subsidies also masked the inefficiency of local agriculture. The government in the case of a staple commodity like wheat was importing at twice the local cost and then selling at subsidised prices. Instead of supporting the foreign farmer, it would perhaps have been more bene-ficial to re-examine local farm gate prices and subsidies. Equally, subsi-dies concealed the wastage in local production: up to $2 billion worth of agricultural production was being lost each year through poor cropping, bad warehousing and inadequate distribution. The Ministry of Agriculture itself estimated that 30 per cent of tomato production and 20 per cent of meat produced was lost in the unco-ordinated chain between supplier and the shop. Meanwhile the farmer was getting as little as 5.5 per cent of the shop price for most products.[48] The govern-ment had stimulated consumption without any proper structural reform of agricultural production.

Reform was attempted in the 'agribusiness' ventures first promoted in early 1969. By encouraging foreign investors with attractive local financial assistance, it was hoped the latest technology could be applied to large-scale farming. The experiment was tried in south-west Khuzes-tan where large tracts of flattish uncultivated land could be irrigated with water from the Dez Dam. Khuzestan was to be the bread-basket of Iran. Four joint ventures were formed with prestigious foreign partners who had the type of experience necessary for the climate — cotton-growing in Ethiopia and Californian agriculture (whose climate was considered similar).[49] By early 1976 three of the four projects had piled up losses of over $5 million; and the Agricultural Development Bank had been obliged to take over the management of three of them, injecting emergency funds into two which were technically bankrupt. Meanwhile only 13 per cent of the land allocated had been brought under cultivation (8,200 hectares out of 60,800).

These ventures lacked proper preparation. Crop choice and crop forecasts were based upon inadequate research: large-scale cotton-growing proved disastrous; while only by accident was it discovered that winter crops like sugar-beet and wheat were the most suitable to the high soil temperatures. The farming units were too large; and no one anticipated the scale of development costs (land-levelling, roads, housing, etc.) which were borne by the companies, not the government or local authorities.

These problems combined with other factors. The vital water from the Dez Dam irrigation scheme was not available in the quantities required. At the end of 1975 only 18,000 hectares were under irrigation: the schedule was for four times this amount. Workers with any mechanical skill quit because wages in the nearby industrial centre of Ahwaz were twice as high. The essential pool of cheap labour dried up. To prepare the land for the large-scale farms 6,530 families had been moved into 13 centres. This had been done in a clumsy way, and many were reluctant to work for others on land which they historically regarded as theirs — especially as most of the work was casual. To cap it all, costs rose by 300 per cent over five years while farm gate prices went up only 50 per cent. In agricultural terms the venture was not a complete failure. In five years up to the end of 1975 wheat yields per hectare rose from 2.2 tons to 4 tons and sugar-beet from 42 tons to 50 tons. But it was a financial and organisational disaster. It left no real model to take forward into the sixth Plan.[50]

The ILO's emphasis on irrigation was reinforced by the experience of Khuzestan and it was allotted an important place in the revised Plan. However, this clashed with the need for more electricity. Hydroelectricity was responsible for almost 18 per cent of power supplies. In the competing demands of water for power generation and water for irrigation in low rainfall years (which was the case in 1976 and 1977) power generation took precedence.

Again extension of rural services was considered an important element of the new Plan's emphasis on social policies. At first the credits were available but the manpower and the materials proved difficult to mobilise for feeder roads, extension of electricity transmission lines, etc. In the competition for scarce skilled manpower, and subsequently scarce materials, the rural areas lost out. In 1976 when budgetary expenditure began to be scrutinised, rural improvements were the easiest to prune.

Meanwhile the difference in urban and rural wage levels increased. Over-all *per capita* income had doubled in three years to $1,600 by March 1976.[51] This had created the illusion that income was being distributed. Rural incomes did rise, true; but only through government spending and not through any clearly defined structural change that would ensure the closing of the urban/rural gap. The rural exodus continued at the rate of 250,000 a year.[52]

Capital-Intense Solutions

In the industrial field the ILO feared that over-emphasis on capital-intense industry would ruin long-term employment prospects.[53] What happened was rather different. With access to new capital, industry opted for capital-intense solutions — attracted by the benefits of high technology in production. In theory the move was logical: better and more efficient equipment would produce a more cost-effective operation. But this was measured against the norms of a Western industrialised country.

In the Iranian context this solution had unforeseen repercussions. The over-all demand for industrial labour was lower than anticipated, yet the need for certain types of skilled and semi-skilled workers, like machine-operators and good managers, increased. Country-wide, capital-intense solutions had been adopted and a key sector like oil competed with construction for skilled labour. Yet if traditional construction techniques had been maintained there would have been little need for skilled labour. The shortage of skilled labour — the difficulty of finding it and retaining it — became the single most important element in delaying projects.

Opting for capital-intense solutions inevitably raised the technology and foreign assistance content. This was willingly accepted by the authorities because it was felt Iranian workers would learn through experience. By and large the presence of foreign assistance discouraged a responsibility to learn; and employers realising that foreign workers performed better — often on lower pay — were reluctant to train Iranian replacements.

Afghans, Indians and Pakistanis were used as the main semi-skilled imported labour — Indians, Pakistanis, Philippinos and South Koreans the main skilled technicians and in the higher-technology fields Europeans and Americans. By March 1977 some 60,000 foreigners possessed work permits.[54] In addition, some 10,000 or more workers were thought to be in Iran without work permits. If all the vacancies were to be filled, the proportion of foreigners in Iran would easily have doubled. At the outset the authorities preferred to let jobs go vacant than allow too high a number of foreigners. As a guideline, the Ministry of Labour in 1975 considered that no more than 10 per cent of the labour shortfall should be made up by foreigners.[55] One of the areas where priority was given to foreign replacement was in the health field, where a target of 20,000 imported doctors was set. (The shortage of medical and para-medical staff was so acute, for instance, that the laboratory of Abadan's largest hospital was forced to close down in February 1976.[56])

Throughout industry, machinery and costly imported technology were often inefficiently employed. This was not entirely surprising. Industry had to make formidable readjustments in a very short space of time and from a narrow base of experience.

> During the years when labour was abundant, financial assistance by the Government and the development banks had placed plentiful resources at the disposal of industrialists, and many of them were making high profits under the protection provided by the Government. Some did not learn to economise in the use of labour, materials and equipment, and the need for careful management of these factors did not seem urgent. Therefore many industrial units had become accustomed to waste of capital, raw materials and surplus labour.[57]

Against this background, industrialists had to cope in quick succession with sudden increases in the cost of imported goods and raw materials, labour shortages, spiralling wage costs, exorbitant land prices, clogged ports, price controls and, finally, serious shortages in power supplies.

The result was extremely uneven performance. Despite domestic demand, it was the rare factory that was able to operate at capacity. A government study in early 1977 found that capacity utilisation was 61 per cent in textiles, 96 per cent in cement, 46 per cent in brick-making, 69 per cent in the automotive industry (51 per cent in the car industry) and 32 per cent in tractors.[58] Quite frequently this was due to factors beyond the control of the individual factory. Arak Machine Tools – the main heavy engineering plant in the country – produced 13,751 tons of goods in 1976/7 against a capacity of 23,000 tons. The low production was attributed to power failures that damaged installations and took a long time to repair. They also suffered from very poor after-sales service on five important boilers and very high absenteeism among the workers. Yet the company was singled out in the revised Plan to have its production raised from 30,000 tons to 75,000 tons a year![59]

One arm of the government undermined the efforts of another. For instance, a company was formed to manufacture road-mending equipment, Hepco. The government had given this company financial support through IDRO (Industrial Development and Renovation Organisation). However, no effort was made to prevent contractors importing foreign equipment. By March 1977 the company was producing at 25 per cent of its capacity, and had accumulated unsold equipment equivalent to 20 times its capital. Or again the country's sole aluminium factory was operating at 43 per cent of capacity largely due to power cuts. In the 12 months to March 1977 it had had its power cut 760 times and in two years had lost $12 million from power shortages.[60]

Some factories suffered seriously from the steep increase in costs after 1973. The Shahriar Industrial Group's steel billet plant at Ahwaz started operations in 1972 using scrap iron as raw material. After three years' satisfactory operation the increasing problems of finding adequate scrap supplies, heavy rises in transportation costs, port congestion and labour shortages forced the plant to close down. The company decided it was more profitable to buy billets abroad and tried to sell its 200,000 ton capacity plant to the government.[61]

Within three years Iran had become an exceptionally high-cost country without the benefits of skilled or efficient labour. General Motors calculated in late 1975 that it took 45 man-hours to assemble their Chevrolet Iran in Tehran against 25 man-hours in West Germany for the same car, the Opel Commodore. GM Iran had managed to reach 45 hours in just over 12 months, having scaled down from 80 hours at the outset of production. The comparative difference of labour costs was 5.2.[62] GM Iran lost $4.2 million in the first two years of operations. In fact the automotive industry's survival depended on high protective barriers (taxes of between 200 and 500 per cent) and a generous pricing policy because so many of the components were imported. (The Chevrolet Iran sold for $8,500 against $4,500 for the Opel Commodore in West Germany.) When price controls were introduced in July 1975, the motor industry was among the first to protest, and indeed was one of the few privileged sectors to have the controls rescinded in early 1976.

The problems of Iranian management centred around the introduction of technology in a country with no tradition of modern technology. For instance, an expensive German press was introduced into an automotive factory with a special device that automatically shut off the machine if the worker came too close. This enabled freer operation of the press by one instead of two people and guaranteed against industrial accidents. An older and cheaper design used a metal guard but needed two operatives. In the Iranian factory the older design was more efficient, since a poorly trained operator found it hard to come to terms with the unseen electronic beam that stopped the machine once he moved beyond a certain point.[63]

A more fundamental criticism of government policy towards industry is that in the three years following the 1973 oil price rises, wage increases were not infrequently three times the annual increase in productivity.[64] Production costs had risen so quickly that Iran's hopes of creating export-orientated industries like automobiles and domestic appliances suffered serious and perhaps irreparable damage.

Another important consequence of the switch to high technology was to suck industry into the urban areas which attracted skilled manpower. Business that ventured into rural areas discovered that the benefits of cheaper land, government grants and cheaper labour were quickly eroded for lack of skilled labour. It was very hard to retain skilled workers once they had been trained. Second, local authorities frequently failed to provide, when required, essential facilities such as telephones, electricity supplies, water or access roads, to say nothing of housing for the work-force. For instance, poultry farms tended to concentrate round Tehran and Qazvin because water supplies were easier to obtain — and in Tehran water connection could take from four to eight months![65]

There was in fact very little real incentive to establish an industry in a rural area or indeed beyond the confines of any large town. With distribution, decisions and communications centralised in Tehran no one really wanted to be located outside the Tehran area: a further factor widening the urban/rural gap and increasing the rural exodus.

In the rural areas traditional industries like carpet-weaving, which employed some 300,000 people, suffered.[66] Labour costs rose sharply and in the Kerman region — one of the principal weaving areas — the expanded mining industry competed for labour. Carpet production declined, producing lower exports in an industry which provided 17 per cent of Iran's non-oil exports.[67]

Finally, the high wages and salaries for qualified personnel in large towns, especially Tehran, made it extremely difficult to attract good people to rural areas. Frequently these were the posts which only foreigners would fill, or disgruntled bureaucrats banished for some form of disobedience. The turnover of personnel was rapid, making continuity of programmes doubly difficult. This was not a problem exclusive to Iran, but shared by all developing countries where the capital and large towns represent the modern world. However, in a large country like Iran, the development of which required a strong element of decentralisation, it was a serious handicap.

Notes

1. *Kayhan International*, 25 October 1976.
2. Plan and Budget Organisation, *Iran's Fifth Development Plan 1973-78*, revised version, May 1975, p. 397.

3. Based on information supplied to the author by PBO officials and Minister of Finance Hushang Ansari.

4. PBO, *Fifth Plan*, p. 46.

5. Ibid., pp. 390-400. The private sector was to build 550,000 urban and 200,000 rural units.

6. International Labour Office, *Employment and Incomes Policies for Iran* (Geneva, International Labour Office, 1973), p. 62.

7. Construction permits dropped 44 per cent in Tehran and large cities in 1973/4. See Bank Markazi annual report, 1973/4, p. 93.

8. Ibid., p. 91.

9. PBO, *Fifth Plan*, p. 246.

10. Bank Markazi annual report, 1974/5, p. 181.

11. *Iran Almanac. Echo of Iran, Tehran*, 1977, p. 316.

12. Ibid., p. 249.

13. PBO, *Fifth Plan*, p. 246.

14. Information supplied to the author by Dr Reza Amin, Chairman of National Iranian Steel Industries Corporation, July 1977, and by executives of foreign steel companies in Iran.

15. PBO, *Fifth Plan*, p. 266.

16. Based on information supplied to the author by NIOC officials, July 1977. See also *Middle East Economic Survey*, 25 October 1976.

17. Information supplied to the author by an executive of Iran Japan Petrochemical Company, July 1977.

18. PBO, *Fifth Plan*, p. 297.

19. *Financial Times*, 28 July 1975.

20. PBO, *Fifth Plan*, pp. 71-3.

21. *Financial Times*, 28 July 1975.

22. Bank Markazi annual report, 1973/4, p. 20.

23. PBO, *Fifth Plan*, p. 459.

24. Based upon information supplied to the author by Cementation.

25. *Kayhan International*, 19 February 1976. These allegations were denied by the companies concerned. Cementation insisted there was no fixed agreement on costs per bed. The British group's three consecutive bids were: £355 million; £210 million; £178 million. The original bid was based upon 2,497 beds.

26. *Kayhan International*, 27 November 1975. That year car production at Irannational was 55,000 units.

27. *Financial Times*, 14 March 1975.

28. *Iran-United Kingdom Investment Conference 1973, summary of proceedings* (London, Times Newspapers, September 1974), p. 4.

29. *Kayhan International*, 12 December 1975.

30. *Financial Times*, 29 October 1975.

31. *Financial Times*, 12 January 1976 and 22 January 1976. Also *Kayhan International*, 23 February 1976.

32. Comment to the author by a member of one of the contracting companies involved at Chah Bahar.

33. Bank Markazi annual report, 1974/5, p. 58.

34. In 1974/5 Iran accelerated repayment of foreign debt, mainly short-term, from $541 million to $1.3 billion.

35. Based on information supplied to the author by Bank Markazi and British officials.

36. Based on information supplied to the author by a GE executive. This project was never publicised.

37. *Financial Times*, 2 July 1975 and 20 July 1975.

38. Based on information supplied to the author by Fried Krupp.

39. The Brazilian subsidiaries were Krupp Metallurgica, Campo Limpo (forg-

ings and castings for the automotive industry) and Krupp Industrias Meccanicas at Minas Gerais (a heavy-machinery plant). Iran bought a 40 per cent direct stake, and in addition 5 per cent of Industrias Meccanicas shares went to a joint Krupp-Iranian investment company set up in Zürich in 1974. See *Financial Times*, 20 October 1976 and 22 November 1976.

40. The price paid was DM178 million.

41. *Business Week*, 13 September 1976. An intriguing aspect of the talks with Occidental is that they also concerned partnership to explore for oil in northern Iran and offshore in the Caspian. This had always been a highly sensitive issue with the Soviet Union; but given Hammer's links with the Soviet leadership this could have been a compromise.

42. Fiat's President, Giovanni Agnelli, is understood to have felt that any equity stake held by Iran would become the focus of industrial action and left-wing agitation. Fiat was one of the few multinationals to avoid Iran during the boom, having sold out its automobile interests in 1971.

43. Cyrus Ansari became the Iranian representative on Krupp.

44. Based on information supplied to the author by Dr Parviz Mina, director of International Relations, NIOC, July 1977.

45. ILO, *Employment and Incomes Policies*, p. 9.

46. Ibid., pp. 13-19.

47. Between 1974 and 1976 European cattle prices rose sharply, making the scheme less attractive. Originally the government undertook to pay for the air freight costs but alienated the companies involved by disputing this commitment.

48. The Iran *Economic Survey*, No. 138, 28 June 1977. The wholesaler (middle man) was getting 44 per cent of the final price; the retailer (shopkeeper) 39 per cent; the transporter 11.5 per cent and the producer 5.5 per cent.

49. The four companies were: Shellcott (foreign partners Shell and Mitchell Cotts); Iran California (foreign partners John Deere, Bank America, Transworld America); Iran America (foreign partners Citicorp International); Iran International (foreign partners Mitsui, Diamond A Cattle Ranch, Chase Investment Company and Hawaian Agronomics).

50. Based on information supplied to the author by the Agricultural Development Bank and foreign consultants familiar with Iran's agribusiness. Shellcott by mid-1976 had accumulated losses of Rs403 million; Iran California had accumulated losses in 1975 of over Rs100 million, and Iran America was wound up in 1975 and restructured with a Rs460 million cash injection from the ADB.

51. Bank Markazi annual report, 1975/6, p. 2.

52. *Financial Times*, 25 July 1977.

53. ILO, *Employment and Incomes Policies*, p. 59.

54. *Iran Almanac*, 1977, p. 379.

55. *Tehran Journal*, 11 August 1975.

56. *Kayhan International*, 25 February 1976.

57. Industrial and Mining Development Bank of Iran (IMDBI) annual report, 1976/7, p. 12.

58. US Embassy, *Semi-Annual Economic Trends Report*, Tehran, May 1977.

59. *Kayhan International*, 13 July 1977; see also PBO, *Fifth Plan*, p. 248. Workers at Arak Machine Tools had taken 20,000 hours' sick leave in one year.

60. Ibid.

61. IMDBI, annual report, 1976/7, p. 61.

62. Based on information supplied to the author by GM.

63. Based on comments by an executive in Irannational.

64. IMDBI, annual report, 1976/7, p. 112.

65. *Iran Almanac*, 1977. p. 217.

66. ILO, *Employment and Incomes Policies*, p. 47.

67. Bank Markazi annual report, 1975/6, p. 56. It has also been suggested

that the value of carpet exports declined following the lifting of foreign exchange controls in late 1974. Previously carpets were the principal means of acquiring foreign exchange for the private sector and carpet sales were used as a means of evading exchange controls. The carpet-dealers and money-changers were closely interlinked.

PART III
THE SYSTEM OF POWER

8 USE AND ABUSE OF POWER

> One can imagine a good man killing himself in the effort to reform the Government of Persia. But success would seem impossible and endurance must lead to compromise with evil and corruption of every sort. A violent death would be the likely end of a good man in such a position, and wealth that of one who would accept the place and swim in the stream of corruption.[1]

Having survived two direct attempts on his life, witnessed the assassination of two Prime Ministers and having experienced a brief but humiliating flight from his country, Mohammed Reza Shah could scarcely pretend that his rise to absolute power has been effortless or his retention of power without challenge. But since the crushing of parliamentary opposition in 1963 he has built up, through the use of force and favours, a position that has proved progressively harder to challenge. He has evolved a system that permits him both to govern and to stay in power.

Government has been fashioned round the principle of sustaining the ruler's power, the hallmark of all authoritarian régimes. The system is successful in sustaining the Shah on the throne but ineffective in handling the dynamic development process.

In theory the present Shah observes the 1906 Constitution, which envisaged a constitutional monarchy with an independent legislature — in the form of the Majles (Parliament) — and an independent judiciary. In practice the Constitution has only served as a point of reference when convenient. The distinction between the executive authority of the Shah and the independence of the legislature and the judiciary has been blurred and all are merely part of the monarch's executive arm. All important decisions are by decree, imperial firman. The monarchy is the country's only institution, around which all power revolves without any formal checks and balances. Nevertheless unconventional checks and balances do exist: namely the self-interest of the Shah in staying on the throne and the self-interest of those who depend upon the Shah as the fountain of all favour. In general the system has encouraged the abuse of power. As Marvin Zonis points out: 'the Government of Iran historically has been and continues to be "of, by and for the elite".'[2]

The Shah observes the traditional and fundamental principle of divide and rule. Power is distributed to a series of individuals or agencies with overlapping functions which are kept fragmented and weak. Loyalty is at a premium in a handful of trusted positions but generally the system is founded on mistrust and mutual antagonism.

The centres of this fragmented power are as deceptive as a Chinese box because the system has two faces — the public or constitutional side, and the covert or unconstitutional side. The former consists of what would seem in a Western society the institutions of democracy: the Prime Minister's office and the Cabinet; the Majles; the single political party, Rastakhiz; the provincial governors and the press. However, the functions of these are either controlled, monitored or duplicated by the covert side which consists of the Imperial Inspectorate, SAVAK, the armed forces, military tribunals, powerful individuals without fixed positions and the economic power of the Royal Family. In some instances these two worlds converge in the Royal Court and the Shah's Special Bureau, which act as a funnel for communication with the Shah. In other instances personalities have connections with both 'worlds'. Yet the one constant factor is the Shah's own direct relationship with all these bodies or individuals. Thus the exercise of power has come to depend exclusively upon the Shah's relationships with a series of individuals either in their function as heads of agencies and Ministries or as individuals.

The Shah has this to say about his own system:

I am a great believer in a plurality of administrative channels and in having alternative channels always available. If through ignorance, laziness or self-interest one official refuses to bestir himself to vigorous action, then I turn to somebody else . . . I do not employ advisors in the usual sense of the term. To do this is, I think, dangerous for any head of state. One of the few mistakes my father made was to rely upon a narrowing circle of advisors. Fearing Reza Shah, they flattered him rather than telling him the truth; and I am sorry to say that they were by no means incorruptible. My system is entirely different. I know that advisors, no matter how technically competent they may be, sometimes make the national interest subservient to their own. Furthermore they are prone to funnel all information through themselves and to seal off independent intelligence channels. So in lieu of advisors I obtain information from many quarters and then try to strike a balance sincerely and solely in the light of the public interest.[3]

This was written in 1961 and since then the emphasis on alternative channels has increased considerably.

The Grand Vizier

Since the experience of Mossadegh, the Shah has turned the Prime Minister into the chief public administrator with rare opportunity to initiate policy of any significance. The last person to try was Dr Ali Amini – and his example stands as a warning to all those who might overstep themselves. He was eased out of office in 1962 (see Chapter 4).

The post has come to resemble more and more that of the old Grand Vizier. The Prime Minister carries out, and occasionally interprets, the Shah's orders. Amir Abbas Hoveida epitomised the Grand Vizier role. He held the post from 1965 to August 1977, the longest uninterrupted tenure since the promulgation of the Constitution. His principal asset was his acceptance of this subservient role, an astute interpretation of what the Shah wanted and a canny feel for the political mood of the country. He was also a solid reassuring figure – pipe-smoking, the quirk of a fresh orchid in his buttonhole – who managed to soften the austere public image of the monarchy. Hoveida seemed to positively enjoy travelling around the country telling the nation the Shah's policies. Yet despite this loyal service, he was shunted aside when the Shah needed a scapegoat.

Hoveida was cast aside because the Shah needed a change of style, a more liberal image, in response to demands from the intelligentsia and the bourgeoisie for greater liberalisation after President Carter's election to office. He was also made the scapegoat for the accumulated failures of the revised Plan, like the power shortages that occurred throughout the spring and summer of 1977. Hoveida was a prime example of the disposability of Ministers and Cabinets who are there in the last resort to protect the royal personage from direct criticism.

Superficially it seemed that someone in Hoveida's position had the means to build a power base. In one sense he could and did. As Prime Minister he had an important area of patronage in influencing appointments to key positions as Ministers, senior civil servants, ambassadors or newspaper editors (he was careful to cultivate the latter). In 1976 the Prime Minister's Office had almost $140 million, available mostly for running expenses and attendant patronage.[4]

Latterly he acquired influence over the choice of Ministers. A foreign diplomat recalled watching a film after dinner with Hoveida. At the end of the film, the lights went on to reveal a room full of men. Hoveida, seeing his guest's perplexity, calmly said: 'I've just reshuffled my Cabinet.'[5] Hoveida also acquired influence through Iran Novin, one of the two 'loyal' political parties until the creation of Rastakhiz. Indeed it was suggested that the creation of the Rastakhiz single party system in March 1975 was intended to curb his power. Hoveida had just been elected party Secretary of Iran Novin at a rousing rally in Tehran; the first time that one man had been Premier and party Secretary in more than a decade. However the party influence remained when he was co-opted into being temporary Secretary-General of Rastakhiz. He was so jealous of his authority that he effectively prevented Finance Minister Hushang Ansari and Interior Minister Jamshid Amouzegar from playing their roles as leaders of the party's two 'wings' — supposedly two ideo-logical groupings for fostering debate within the party. In fact even after Amouzegar was elected Secretary-General in October 1976, Hoveida still sought to obstruct him and control the party.

The Prime Minister's main task within the Cabinet is to orchestrate a result that has been agreed in advance. The Cabinet takes no import-ant decisions. These are reached in advance by the Shah in private audi-ence either with the Prime Minister or with individual Ministers or heads of agencies. At best the Cabinet acts as a forum for working out the application of a decision. Hoveida tended to dominate all discussion. One Minister recalled the unedifying experience of his first Cabinet meeting with Hoveida:

> At my first Cabinet meeting I was very nervous; but then I almost laughed when I saw how frivolous the whole thing was. No one talked very much. They [the Ministers] just sat there signing docu-ments or listening to Hoveida. I remember one day a Minister got up and asked something like 'Why do we bother to come here if no one discusses anything?' This created little reaction and changed nothing.[6]

The weakness of the Prime Minister, and the Cabinet, stems from the Shah's control over their appointment and dismissal. Although the Con-stitution would have it otherwise, Parliament has no say in appoint-ments. The Prime Minister and the rest of the Cabinet have no institu-tional protection for their positions or recourse to popular opinion except in the most indirect way: the dismissal of a certain Minister might reflect unfavourably on the Shah's ability to govern. Damage to the Shah's credibility is the sole effective check on his power of hire and fire.

Individual Ministers do develop their own area of influence; however, it is always strictly circumscribed. Even more than the Prime Minister,

Ministers are a disposable commodity: scapegoats for any unpopular policy of the Shah. Initiative is discouraged and the delegation of authority inhibited. Ultimately it becomes unavoidable that the men chosen, and willing to serve, as Ministers have to emasculate themselves if they wish to survive in their posts.

Ministers tend to use influence defensively, to protect their own position from the rivalries of other Ministers or heads of government agencies. This creates considerable antagonism between Ministers, often deliberately fostered by the Shah. An important by-product of this antagonism is that Ministers continually seek to ensure their Ministries are seen in a favourable light by the Shah. Facts and figures are distorted to protect individual positions in every Ministry because Ministers have no means of self-protection outside the Shah's favour.

The Shah, knowing full well that facts are withheld or doctored, counters by reinforcing his parallel government, which duplicates with little efficiency the institution it is monitoring. In 1975 the Shah created an Energy Ministry to be responsible for Iranian energy policy. However, this Ministry has no control over the management or policy of the National Iranian Oil Company which produces, markets and refines Iranian oil and which also coordinates the development of gas through its former subsidiary, the National Iranian Gas Company. The Ministry of Energy equally has no control over the Atomic Energy Authority, whose expenditure has become the largest single item in the energy budget. The decisions on the purchase of nuclear power stations are made by the Shah in co-ordination with the Atomic Energy Authority. Both NIOC and the Atomic Energy Authority report direct to the Shah, never to the Cabinet. NIOC is not consulted on oil price policy. This is decided by the Shah in conjunction with another Minister – for several years until his appointment as Prime Minister in August 1977, it was Jamshid Amouzegar, Minister of the Interior. Thus the Ministry theoretically responsible for energy matters has its empire broken up into separate parts which can only be co-ordinated through the Shah. Even in such a vital area, the Shah still feels obliged to adopt an inefficient, but protective system in terms of his own power.

In many developing countries the one Ministry that provides a separate power base is Defence. In Iran, the Ministry of War (Iran is one of the few countries not at war to call a Ministry by this name) has been kept in the hands of the military since defence is considered to be outside the sphere of civilian Ministers. Defence policy and foreign affairs are exclusive spheres for the Shah. On paper the Ministry of the Interior is powerful since it controls both the police and the 70,000 strong paramilitary gendarmerie equipped with light weapons and using its own communications systems.[7] However, these two bodies have limited investigatory powers and on key issues they report not to their Minister but direct to the Shah. The same applies to provincial governors who are nominally under the Ministry of Interior but since they are appointed personally by the Shah they report direct to him on important matters.

The Rastakhiz Party

The creation of the Rastakhiz Party finally dismissed the masquerade of a Western-style political system in Iran. At the time the Shah declared: 'Every Iranian who has clarified his position, that is who believes in the Constitution, the Monarchy and the Sixth Bahman Revolution [the White Revolution of 1962] must definitely join this political organisation.'[8] From now on there would be one political party grouping all loyal Iranians.

Yet if he was disillusioned with Western democratic structures in Iran, the Shah was nevertheless anxious to generate a sense of participation in the modernisation of the country. The party was intended to be an important element in his system of government; the link between the Shah and the nation, cementing the mystical union. In practice the party has proved, as all single-party systems under an authoritarian régime, to be just another extension of the executive.

The party has been used in three main ways – to channel and depoliticise public debate, as a parallel watchdog organisation of the administration and as a sort of popular police force. It was used to police the anti-profiteering and prices campaign in the summer of 1975. Youths were recruited in the name of the party to check out shop prices and where necessary were used to break up supermarkets that overcharged. This was later admitted to be a mistaken policy.[9] In the name of the party, groups of 'loyal' students and workers still pack rallies staged to counter the religious or political gatherings which the Government dislikes. In the provinces people use the party as a kind of ginger group to activate otherwise lethargic local administrations. But equally the party serves as another source of information for the Shah reporting on rural affairs.

The party's principal function has been to channel public debate in Parliament.

There is no majority or minority as such and the wings [of the Party] are not in the status of majority or minority. For this reason the

Budget Bill for the year 1976/77 was approved unanimously. Those who took part in the debate had not registered to speak in the debate as 'against' it and in their speeches therefore they just made a certain statement. For the first time, the list of speakers had not been drawn into two sections — 'for' and 'against'.[10]

The party's real power is negligible, not least because the Shah sought to prevent it being used as a potential threat to his own authority. Although Hoveida was put in overall charge, the party was split into two 'wings', in theory to orchestrate internal debate. In practice the Shah was much more concerned with balancing power. The wings were placed under the separate command of Hushang Ansari at the Finance Ministry and Jamshid Amouzegar at the Interior Ministry. Not only were these the two most powerful civilian Minstries but also their Ministers were the two chief contenders for the premiership. Amouzegar and Ansari were also personal rivals with no great affection for each other. The power-sharing was reflected in the names applied to the two wings — the 'progressive liberals' (Amouzegar) and the 'constructive liberals' (Ansari). Both sides apparently wanted to call themselves liberal but the distinction was between those like Amouzegar who believed in high growth but not at any price and those like Ansari who believed in high growth no matter what the consequences.

In the party's brief history there has been no evidence of it taking the initiative. In Parliament it has encouraged the idea of debate — but on non-contentious issues like rents, traffic and the role of women. Key issues that affect national life like freedom of expression, internal security, defence or oil policy are never touched. The Majles is even expressly excluded from debating the budget of public corporations (like NIOC) whose expenditure amounts to over half the total budget and whose foreign borrowing requirement is the most significant.[11]

The distinction between the party executive and the government is deliberately obscure. One way or another, the majority of the Cabinet is represented in the party's Political Bureau. The party newspaper, *Rastakhiz*, has come to be regarded as the official organ of the government — incidentally claiming a daily circulation of 150,000. This is in spite of all newspapers and reporters being affiliated to the party.

This lack of a clearly defined role and its ambiguous relationship with the government is merely a reflection of Rastakhiz' inherent disposability. There is no sense of permanence about the party since it is so clearly a child of the Shah's creation and it lives or dies at his whim. Not surprisingly membership has been prompted more by a cynical Iranian belief in political convenience than by genuine feelings that Rastakhiz is a new dimension in the political process. Total membership at the end of 1976 was just over 5 million.[12]

The creation of Rastakhiz has further obstructed the growth of an independent-minded press. The press plays a wholly subservient role and is effectively absorbed into the executive. Its main function is to propagate and propagandise the activities of the monarchy and the monarch's policies as carried out by the government. It is a government public relations agency, only allowed to trespass into criticism where the issues are deemed inessential – like Tehran traffic or rents. When more contentious issues are discussed it usually means a change in policy is being floated. Censorship exists but this usually takes the form of self-censorship, which is more invidious. No proprietor is willing to risk going against the government since this means closure.

In the absence of a free press, the Shah on occasions uses rumour as a means of testing opinion. Tehran has developed a fast bush telegraph that is frequently accurate. This is tolerated partly because it mollifies to some extent the élite's frustration over censorship but mainly because it enables the Shah to float ideas. In mid-July 1977 rumours began to circulate that Hoveida would be replaced as Prime Minister (Hoveida was holidaying in Corsica) by Hushang Ansari. Reaction was extremely hostile to Ansari; if a change was to be made, Amouzegar was considered a more apt choice. Perhaps it was no accident that ten days later Amouzegar was chosen as the new Premier.

The Judiciary

The judiciary has been absorbed almost completely into the executive. Judicial decisions now reflect the will of the government. Moreover the area of competence of the judiciary has been gradually eroded by military tribunals and by special civil service tribunals. Under both Reza Shah and Mohammed Reza Shah the legal system has been based on the principle that the state can do no wrong.

Military tribunals have since the late 1950s acquired a growing importance. These are staffed by military personnel (retired or serving), held on military premises and follow military rules. Martial law effectively extends over a large area of national life. Any member of the armed forces, whether in uniform or not, automatically goes before a military tribunal even if the offence is a civilian one. Any crime that involves the use of a gun comes within the competence of the military. More importantly, the military courts are concerned with all cases affecting national security – a blanket term which is loosely interpreted.

In addition the military courts have arrogated to themselves a host of vaguely defined offences. For instance military courts were used to try some of the offences in the anti-profiteering campaign of August 1975. In another instance the former head of Iran's civil aviation authority, Abdolqassem Hushang-Arbabi, was tried by a military court for alleged misappropriation of funds. The trial was *in camera*, the charges were never detailed and only the sentence published – a Rs111 million ($1.5 million) fine.[13] The military argued that civil aviation was a military matter. Some felt that Arbabi had been framed out of political vindictiveness and the military trial was a means of preventing proper legal challenge.[14]

Where the judiciary has not lost out to the military, its authority is usurped by special tribunals serving the executive. These are only partially staffed by qualified legal personnel. They have unlimited powers to fine and sentence, powers that cannot be challenged by appeal within the normal law courts. The most powerful are the civil service tribunals that have the right to try – or rather have developed the practice of trying – all infringements of civil service rules in addition to common law crimes like embezzlement, fraud and bribery. These courts also have a loose definition of what is a civil servant. For instance, the managing director of a development corporation set up by Tehran municipality was tried and sentenced to four years' imprisonment after a civil service court had found him guilty of mismanaging municipal funds.[15]

Tax courts have acquired considerable importance since 1973. They are administered by the Ministry of Finance, held on Finance Ministry premises and two of the three members of the bench are Ministry nominees. The third is a qualified judge on loan from the Justice Ministry who has a special salary paid by the Finance Ministry (on top of his normal Justice Ministry one). It hardly needs to be said that the Finance Ministry represents one of the parties in litigation.

In late 1976 the government began to prepare a major overhaul of legal procedures to streamline antiquated practices and cover some of the lacunas in the law. A number of progressive lawyers saw these moves, which included the downgrading of some of the activities of the Supreme Court, as a further shackling of the judiciary. One reform proposed to enlarge the competence of Arbitration Councils, a type of magistrate's court dealing with neighbourhood problems such as property title disputes. It was intended to raise the competence of these courts to try cases involving sums up to Rs200,000. An important group of lawyers protested that this would deny the ordinary citizen qualified legal opinion as the Arbitration Councils were staffed by government-selected personnel without legal training. The Bill was none the less accepted by the Senate judicial committee after a debate of less than five minutes.[16]

The credibility of the legal system is now very low, and the rule of law is non-existent because, of course, to admit the existence of the rule of law would undermine the Shah's authority. However, by castrating the judiciary the government to some extent has hurt itself because there are whole areas, like commercial practice, where laws are needed but not provided, so complicating the development process.

The Imperial Court

The Imperial Court and its executive arm, the Special Bureau, act in some ways like a White House staff. These are the carefully selected men responsible for the smooth functioning of the monarchy, both in its ceremonial and executive functions. Through the Court the Shah's schedule is planned and most people have to pass through the Court to reach the Shah. Because it has the full weight of royal authority behind it, the Court is extremely powerful: its officials can cancel or overrule orders from all other bodies or individuals in government and they have considerable authority over the Shah's parallel government. The Court Minister ranks on a par with, if not above, the Prime Minister, though he never sits in on Cabinet meetings. Quite often the Court Minister himself has been a former Prime Minister.

One branch of the Court Ministry is devoted exclusively to looking after the private affairs of the Shah and the Pahlavi family. The other main branch concerns the organisation of the Shah's daily schedule. While the official duties of the Court Ministry are more ceremonial, the Special Bureau has the primary responsibility of ensuring that the Shah's orders are carried out. It also acts as the final filter for all the multiple channels of administration and control that the Shah employs.

The current head of the Special Bureau, Nasratollah Moinian, is a man of modest origins and is regarded as a technocrat. Both the Special Bureau and the Court have small staffs although they can rely upon secondment either from the military or civilian sectors where necessary. Their budget is treated as part of the operational expenses of the monarchy which in 1976/7 was $40 million.[17] This figure may not reflect actual outlays, which can easily be grafted on to the expenditure of other government agencies, and probably frequently are.

The Court Minister has responsibility over the Special Bureau and he is the man with the most privileged access to the Shah. The Court

Minister usually acts as the royal intermediary whenever the necessity arises. Assadollah Alam, Court Minister for a lengthy period until August 1977, was an archetypal figure in this position: discreet, diplomatic and utterly loyal. He was a boyhood friend of the Shah, and wealthy in his own right. He had also direct experience of government as Premier in the wake of Ali Amini's dismissal. Even though weakened by illness from 1975 onwards, Alam was regarded as the one man who was not a member of the Royal Family capable of giving objective advice, and when Hoveida became Court Minister in August 1977, he remained as an elder statesman until his death in May 1978.

Associated with the Court are the activities of Empress Farah, the Shah's twin sister Princess Ashraf and other members of the Royal Family. The Empress has her own special bureau and staff which has an important area of patronage within the fields of the arts, charity, culture and education. Over the years the Shah has delegated more and more of his responsibilities to the Empress in these marginal areas so that they have become almost exclusively her domain. The Ministry of Culture and Information, the museums, the various arts festivals and national television are all used as a means of royal patronage and extending the individual importance of those within her office (many of whom are often related to her and the Diba family).

However, the position of the Empress is deceptive. She is not just the ceremonial adjunct of the Shah. Because she is known to be one of the handful that can speak frankly with the Shah and who has regular access to him, she has acquired importance as an alternative means of gaining access to the Shah. She would also technically be regent in the event of the Shah's death and his son still being a minor. Access to the Shah immediately confers influence in its own right. Channels to the Shah are so limited that visiting foreigners are sometimes asked to raise issues in their audiences. For instance, when a senior ranking envoy of President Carter visited Tehran in early 1977, he was asked by several Iranians to raise issues on their behalf.[18] Foreigners are also considered more impartial and in the past the American and British Ambassadors have enjoyed a privileged role.

Princess Ashraf's role has been less evident since the early 1970s; but she nevertheless remains an integral part of the Shah's system of government. She is credited with having the most astute brain in the Royal Family, and, though whimsical, of being the most determined in-fighter. She has been used for delicate foreign policy missions as far back as the end of the Second World War when, still a young woman, she was sent by her brother to parley with Stalin. In a public role outside

Iran, the Shah has relied upon her to act as chief spokesman on human rights and on the emancipation of women. She was, until Empress Farah took over, heavily involved in promoting the Pahlavi dynasty image of philanthropy and remains the titular head of the Imperial Organisation of Social Services.

More recently Princess Ashraf's special bureau has acquired significance, collecting Ministers and senior officials who for reasons of political expediency have been obliged to leave their jobs yet whom the Shah does not wish to have excluded from the system. For instance Iraj Vahidi, removed as Energy Minister in February 1977 as a sop to public opinion over drastic power shortages, ended up in her special bureau. The bureau has so many ex-government heavyweights that it has become known as the 'elephants' graveyard'. The activities of the bureau itself are obscure apart from running the Ashraf Pahlavi Foundation established in April 1976 as a charity, which for instance has donated £250,000 to Wadham College Library, Oxford. According to one report the bureau is used by the Shah as another parallel organisation monitoring projects in the civilian and non-security sector.[19]

Princess Ashraf is also useful to the Shah for her wide network of friends who have now gained important jobs in the administration — ambassadors, senior civil servants, etc. These can also serve as alternative channels of information for royal ears. In the jealous world of Court intrigue Princess Ashraf, although frequently away from Iran, maintains a hand in important changes and decisions. Her third husband, Mehdi Bushehri, who lives in Paris, is used by the Shah as an important contact with French business interests. Bushehri is credited with having been the Iranian intermediary in arranging the sale of French nuclear reactors to Iran.[20]

The Unconstitutional Side

The least-known and the most unconventional of the agencies created by Mohammed Reza Shah is the Imperial Inspectorate. Created in 1958, one year after SAVAK, its functions have gradually expanded as the complexity of the Shah's own needs have grown. It is answerable neither to the Majles, the Rastakhiz Party, the Cabinet, the police, SAVAK nor the armed forces — only to the Shah. There is no check on its use of power other than the Shah's will. Its competence extends over and above SAVAK.

There have been only two heads of the Inspectorate since its creation, both drawn from the military — the Shah prefers to trust power in the hands of the military. The present head of the Inspectorate,

General Hussein Fardust, has known the Shah longer than almost any other close associate. As a boy he accompanied the Shah when as a Crown Prince he was sent to boarding school at Le Rosey, Switzerland. Fardust then followed a military career, instructing at the Tehran Military College and then running the Imperial Guard.[21] He is also one of the few outside the Royal Family whom the Shah sees socially.

As its name suggests, the Inspectorate is primarily investigative — probing into political, economic and social matters. The staff is small and select, although it can be augmented by seconded personnel from the Ministries, the armed forces or SAVAK. The Inspectorate had a published budget of $8 million in 1976/7 but its size bears no relationship to its importance.[22] Every organisation in Iran is under orders to co-operate with it and it is empowered to carry out regular, but unannounced, inspections in every sphere of government, central and provincial.[23] Its prime concern is monitoring how Ministries and individuals are carrying out the Shah's policies and investigating sensitive cases of misconduct or suspected disloyalty among high officials. It also appears from time to time to monitor the activities of other members of the Royal Family, especially their business involvement. It seems it is most frequently used when civil servants are thought to have become too obviously corrupt.[24]

The Shah has described its purpose:

> Although the gendarmerie as well as other agencies of the Government often handle internal self-discipline very well, experience showed the need for an independent investigating authority. That is what *my* Imperial Investigation Organisation provides. Its staff can go anywhere, and without fear or favour investigate any alleged injustice (author's italics).[25]

The suggestion here is that it is at the service of the nation but this is largely cosmetic. In March 1976 the Inspectorate was called in to investigate allegations of corrupt practice involving two Under-Secretaries in the Ministry of Commerce and the British sugar company, Tate and Lyle. The allegations, made at the beginning of an anti-corruption drive, concerned attempts to overcharge the government on sugar purchases totalling 250,000 tons. The Inspectorate drafted in the assistance of a former deputy governor of the Bank Markazi and sent him with an investigatory team to London to examine Tate and Lyle's books. Interestingly, their investigations came to the embarrassing conclusion that the allegations were untrue. To save face, the officials were brought to trial only to have the charges quashed. One suspects the trial was held in the knowledge that the charges would not stick, just to show that justice exists in Iran.[26]

The Inspectorate has acquired new importance as the Shah does not trust his own Ministries to provide accurate information on the state of the economy. He turned to the Inspectorate to investigate the failings of the revised Fifth Plan. In November 1976 a new body, the Imperial Commission, was created by special decree to monitor the economy. Moinian in the Shah's Special Bureau was designated a co-ordinator, assisted by representatives of the Inspectorate and SAVAK.[27] The Commission also contains representatives of all Ministries and has eight subcommissions reporting on specific topics.

When still Prime Minister, Hoveida described the Imperial Commission as 'the most powerful arm of the executive'. He hoped that it would considerably streamline government.[28] At the PBO, the Director-General, Abdol Majid Majidi, claimed that the Commission gave him, for the first time, the capacity to cut through inter-Ministerial rivalry and properly evaluate the progress of projects.[29]

The Imperial Commission marked an important departure in policy by the Shah. For the first time he established a body that spanned the public and covert sides of his administration. It was designed to weed out inefficiency and incompetence in individual Ministries and agencies. A local newspaper commented that the Commission introduced into the government machinery the Shah's dual role of guide and critic: 'It provides a mechanism by which the Government can engage in a continuous exercise of self-evaluation and self-criticism.'[30]

The creation of the Commission underlines how difficult it is to have an efficient administration with so much overlapping authority and parallel power. By including all these different bodies in one commission the Shah hoped to achieve a measure of co-operation from what are often mutually antagonistic agencies. The Commission is thus the furthest that the Shah's system will permit 'independent' criticism. As such, it is eloquent testimony of the nature of the system that the Majles is ignored and that the strength of the Commission derives solely from the Shah's direct backing and the presence of senior members of the Inspectorate, SAVAK and the armed forces.

The Security Services

Over twenty years the security services have become a central pillar of the Shah's system of government. The armed forces may be the ultimate guarantors of power; but the security services ensure that the armed forces are never used in this role. They are the Shah's eyes and ears and, where necessary, his iron fist, neutralising all those disloyal to the régime. Since the establishment of SAVAK the armed forces have twice been called upon for a major internal security operation to suppress religious riots in 1963 and May 1978.[31]

SAVAK thrives on Mohammed Reza Shah's deep-felt need to insulate himself and his régime from all potential enemies. For SAVAK there are only those who approve of Mohammed Reza Shah and those who disapprove. Disapproval is potentially subversive and in need of frequent surveillance to check whether it has crossed over into outright opposition. SAVAK alone defines opposition.

SAVAK acts as both an intelligence service and a political police force concentrating on Iranian dissidents. Espionage and military intelligence are the concern of another organisation, known as J-2, which is also believed to be a watchdog of SAVAK – even in the security field the Shah wants to have overlapping authority and alternative channels.[32] In fact the Imperial Inspectorate is the only superior agency and normally SAVAK is answerable directly to the Shah. In the name of protecting the interests of state, SAVAK can arrest, interrogate, imprison and eliminate individuals without challenge or scrutiny.

The Shah regards SAVAK as a necessary arm of government. Not long after the organisation's establishment, he commented:

In counteracting subversion, we have also found that the main emphasis should always be placed on social justice rather than on coercion and control measures. It is true that, especially in a country as strategically placed as we are, there may be a need to act quickly and decisively to combat attempts to topple the Government by unconstitutional means, particularly those which are foreign inspired. Today every free country needs a political security agency which, in cooperation with other Government departments, can detect and neutralise attempts of that kind. In present day conditions any other course would be reckless.[33]

SAVAK operates under the protective cover of the military. All public discussion of its activities is prohibited since this would be a breach of the military secrecy regulations. The civil courts have no power over SAVAK's investigations since its prosecutions come within the sphere of military tribunals where the judge and personnel are military. In June 1977 some amendments were made to the regulations governing military tribunals, including an obligation to hold public trials and the institution of a sort of minimal habeas corpus once a detainee had appeared before a military prosecutor.[34]

These changes were essentially cosmetic and made no attempt to bring the tribunals under the control of the judiciary. Much also depends upon interpretation. For instance Article 192 has been revised allowing public trials:

> Sessions of military courts shall always be public. However, if the prosecutor shall exceptionally feel that a public trial is prejudicial to public order and public interest, he may request the court for a secret trial. If the court accepts the prosecutor's request, it shall issue the order for a secret trial. At the end of the trial, the judgement of the court shall be read only to the prosecutor, the accused and the defence lawyer.[35]

Within three weeks of this new provision coming into force a well known opposition figure associated with the former National Front, Ayatollah Mahmoud Taleghani, was sentenced to ten years' imprisonment on unspecified charges in a secret trial. Not even the sentence was published.[36]

The links between SAVAK and the military establishment are still not entirely clear. The four persons who have run the organisation from its inception have all had military backgrounds. The previous commander, General Nematellah Nassiri, graduated to SAVAK from running the Imperial Guard.[37] It is also known that the senior personnel within SAVAK have military backgrounds.[38] Further it seems − although there is no hard evidence − that SAVAK is financed either from secret state funds or more probably from within the overall defence budget. The budget does contain a classification 'establishment of internal order and security'; but this covers the gendarmerie and the police and allocations from these items is most unlikely since it would compromise SAVAK's autonomy and one of the Shah's cardinal principles of separation of powers.[39]

The absence of a published budget has led to some wild estimates on SAVAK's size. In the past the regularly employed members of SAVAK have been guessed at between 30,000 and 60,000.[40] The lower figure is almost certainly more accurate. However, SAVAK relies extensively on part-time informers and personnel already employed by other government agencies. If these are included, then the figure of SAVAK personnel rises to even beyond 60,000.

SAVAK's all-embracing brief means that it can overrule Ministries and other government agencies. For instance in the field of labour, both the Ministry of Labour and the Ministry of Interior are responsible for work regulations and the running of the state-controlled labour syndicates. Nevertheless SAVAK has the task of ensuring that labour does not become politicised or does not exploit industrial action for political ends. This therefore gives SAVAK an important say in labour policy. Frequently, SAVAK intervenes in petty issues in the affairs of the Ministries. For instance, Iranian delegations travelling on official business to Eastern Europe are obliged to go through special security vetting that results on occasions in government officials being refused visas.[41]

SAVAK also interferes extensively with the Ministry of Information and Culture on matters of censorship and artistic control. The banning of plays, films or the refusal of permission to publish books are an integral part of SAVAK's function. SAVAK can also overrule decisions of the Ministry of Posts and Telecommunications regarding communications equipment – the installation of telex machinery requires SAVAK approval and those who operate the machine need to be named. It is rare, however, that directives are issued in the name of SAVAK: rather SAVAK operates from behind, telling Minstries to act, and so avoiding a direct connection with a specific action or decision.

Over all, SAVAK's activities clog up the administrative machine and considerably reduce its efficiency. SAVAK can, for instance, even have a say in the granting of industrial licences, in the right to import certain equipment (short-wave radios and paging systems are banned from sale to the general public on security grounds which always leads to conflict with the Health Ministry over hospital systems) and in the clearance of goods from customs. In any area remotely connected with national security, SAVAK has the final say on employment. This has led, for instance, to great difficulties at Tehran airport in finding qualified technical personnel who can pass the security muster.[42]

This constant interference, or threat of interference, has led to a good deal of friction between SAVAK and senior civil servants. Because the civil servants are afraid of SAVAK they hide behind instructions and regulations, unwilling to venture beyond the strict limits of bureaucratic responsibility. It is not a situation which encourages individual initiative. Although in many important respects counter-productive, these results are the price paid for a blanket approach to security. Given the Shah's sense of insecurity and the unchecked nature of SAVAK's power, there is a built-in tendency to overreact. Over the years the focus of SAVAK's attention has shifted. Initially it was primarily directed against anyone connected with Mossadegh and his banned National Front Party or those connected with the Tudeh (Communist) Party. By the mid-sixties SAVAK could claim to have rounded up, chased into exile or effectively silenced the majority of these; and so it began to focus on the opposition in exile, and at home the students, intellectuals, religious leaders and underground extremist groups. It has been particularly concerned with Iran's rapidly expanding student population: those capable of seeing the cracks in the Shah's vision and the most fearless of protest. Student surveillance is all-embracing. At the universities, especially in Tehran, there are probably two to three informers per class. Academics are carefully vetted for their political affiliations and as part of a teacher's contract discussion of politics is expressly forbidden. Textbooks and courses, especially on history and sociology, are doctored. All this is done ostensibly in the name of the governing body of the university; but the directives to the governing body come from SAVAK. To forestall the interference of SAVAK, the university authorities also censor themselves — a more insidious form of control.[43]

Dissidents face the prospect of intimidation, interrogation, torture and imprisonment without trial.[44] A report prepared by William Butler, head of the executive committee of the International Commission of Jurists concluded in 1976 that over the past years torture had been systematically used to extract information. 'The number of detailed allegations made, the absence of any impartial investigation and the fact that the SAVAK knows that it is the law inevitably leads to this conclusion.'[45] Two years earlier the Secretary-General of Amnesty International described Iran's human rights record as worse than any other country in the world.[46] Latterly the Shah himself has made no secret of the use of torture, though insisting it is refined to psychological, not physical, methods.[47] There is, it seems, a connection between increased resort to torture in the late sixties, early seventies, and the upsurge of a well organised urban guerrilla movement.

SAVAK's basic weapon has always been intimidation. If a person is considered troublesome but has committed no offence, exit visas and passports are denied. A number of persons active under Mossadegh and again under Dr Amini have been denied passports for over fifteen years.[48] Alternatively, job promotion is denied. Pressure is brought to bear upon students with the threat of refusal or withdrawal of grants to study abroad. At the time of the creation of the Rastakhiz Party, inspired rumours circulated that those who did not register would be denied exit visas. The rumour proved groundless but people did register out of fear of this reprisal.

Pressure on family or friends, or the threat of charges which a person is powerless to disprove, are the standard methods of obtaining collaboration. Even military defence lawyers in military tribunals are under pressure not to sympathise with their clients; and there have been instances of prosecution of military defence counsel.[49] Any defence counsel honestly defending his client is invariably called upon to challenge the legality of the process, the validity of evidence, or both — itself an inherent criticism of the system. A more direct form of intimidation has been lengthy detention without trial. This has been applied to recalcitrant writers as well as politicians. For instance, Dr Shahpour Bakhtiar, who has been associated with the National Front, has been imprisoned on six different occasions, but only tried once.[50] SAVAK also has at its disposal a series of nation-wide security commissions that can send people into exile in various remote parts of the country. Ironically these commissions were formed under Mossadegh to prevent sabotage of oil installations and to protect the régime from subversion. They have subsequently been refashioned into 'exile courts'.

The security commissions are composed of representatives of the police, gendarmerie, the judiciary, the local town governor and SAVAK, which is responsible for bringing people before the body. They have been mainly used to deal with rebellious religious figures, like the 40 leading mullahs from the religious city of Qom who, in late 1973, were banished to various parts of the country, like Bandar Langeh, for periods of up to three years.[51] The ultimate form of intimidation is the threat of death. Among the educated there are few who cannot cite the names of people they know either directly or indirectly, who have disappeared without trace. Occasionally this can be attributed to deliberately going underground; but more often it is the work of SAVAK.[52] Perhaps just as important, it is believed to be the work of SAVAK. For instance, in July 1977 an exiled opposition figure died unexpectedly in London and his friends immediately suspected SAVAK. In fact he died from a heart attack.

Because SAVAK is a law unto itself, there is no way of checking the limited information that comes out about its activities. Descriptions of the capture of urban guerrillas that appear in the local press read unconvincingly. A surprising number of well trained and determined 'terrorists' manage to die from a grenade going off prematurely in their hands, and even this doctored information filters out several days late.[53] Relatives are rarely allowed access to autopsy reports, and besides, medical evidence can be rigged and is frequently thought to be so. In March 1975 nine political prisoners, tried in 1969 and serving ten-year terms, were alleged to have been shot while attempting to escape. Two French lawyers subsequently came to the conclusion that they had been tortured to death.[54]

All this begs the vital question of SAVAK's efficiency and effectiveness. Judged at its simplest level, SAVAK is effective because it enables the régime to survive. SAVAK has succeeded in intimidating all except the hard-core guerrillas, a few determined intellectuals and religious figures, and the exiles abroad. Its activities – real and imagined – have created a fear of authority and have cowed Iranians into being afraid of the mere threat of SAVAK's intervention.

This said, the aura of efficiency that tends to surround SAVAK is exaggerated and misleading. SAVAK is clumsy, interfering and cruel; and, as an organisation, riddled with administrative and personal pettiness, frequently blinded by a bully-boy mentality. Though effective, the blanket approach to security that SAVAK has adopted is inefficient. For fear of one individual escaping, the net is cast very wide. Arguably the large number of political prisoners in Iranian jails results from precisely this fear that it might not arrest the right person. Since 1973 there have been at any one time between 3,500 and 7,000 political prisoners, of which less than half were formally charged.[55] For instance, in December 1976 over a hundred persons were arrested in what SAVAK later claimed to be a major breakthrough in cracking Marxist subversion. However, only eleven were eventually put on trial in April 1977.[56] Other examples of SAVAK's efficiency are more mundane. To prevent the inflow of subversive literature into Iran, all books entering the country are liable to confiscation. Some 700 books belonging to the author were only prevented from being confiscated by a senior official intervening with the customs under instructions from SAVAK. Mail is opened with a lack of subtlety that would appal most detective agencies – opened and then clipped together with staples. (Iranians argue that this is because SAVAK is so arrogant it does not have to pretend.) In another instance, SAVAK asked the Foreign Ministry to obtain the names of all Iranians granted visas by Arab countries. A letter was duly sent out to all Arab embassies in Tehran with this request. In the case of Tunisia no one in SAVAK realised that a consular convention between Iran and Tunisia in 1972 abolished visas.

However, in the end SAVAK is judged not by its competence but its effectiveness. To the Shah, it is effectiveness that counts, not competence. Undoubtedly SAVAK serves its purpose but it makes a mockery of the rule of law which the Constitution established. SAVAK's activities are at the expense of all politically minded Iranians, and are responsible in large measure for the cynical indifference of the Iranian élite. Last but not least, SAVAK's presence reduces the efficiency of the administration through cumbrous duplication and makes officials unwilling to shoulder responsibilities or take initiatives.

Notes

1. Arthur Arnold, *Through Persia by Caravan* (London, Tinsley Brothers, 1877), Vol. I, p. 219.

2. Marvin Zonis, *The Political Elite of Iran* (Princeton, N.J: Princeton University Press, 1971), p. 133.

3. Mohammed Reza Shah Pahlavi, *Mission for My Country* (London, Hutchinson, 1974 edition), pp. 321-2.

4. Plan and Budget Organisation, *The Budget 2535 (1976/77)*, Part III, p. 16.

5. Recounted to the author by a Western ambassador in Tehran.

6. Recounted to the author by an Iranian of Ministerial rank.

7. The combined budgets of these bodies were $700 million in 1976/7. See PBO, Budget, Part III, pp. 18-19.

8. *Iran Almanac. Echo of Iran*, Tehran, 1977, p. 16. The creation of the Rastakhiz was a complete surprise and appeared to contradict the Shah's previous philosophy of wanting to have at least two loyal parties to manipulate.

9. *Kayhan International*, 23 April 1977. Interview with Darioush Homayoun, deputy Secretary-General of Rastakhiz.

10. *Iran Almanac*, 1977, p. 91.

11. PBO, *Budget*, Part I, p. 7. This percentage is smaller when double counting is taken into account.

12. *Iran Almanac*, 1977, p. 119.

13. *Kayhan International*, 28 April 1977.

14. This was the view of both Iranians and foreigners involved in civil aviation. Arbabi was removed from office in January 1977; but no mention was made in the press of this or of any charges until the brief trial result.

15. *Kayhan International*, 3 March 1977.

16. Recounted to the author by one of the 47 lawyers involved in the original protest. At a subsequent meeting at the Park Hotel on 12 July 1977, 64 lawyers signed a protest letter to the Shah calling for the independence of the judiciary, observance of the rule of law and respect for the Constitution.

17. PBO, *Budget*, Part III, p. 44.

18. The official referred to was Jim Akins.

19. Another theory is that this bureau is used as a means of keeping officials so that after a suitable period of time they can be once again reintegrated.

20. Recounted to the author by an expatriate involved in the reactor contract.

21. Mohammed Reza Shah Pahlavi, *Mission*, pp. 54-5.

22. PBO, *Budget*, Part III, p. 20.

23. In June 1977 a special decree extended the Inspectorate's powers to carry out on-the-spot provincial inspections. *Kayhan International*, 12 June 1977.

24. Perhaps it is wrong to talk of the Inspectorate having a main use as its value depends upon its total flexibility.

25. Mohammed Reza Shah Pahlavi, *Mission*, p. 177. At the time the Shah also conceived the Inspectorate as a sort of Ombudsman for complaints about his administration; but it has not been used convincingly in this role.

26. *Financial Times*, 4 May 1976 and 14 November 1977. See also *Kayhan International*, 11 December 1976. These proceedings were believed to have been politically motivated. The Inspectorate team who went to London revealed a very bureaucratic approach to investigation and found it hard to understand the intricacies of commodity trading.

27. *Kayhan International*, 9 November 1977; *Iran Almanac*, 1977, pp. 114-15.

28. *Kayhan International*, 22 May 1977.

29. Comment to the author by Abdol Majid Majidi, 16 June 1977. In a report on Iran released by the International Labour Office in Geneva in 1973, one of the main conclusions was that the PBO carry out inspections 'to check on the reliability of the information received'.

30. *Kayhan International*, 23 May 1977.

31. See Chapter 4. SAVAK stands for 'Sazemane Ettela'at va Amniyate Keshvar'.

32. See Zonis, *The Political Elite*, p. 85. There appears to be a grey area where SAVAK competence ends and that of J–2 begins. Iran's increased defence capability and regional military role suggests that J–2 has its hands full dealing with military intelligence matters.

33. Mohammed Reza Shah Pahlavi, *Mission*, p. 129.

34. *Iran Almanac*, 1977, p. 486.

35. Ibid.

36. Recounted to the author by lawyers connected with the case.

37. Gen. Nassiri was replaced in June 1978 by Gen. Mohammed Moghadam, formerly director of military intelligence. Nassiri was appointed Ambassador to Pakistan, the same post given to his predecessor, Gen. Pakravan, when he was replaced.

38. SAVAK is organised on army lines with army ranks applied to officers.

39. PBO, *Budget*, Part III, p. 45.

40. Exiled opposition sources talk of SAVAK numbering 100,000.

41. Recounted to the author by an Iranian official. The author has witnessed a telephone conversation in a Ministry during which an official remonstrated with SAVAK to permit someone to travel on an official delegation.

42. Recounted to the author by the manager of an international airline in Tehran. Airline managers are also requested not to fraternise with Aeroflot or Chinese National Airlines staff.

43. Based on information supplied to the author by persons who have taught at Tehran University and Aryamehr University.

44. SAVAK also has an unpleasant habit of employing 'loyal' workers to break up demonstrations. This was done particularly blatantly on two occasions in October 1977, when busloads of workers 'happened to be passing' by the university campus in Tehran, and 'incensed' by anti-Shah demonstrations, attacked the demonstrators with clubs.

45. *Le Monde*, 3 October 1976.

46. *Observer*, 26 May 1974.

47. Shah interview with Lord Chalfont for BBC, 17 June 1975; and also Shah interview with David Dimbleby, BBC, reproduced *Kayhan International*, 18 December 1976.

48. This is one of the least publicised measures adopted by SAVAK but is an important human rights violation. The author knows of at least two persons affected. Even with a passport there is no guarantee of leaving the country. All passports are surrendered 24 hours before departure and collected at the airport.

It is not infrequent for people to arrive at the airport and discover they have no passport.

49. Under the new regulations of June 1977, a lawyer is now theoretically exempt from prosecution (see note to Article 182). However, the basic problem of the legality of the military tribunals remains unchanged.

50. Recounted to the author by Dr Shahpour Bakhtiar.

51. Little is known about these Security Commissions. This information is based on facts supplied by a group of lawyers who have appeared for clients in these 'courts'. In one incident a judge on submission from a lawyer ruled that an elderly mullah exiled to Zabol could have his place of exile changed because he should not suffer undue hardship. This loophole was subsequently closed.

52. This assertion is based on conversations with both the Iranian Establishment and opposition figures. Typical of the suspicion prevalent was the reaction to the death of Mostafa Khomeini, the 45-year-old son of the famous Ayatollah who sparked the riots of 1963 and who was subsequently exiled. Mostafa died in unexplained circumstances at the holy shrine of Kerbala, Iraq. See *Le Monde*, 31 October 1977.

53. Compare the account of *Kayhan International*, 22 February 1976 and *Kayhan International*, 18 November 1976.

54. *The Times*, 22 May 1975.

55. The Shah's own figure has varied, but he has never admitted a higher figure than 3,300. See *Kayhan International*, 18 December 1976.

56. *Kayhan International*, 10 April 1977. This was the first political trial of persons charged with anti-state offences open to the public and international observers for many years.

9 CONTROL THROUGH MONEY

> I am hopeful that the Pahlavi Foundation will develop into one of the great charitable institutions of the world. While it is less wealthy than the larger ones of Europe and America, it is steadily expanding the scale and scope of its activities.[1]

More than any other single factor, money and wealth are the cement for Mohammed Reza Shah's system of government. He has refined and adapted time-honoured practice. In 1910, when an American, Morgan Shuster, was brought in as Treasurer General in the first attempt to organise the state's chaotic finances, he discovered that some 100,000 persons received special annual handouts, most of which he considered 'pure graft'.[2] On one authoritative estimate almost a quarter of all state revenue at the turn of the century was devoured by these so-called pensions.[3]

In the past the monarchy was able to bind its power base with money either by controlling state revenues or by amassing a large private fortune. More often than not these two alternatives were indistinguishable since there was little practical division between the private wealth of the Shah and state funds. Moreover, the Shah did not have to make such a distinction since he regarded himself as embodying the state. The modernisation of the administration and the advent by the mid-fifties of a regular and sizeable income from oil, coupled with the expansion of the economy, has inevitably made the reward system more complex. Of necessity the distinction between state funds and the private wealth of the Shah, albeit on paper, has become more clear-cut. The budget has become institutionalised so that a specific allocation is now made for the 'Supreme Leadership of State' which in 1976/7 amounted to $43 million.[4]

More importantly, the expansion of the economy and the increased revenue from oil has resulted in a shift in the direct burden of reward — away from the royal purse and on to state funds. The budget is even used quite unashamedly to bankroll operations which the monarchy would have supported out of its own pocket in the past. For instance, the budget provides annual cash backing for such things as Tehran's privately owned exclusive Imperial Country Club, the Imperial Horse Society and the Imperial Aviation Club.[5]

The expansion of the economy has also provided the Shah with a greatly diversified set of rewards. He has utilised the granting of trading and manufacturing monopolies and restricted licences or agencies for international companies as a means of making people beholden to him. In a heavily protected and fast expanding economy like that of Iran such concessions are highly profitable. The most profitable arrangements permitted have been the acceptance by the Shah of certain trusted individuals as intermediaries in large-contract negotiations with international companies in the defence and civilian fields. In return for permitting the intermediary a 1 per cent commission, the Shah is kept fully informed on negotiations. For instance, in 1971 a £1 million commission was paid to Sir Shapoor Reporter for his part in arranging for the sale of British Chieftain tanks to Iran. This money was paid by the British government with the Shah's knowledge on what was essentially a government to government sale.[6] Granting of licences or asking select individuals to establish monopoly industries also allows the Shah an important form of personal control. For instance, the establishment of the most important modern defence industries has been entrusted to one man – Abdol Hassan Mahvi. He has assisted in the creation of military electronics industries, the aircraft servicing and repair industry and a naval servicing company.[7] Thus while Reza Shah was concerned (some would say obsessed) with building up a huge fortune for the Pahlavi dynasty as a means of control and reward, his son has had less need simply because money has become available in more diversified forms. It has been sufficient for Mohammed Reza Shah to exercise ultimate control over the state economic apparatus. Nevertheless, he has been careful to maintain a certain blurring of the distinction between state funds and royal funds to ensure that, when necessary, the former are at the disposal of the régime.

The Role of NIOC

The ambiguity between state funds and the royal purse is most evident in the National Iranian Oil Company (NIOC). The Chairman of NIOC holds one of the most important posts in the country – the equivalent of a senior Cabinet rank. He is appointed by the Shah and answerable only to him. During NIOC's formative years this post was held by Dr Manouchehr Eqbal, a man close to the Shah with a proven record of loyalty. He was Prime Minister for over three years until forced to resign in 1960 over allegations of pro-Shah vote-rigging.[8] NIOC, as the most important national agency in the economy, is directly beholden to the Shah. Its budget is presented to the Plan and Budget Organisation, but never discussed in detail. Its full accounts (which follow a calendar year, not the Iranian year) are seen by only a few of its directors and never by any member of the public. It is doubtful if more than three Cabinet members have seen or are allowed access to its accounts.

No conclusive evidence exists, but a number of well placed persons, both Iranian and foreign, familiar with NIOC are convinced that the national oil company acts as a source of supplementary and secret funds for the régime — not for the personal enrichment of the Shah but to sustain him in power.[9] State Department analysts in Washington have consistently been puzzled by an apparent discrepancy between NIOC's statement of its income from its own sales and the foreign exchange earnings as reported in the balance of payments by the Bank Markazi. Because NIOC accounts are made up on a calendar year and those of the Bank Markazi on an Iranian year (March to March), it becomes more difficult to match up the bank's statement of receipts and NIOC's own statement of sales. However, even with this difference in accounting, the discrepancy is considerable.

In the balance of payments figures for the year ending March 1977, NIOC's foreign exchange receipts are listed as $3.14 billion. In the calendar year ending December 1976, NIOC foreign exchange earnings from direct sales were $4.6 billion.[10] This gap can be accounted for only in small part by the drop in sales during the first quarter of 1977, since the system of delayed payments for crude oil bought from NIOC means that the effect of lower sales is spread out. On conservative accounts there is $1 billion unaccounted for — even allowing for NIOC selling oil at a discount.

Dr Parviz Mina, head of international relations at NIOC, admitted in July 1977 a discrepancy between NIOC sales and balance of payments published receipts. However, he would only concede that these extra funds were retained by NIOC for 'its own use'.[11] Retention of undisclosed funds by state oil companies is not an uncommon practice within OPEC. The Abu Dhabi National Oil Company, for instance, retains funds for its own use without including them in published state revenues.[12] In the case of Iran, the uses of these retained funds are mysterious. Some almost certainly are used for investment and a strategic reserve.[13] However, a substantial part is believed to be set aside for special state uses. In short, NIOC contributes to a glorified slush fund.

In this respect an interesting document was published by *Le Canard Enchaîné* in 1976. The document purported to show a 1962 monthly excerpt from a Swiss bank account of the Pahlavi Foundation. The main income on the balance sheet for the month was a $12 million transfer from NIOC.[14] Although the motive for publication appeared deliberate embarrassment of the Shah, the veracity of the document has never been challenged. Though clearly unsatisfactory, this document is the closest published proof of what many believe to be both a use for secret NIOC funds and a link between NIOC and the Pahlavi Foundation.

The Pahlavi Foundation

Officially the Pahlavi Foundation is a charity organisation sponsored and financed from Mohammed Reza Shah's wealth. It is listed as such in all Iranian publications.[15] In practice it is nothing so straightforward. Behind a smokescreen of charity, the Foundation is used in three key ways to assist the régime: as a safe and institutionalised conduit for 'pensions'; as a means of exerting economic control or influence by investing in specific sectors of the economy; and as a source of funds for royal ventures. In a hard-hitting assessment, Marvin Zonis had this to say about the Pahlavi Foundation:

> It is unquestionably true that the Foundation plays a crucial role in all areas of Iranian public life. After the government itself, it is the most powerful economic force in the country. It seems certain, however, that a great deal of its resources are spent maintaining and enhancing that economic power. Resources devoted purely to charity rather than commercial undertakings appear relatively slight.[16]

According to the Shah, he established the Foundation in 1958 as a non-profit-making organisation to co-ordinate a group of social services in which he was interested.[17] The Foundation replaced what was known as the Pahlavi Estates Office, created in 1951 to handle the proceeds of the sale of Crown land to tenant farmers. These estates comprised over 830 villages with a land area of more than 2.5 million hectares, all of which was acquired in under twenty years by Reza Shah. Although established in 1958, it was not until 1961, when the topic of royal wealth became politically sensitive, that the Shah chose to transfer the more substantial Pahlavi assets to the Foundation. At the time, these assets were valued at approximately $135 million. This, the Shah claimed, represented 90 per cent of his personal fortune: put another way, the Shah still possessed about $15 million worth of personal assets.[18]

Such a claim was almost certainly an overstatement. Back in 1947, when the Shah established the Imperial Organisation for Social Service (IOSS) to pioneer mass welfare in Iran, he was reported to have allocated Rs60 million (under $1 million) to this new body which was said to be equivalent to half his fortune.[19] Nevertheless he has vested more of his personal assets in the Foundation than he is generally credited with doing by his opponents.

The reason for this is twofold. In terms of political propaganda the divestiture of his wealth to a supposed charitable organisation has relieved some pressure on the Shah from those who regard Pahlavi assets as ill-gotten, or in reality belonging to the State. More important, by transferring his wealth to the Foundation, it can still be used for the very same purpose for which it was intended under previous monarchs – to keep the Shah in power. All he has done is to institutionalise the extensive wealth of the Pahlavis – a collective wealth exceeded in the Middle East only by the House of Saud in Saudi Arabia and the al-Sabah ruling family in Kuwait.[20] The Foundation operates under the aegis of the Court. The Shah from the outset appointed himself chief Custodian. As such he is entitled to 2.5 per cent of the net revenues, but this he has waived. He also appoints the ten Custodians, five of whom are state office-holders – the Prime Minister, the Court Minister, the head of the Senate, the Speaker of the Majles and the Supreme Court Justice (all posts appointed by the Shah anyway) – and five direct nominees. The latter are all entitled to 2.5 per cent of total net income 'equally shared'.[21] At present the deputy chief Custodian is Jafar Sharif Emami, who is also head of the Senate. Though once associated with Mossadegh's National Front, Emami is now considered a loyal servant of the Shah.

The front of a charity organisation is an impressive one. The Foundation is involved in a large number of charitable causes and good works ventures. Since its inception up to March 1977, the Foundation financed the education abroad of 12,000 students with direct cash grant or loan assistance. Only 25 per cent of the total sum loaned to each student is reimbursable. The Foundation puts great store by this activity and estimates now that the average *per capita* cost each month is $500 for students studying abroad.[22] The Foundation provides assistance to the deaf, dumb and blind; clothing for certain especially needy; supports the cost of food for the faithful during the fast of Ramadan in certain cities; and assists orphans. It provides pensions and assistance to the families of those who have lost their lives for the country – this includes members of the police and security forces killed by urban guerrillas.

The Foundation also runs a book translation and publishing company that reprints Persian and foreign classics. Up to March 1976 this company had printed 476 titles.[23] Through other institutions the Foundation is involved with more charitable organisations like the Farah Pahlavi Foundation, which operates 87 boarding houses, nurseries and youth centres; the Queen Pahlavi Foundation (a charity founded in the name of Mohammed Reza Shah's mother); the Ashraf Pahlavi Foundation and the Shahnaz Youth Clubs. Largest of all these is the Imperial Organisation for Social Service (IOSS), which operates over 250 clinics and 10 hospitals.

These charitable activities are carried out in the name of the Royal Family and are used as a means of royal patronage. Nevertheless the Pahlavi Foundation and the royal purses are not always the prime contributors. The burden has been shifted on to the state. The state budget, unbeknown to most Iranians, provides direct assistance in a substantial way. Almost half the IOSS budget is met from the Treasury ($80 million); the book translation and publishing company receives $700,000; the Queen Pahlavi Foundation is given $10 million; the Farah Pahlavi Foundation $22 million; and the recently established Ashraf Pahlavi Foundation $105,000. The combined annual subsidy from the budget for these philanthropic and charitable activities – for which the Pahlavi family draws kudos – is over $100 million.[24]

These philanthropic activities could not claim to be entirely altruistic. The Foundation has built up directly, via the book translation and publishing company, and indirectly, via the 25th Shakrivar Publishing Company, which is owned by the IOSS, the biggest single controlling interest in Iranian publishing. In particular the Shahrivar Publishing Company supervises the printing of all school textbooks in Iran: some 50 million copies of 428 titles each year.[25] These textbooks can easily be controlled to present material favourable to the régime, and frequently are. This stranglehold on educational publishing is a formidable potential weapon of control. In a lesser vein the orphanages run by the Foundation, or its adjunct the Farah Pahlavi Foundation, are used as recruiting grounds for the police and gendarmerie.[26]

The Extent of Assets

To appreciate the full extent of the Pahlavi Foundation's all embracing presence in Iran, it is essential to have an idea of its assets. Just after its creation, the Shah described the Foundation's assets as shares or interests in a 'number of hotels (mostly constructed by my father); cement factories, sugar factories, our Iranian National Insurance Company, a bank, merchant ships and various other industrial and commercial undertakings'.[27] This in itself demonstrated how deeply involved the Pahlavi family had been in the country's economic affairs.

The original list of assets has never been fully published. Since 1961 there has been no mention of new acquisitions or any changes in the nature of the investments. The Foundation did not even choose to disclose that it had off-loaded to NIOC one of its bigger activities – the ownership and operation of the National Iranian Tanker Company. This was sold off gradually but completed in 1970. The Foundation itself refuses to part with any information concerning the value of its assets, annual income or the composition of investments.[28] Even foreign bankers who have been invited by the Foundation to do business are merely presented with an unsatisfactory list of the original assets at historic book value.[29] Thus, to provide an accurate, or even a reasonably accurate estimate, is impossible. It is more than likely too that the Foundation itself has no accurate idea either. One can therefore only arrive at a conservative guesstimate of between $2.8 billion and $3.2 billion. This excludes liabilities and does not fully take account of the enormously variable element in the value of property.[30] In the last resort, however, the value of the assets makes little difference so long as the Shah's control over the country's economic apparatus is not challenged.

The Foundation's charter sanctions diversification 'to supplement the endowment revenues'. To this end, investments can be made 'in productive and profitable development ventures and purchases of new properties'.[31] This has enabled the Foundation to further strengthen the Royal Family's close association with most major economic activities, fostered by Reza Shah.

The most important asset held by the Foundaton is its 100 per cent ownership of the Bank Omran, the fifth largest commercial bank in Iran. The bank was founded in 1952 and intended to finance the development of agriculture on Crown lands and assist the peasants in the purchase of these lands. The more cynical regarded the bank's creation as debt collector of funds owed to the Crown from the sale of land; and there is more than a grain of truth in this. In any event, what was conceived as a development bank quickly grew into the bank of the Royal Family.

The nature of the Bank Omran is aptly illustrated by the composition of its seven-man higher council. It is headed by Emami, who runs the Foundation. He is assisted by the Court Minister, and Alam, the Shah's closest associate, who was for many years on the council. Also on the

board until his death in November 1977 was Eqbal of NIOC, the head
of Iran Air, Lieutenant-General Khademi; the head of the Iran Chamber
of Commerce, Taher Ziyaee, and Mehdi Samii, a former Governor of
the Bank Markazi and now head of the Agricultural Development
Bank. Samii is the only person with proper banking experience. The
Shah has also ensured that Mohammed Jafar Behbanian is on the
council. Behbanian, who has served the Court for 33 years, acts as the
Shah's private treasurer and has been used as a front man for royal
financial activities.[32]

In July 1977, at the time of the publication of the bank's latest
results, it had assets totalling $1.05 billion and a capital that had been
increased to Rs5 billion, equivalent to $81 million.[33] That year the
bank declared a dividend of $4.2 million, which went directly to the
Foundation. On its own admission the bank is now scarcely involved
in agricultural loans and has switched into property development. It
has for instance a 30 per cent stake in 22,000 upper-income housing
units being built at Farahzad in north-west Tehran, for which it is also
providing financing. Total costs are in the region of $200 million.[34] It
is also financing for the Pahlavi Foundation three of the biggest tower
blocks in Tehran at Vanak.

This heavy involvement in middle- and upper-income property
development contrasts with the Shah's strictures about an over-emphasis on such activity in Tehran to the detriment of lower-income groups.
However, in this way the Royal Family has direct access to, and knowledge of, the most profitable activity in Iran.[35] Bank Omran also acts as
financier for a number of fringe projects for Iran's élite. The bank is
financial comptroller of, and has a 20 per cent interest in, the development of the resort of Kish Island, off the Iranian coast of the Gulf.
This is being developed at huge cost, conservatively estimated at over
$100 million, as a winter playground for the very rich. The Shah
already has a villa there with houses for select friends. The development
envisages the construction of 1,200 villas, three luxury hotels and a
casino, a golf course and duty-free shopping facilities (for the first
time in Iran).[36] The viability of such a project is questionable. Due to
the heat in the Gulf the resort can be utilised for under six months a
year and must import everything, including 3,000 foreign personnel
to operate it. However, financial viability appears less important than
keeping Iran's privileged class content. Interestingly, 80 per cent of
the project is owned by SAVAK; and SAVAK has a represantative
on the board. This Savak involvement dates back to the time when
General Bakhtiar ran SAVAK and acquired the island with SAVAK

funds for $2 million. When he was dismissed from SAVAK the island became SAVAK property.[37] The Foundation's banking interests are not restricted to owning the Bank Omran. One banker's estimate is that, directly or indirectly, the Foundation controls over 15 per cent of the commercial banking system. It has a direct holding in at least three other commercial banks, including 30 per cent of the Bank Iranshahr, whose assets are worth $535 million. It has much smaller holdings in the Irano-British Bank and Bank Etebarat (see Appendix A). It also has a 1.6 per cent share of the development bank, DIBI, worth $700,000.[38]

The Foundation's involvement with insurance is equally large. The Bimeh Melli, officially owned 80 per cent, but perhaps more, by the Foundation, is the third biggest insurance company in Iran. It is primarily concerned with insuring the Foundation's interests and has premiums of around $5 million a year. In addition there are an almost equal amount of premiums coming from Bimeh Melli's lucrative insurance contract with Iran Air, for which it is the sole local insurer.[39] This is the second key link with Iran Air, as its chief is also on the council of the Bank Omran.

Conservative Approach

On the whole, the Pahlavi Foundation has been conservative in its approach to investment with a pronounced emphasis on vertical integration of construction interests, so assisting its main activity: property development. The Foundation has important shares in two of the country's ten cement plants, including 25 per cent of the Tehran Cement Company — Iran's largest plant, accounting for 18 per cent of national production. It has a 30 per cent share in Iranit, a company that imports cement and building materials and recently established a company, Sangarveh Mining, to provide quarry products for the building trade.[40] Ironically cement and building materials have been the items in the shortest supply since the 1973 oil price rises, and for which the biggest black-market prices have been paid.

The Foundation has been wary about large-scale involvement in heavy industry. Nor has this really been necessary since the Shah has preferred to use state-owned companies for the strategic sectors; and the main appointees in these companies report direct to the Shah. The Foundation's principal holdings are in the motor industry (see Appendix A). Through a 10 per cent stake in GM Iran that has the licence for six to eight cylinder cars, it controls 8 per cent of the car market. If GM's plans for a truck plan materialise it could control 50 per cent of Iranian truck assembly. There are unconfirmed reports of a Foundation holding in Irannational, the largest automotive concern. Other important industrial holdings include shares in tyre-making, road construction machinery, leather, office machinery and pharmaceuticals.

The Foundation is strongly involved in agribusiness. This dates back to Reza Shah's establishment of a local sugar industry in the mid-thirties to lessen dependence upon what was then one of the country's main imports. The Pahlavi Foundation now has a share in at least six sugar mills and sugar-beet factories, responsible for about 15 per cent of total capacity. For instance, the Ahwaz Sugar Beet Factory has a monopoly of operations in Khuzestan; while the Kermanshah plant in which it also has an interest is one of the three largest in Iran. Latterly the Foundation's involvement has been indirect via equity participation of the Bank Omran. The bank holds 20 per cent of a $14 million venture to process meat near Qazvin; and is further involved in Khuzestan agribusiness via an interest in Iran Shellcott, one of the major large-scale ventures in this field with an allocation of 14,700 hectares.

Also dating back to Reza Shah's time is the Foundation's ownership of the country's largest chain of hotels. The hotels are primarily in the luxury or first-class category and in this sector the Foundation owns over 70 per cent of Iran's total bed capacity. In Tehran itself, the Pahlavī Foundation owns four leading hotels – the Hilton, the Vanak, the Evin and the Darband. Of these the Evin is being expanded with a new tower block, the Vanak is being completely rebuilt and the Hilton has plans for a third wing. Outside the capital, the main hotels are concentrated round the Caspian, where it also owns the Caspian's two casinos. Directly or indirectly through Bank Oman, it has a monopoly of casinos.[41]

Until recently the Foundation eschewed foreign investment, and where money was placed abroad it sought a low profile. However, in 1973 the Foundation made a public entry into the international property market by buying the DePinna building on Fifth Avenue, New York. To do this, the Foundation was obliged to register as an American charitable institution with the declared aim of using the rental to pay for Iranian students studying in America. The advantage of charitable status in the US is that tax is avoided and the US authorities cannot investigate the books of the parent Foundation in Tehran. In 1975 the building had a book value of $14.5 million. A new 36-storey building is due for completion on the site sometime in 1978. The main clients will be Iranian state agencies – the Iranian New York consulate, an information office, the NIOC and Iranian banks. Their rental payments are expected to provide an annual income of $5 million. This arrangement illustrates the neat interlocking of the Foundation with the rest of the state apparatus.[42]

In addition to financing Iranian students, the large rental income is expected to take the burden off the Foundation in Tehran of financing grants to American universities for studies on Iran. For instance, Princeton University receives some $500,000 a year and Columbia University $18,000.[43] This financing of Iranian studies or outright Iranian gifts to American academic bodies has been criticised in the US as an attempt to obtain tame academics and buy respectability in the academic world.[44]

The Pahlavi Foundation is now actively searching the international property market for investment opportunities; and even employs a senior Member of Parliament, Senator Foroughi, to act as an international adviser in this respect. Bank Omran has also begun to turn to international property development. Through a long-standing association with a small US bank, First National Wisconsin of Milwaukee, Bank Omran has become involved in a huge three-phase neighbourhood development — the Canal Street project — in New Orleans.[45]

The full extent of the Pahlavi Foundation's national and international assets are impossible to describe. For it is not always a question of the Foundation being called upon to invest. It has been and still is a practice in Iran for those establishing industrial and commercial ventures to offer small stakes to members of the Royal Family or to the Pahlavi Foundation direct. Usually this has involved no more than 1 per cent but it can be more. This practice grew up out of the generally well founded belief that royal patronage was the most effective guarantee of profitability. This was the basis for part of Reza Shah's fortune. Latterly these interests offered to the Royal Family have tended to be referred back to the Foundation. In the same way the commissions on contracts, especially defence contracts, paid to intermediaries have been channelled to the Foundation on the Shah's instructions — though presumably with some cut for the intermediary.[46]

Those companies with Foundation equity tend to rely upon Emami to intercede for them, outside the normal administrative channels, if they have problems.[47] Within the business community there is a general assumption that Foundation associated companies and ventures enjoy a privileged status. For instance, B.F. Goodrich was prompted to sell up its share in its Iranian subsidiary partially because of a two-year price freeze. No sooner had the sale gone through to Iranian shareholders, which included the Foundation, the price freeze on Goodrich products was lifted.[48]

Yet it would be wrong to assume that royal involvement can always protect poor planning, bad management and international competition. For example, Bank Omran set up an investment company, Omran Trinwall, in 1974. Bank Omran took a 30 per cent share; and the intention was that Omran Trinwall handle overseas investments and act as a merchant bank. By July 1977, Omran Trinwall had exhausted most of its original Rs12 million capital and Bank Omran had only succeeded in alienating its partners.[49] In another instance a company formed by the Foundation with Krupp to build steel structures, Montex, was liquidated in June 1977 after never having become fully operational. Having formed the company, the Foundation seemed unable to decide what it should do and how it should operate — except provide sinecure jobs.[50] On occasions too the state is obliged to provide direct budgetary assistance to Pahlavi Foundation ventures like a $1 million cash injection given to the Ghahestan Sugar Corporation in 1976.[51]

Uses of Income

The economic power that comes from controlling the Pahlavi Foundation is therefore obvious enough. Less obvious are the more clandestine uses of Pahlavi Foundation income. Here proof of Pahlavi Foundation activities relies more on hearsay than fact. Marvin Zonis, commenting on the Foundation's role of paying 'pensions', says: 'Outright pensions are still granted to elites and counterelites, the monarch's Pahlavi Foundation frequently serving as a conduit.'[52] Although written seven years ago, this still seems to hold true.

With a growing gap between civil servants' salaries and those of the private sector as a result of the 1973 oil price rises, the Foundation has become an important source of fringe benefits to entice them into staying in their jobs. In particular, the Foundation is believed to be the conduit for end-of-year bonuses.[53] These bonuses are paid nominally out of the Shah's private purse. Foundation funds are also used to provide what are in effect straight cash grants in return for special favours, or on occasion low-interest loans — although the latter are usually channelled through the Bank Omran. The extent to which this type of activity is carried over into the military sector has never been satisfactorily clarified. There is a suspicion, based upon the Shah's overriding concern for the well-being of the military, that the military side gets more of Foundation hand-outs than the civilian side.

The Foundation is also used to provide extra income for various members of the Royal Family, either as regular payments or as special funds for specific undertakings. A revealing passage in an unpublished book written by a member of the Foundation Secretariat has this to say:

> The last and by no means least service of the Social Affairs Department [of the Foundation] is to seek out the near and distant relatives of the founder of the Pahlavi dynasty and see to their basic needs and requirements; for welfare begins at home and no foundation could be expected to ignore the essential requirements of its own flesh and blood relatives.[54]

The Swiss bank account of the Foundation quoted earlier showed payments to ten Pahlavis and two other persons associated with the family by marriage.[55] The extent of this assistance is believed considerable. Even minor and distant members of the Royal Family are now reckoned to need $1 million a year to cover their basic needs, to say nothing of capital expenses like new houses.

The expansion of the economy since the early seventies has, however, meant that proportionately Foundation support of the Royal Family has lessened. Royal Family business interests prospered with the boom, especially property; and money has become easier to borrow. As a whole the Royal Family have preferred to act as sleeping partners in business – a *rentier* approach. Among the more speculative has been Prince Shahram, a son of Princess Ashraf.

By all accounts there is a good measure of inefficiency in the handling of Foundation affairs. Discretion and loyalty are prized more than brilliance.[56] This inefficiency has little overall impact on income, however. At one end the Foundation's financial needs – or rather the régime's needs from the Foundation – are underpinned by the budget. At the other it has the ability to draw on secret funds from NIOC. The scale of the Foundation's activities suggests that its income alone would be unable to provide the necessary liquidity, and the most natural covert source would be NIOC. Moreover, use of NIOC in this respect is in line with the Shah's favoured strategy of always having an alternative channel. It means he does not have to rely too much on the budget of the state.

The proportion of income devoted to charitable and philanthropic activity has not increased over the years; and most believe that it has contracted, especially as the state has made a more conscious effort to adopt welfare policies. One person involved in an abortive commercial venture with the Foundation commented:'You can remove the word Foundation'.[57] Certainly there is little doubt that were the Foundation obliged to pay in full for all charitable activities it supports in its name, or those of the related royal foundations, spare income would be very limited – it would probably be unable to support any other activity outside charity.

Notes

1. Mohammed Reza Shah Pahlavi, *Mission for my Country* (London, Hutchinson, 1974 edition), p. 190.

2. W. Morgan Shuster, *The Strangling of Persia* (London, T. Fisher Unwin, 1912), p. 267-8.

3. Julian Bharier, *Economic Development of Iran: 1900-1970* (London, Oxford University Press, 1971), p. 19.

4. Plan and Budget Organisation *The Budget 2535 (1976/77)*, Part III, p. 19.

5. Ibid., p. 70-2. The Imperial Aviation Club gets Rs390 million; the Imperial Horse Society Rs490 million; the Imperial Country Club (called the Imperial Sport Club) Rs130 million.

6. The Shah's official policy is against intermediaries in government-to-government contracts. Agents were specifically barred in US weapons sales as a result of a letter from US Defense Secretary James Schlesinger sent on 23 November 1973 to General Toufanian, Vice War Minister. A major controversy arose over the payment of a $28 million commission. See *International Herald Tribune*, 2 February 1976. On the Reporter commission, see *Financial Times*, 17 December 1977.

7. Abdol Hassan Mahavi, whose family is linked to the former Qajar dynasty, has established for the Shah: Iran Electronics Industries (which eventually plans missile assembly); Iran Marine Services; Iran Aircraft Industries; and a nuclear service company, Iran Nuclear Energy Corporation. He also took part in negotiating for the purchase of AWACs from the US.

8. Eqbal died in November 1977 and was succeeded by Hushang Ansari, former Finance Minister.

9. This view has been recounted to the author with a remarkable degree of consistency by foreigners in the oil business, and Iranians and foreigners involved in analysing the economy.

10. Figures supplied by Bank Markazi on balance of payments. NIOC sales figures supplied by Dr Parviz Mina, head of NIOC's international relations, 13 July 1977.

11. Comment to the author by Dr Mina, 13 July 1977.

12. The Abu Dhabi National Oil Company retains income for operational expenses. Also about 7 per cent of oil income goes direct to the Ruler's purse. *Financial Times*, 11 February 1976.

13. NIOC receives direct budgetary assistance but this covers only part of investment needs and operating costs. See PBO, Budget, Part III, p. 31. In 1976/7 the budgetary assistance was Rs34 billion.

14. *Le Canard Enchaîné*, 21 January 1976. The extract shows a statement from Union de Banques Suisses.

15. See *Iran Almanac, Echo of Iran*, Tehran, 1977, Index.

16. Marvin Zonis, *The Political Elite of Iran* (Princeton, N.J., Princeton

University Press, 1971), p. 49.

17. Mohammed Reza Shah Pahlavi, *Mission*, p. 197.

18. Zonis, *The Political Elite*, p. 48.

19. Pars News Agency daily bulletin, 20 July 1977. An indication of the Shah's continued large personal wealth was his donation of $4 million towards the renovation in 1976 of a Tehran hospital taken over by the Knights of Malta. This primarily represented the price of the land.

20. Perhaps the al-Thani family of Qatar and the al-Nahayyan of Abu Dhabi are also wealthier than the Pahlavis. But such comparisons can only be very approximate.

21. *Pahlavi Foundation Statutes*, Chapter I, Article V.

22. Information supplied to the author by the Pahlavi Foundation.

23. *Iran Almanac, Echo of Iran*, 1977, p. 445.

24. PBO, *Budget*, Part III, pp. 70-1.

25. Pars News Agency daily bulletin, 20 July 1977. The same publishing company was also entrusted with reprinting 50 rare books on Iran to celebrate the 50th anniversary of the Pahlavi dynasty in 1976.

26. A substantial proportion of Iranian policemen are recruited from orphanages.

27. Mohammed Reza Shah Pahlavi, *Mission*, pp. 187-8.

28. The Minister of Information Karim-Pasha Bahadori wrote a letter in May 1977 on the author's behalf requesting assistance from Emami in supplying these details. The Foundation's view was that it took orders only from the Shah and that it was a private – not a state – institution.

29. Based upon the experience of two foreign bankers.

30. Property holdings constitute a major problem in reaching any evaluation of the Foundation's assets. Since 1970 and through to mid-1977 property values rose in the main urban areas between 400 per cent and 1,000 per cent. In many instances this has given inflated values. This estimate takes account of a tripling of property values but it takes no account of the Foundation's ability to influence in its favour (which it can) decisions on urban zoning or the incorporation of agricultural land for urban development.

31. *Pahlavi Foundation Statutes*, Chapter V, Article IX. Also the Ashraf Pahlavi Foundation into which Princess Ashraf claims to have placed all her wealth is entitled to carry out commercial ventures.

32. Behbanian has acted as a deputy Court Minister, and appears to have particular responsibility for the Shah's financial affairs in Europe.

33. Bank Omran annual report, 1976/7.

34. The bank is also linked to Omran Construction, which is involved in a $500 million project for middle- and upper-income units in a Tehran suburb to be called Levittshahr. See *MidEast Markets*, 9 May 1977 and 4 July 1977.

35. The Ashraf Pahlavi Foundation is also involved in property development. In early 1976 a fifty/fifty venture was formed with the Italian state concern, Condotti d'Acqua, to build luxury high-rise apartments near Vanak in Tehran.

36. *Kayhan International*, 20 April 1977.

37. Information supplied to the author by a former sympathiser of General Bakhtiar. There is no independent confirmation for this unusual SAVAK property ownership other than Genral Nasseri's presence on the board of the development company, which itself is only explained by the latter facts.

38. Based on information supplied by a Pahlavi Foundation official.

39. Bimeh Melli refuses to discuss details of any of its activities. This information was supplied by other insurance companies operating in Iran.

40. IDRO annual report, 1975.

41. The Foundation is not directly involved in running the casinos but uses a group of foreign businessmen with South African and British connections –

allegedly because they are not tainted by involvement with big crime.

42. This information is based extensively on a lengthy article in the *New York Times,* 26 September 1976.

43. Ibid.

44. *Washington Post,* 10 May 1977. This cites the case of the American university endowed with an Aryamehr chair of management studies worth $1 million.

45. Bank Omran employs a number of advisers from this bank in which it now has a 5 per cent stake.

46. The proceedings of a bribery trial at the Old Bailey, London, concerning arms sales to Iran, produced the following comment by a witness: 'Sir Shapoor Reporter told me that the Shah had set up the Pahlavi Fund to receive bribes which otherwise would have found their way to officials.' See *Financial Times,* 17 December 1977.

47. Based on information supplied to the author by a company with a Foundation shareholding.

48. Based on information supplied by a former B.F. Goodrich executive. See also *Kayhan International,* 7 July 1976. In other instances the regulations on limits to foreign shareholding are waived. In the Ashraf Pahlavi property venture (cited in note 35) the foreign shareholding was well above the 35 per cent maximum which applied to partnerships involving high technology.

49. Based on information supplied by the Mercantile Bank of Iran and Holland, a partner along with F. Eberstadt in the venture.

50. Based on information supplied by Krupp. Montex had a Rs12 million capital in which the Foundation held 35 per cent.

51. PBO, *Budget,* Part III, p. 34.

52. Zonis, *The Political Elite,* p. 24.

53. Based on information supplied to the author by a senior civil servant. There is no firm proof of this, however.

54. Written by Siavash Danesh, public relations director of the Foundation and assistant to Emami. The Foundation apparently considered publishing a booklet on its activities but had second thoughts on its value and content.

55. *Le Canard Enchaîné,* 21 January 1976.

56. Based on comments by those bankers who have had dealings with the Foundation.

57. Comment by a person involved in the abortive Montex venture.

10 INFLUENCE OF THE MILITARY

I know many people say the Shah wants to have troops to hold a big parade once a year. But you see every day proof that an unprepared country is almost a dead duck. That is not going to happen to us.[1]

More than any other shah, Mohammed Reza Pahlavi has lavished attention on the armed forces. With some justification he could claim to have been one of the few Iranian rulers to have appreciated the need for a strong and credible defence force. The Iranian armed forces, as under most authoritarian régimes, are called upon to play the dual role of guarantors of national sovereignty and guarantors of the ruler's power. Mohammed Reza Shah sees no distinction between these roles but there is an essential duality, and one role exists at the expense of the other.

The armed forces are the keystone of the Great Iranian Civilisation. Military strength is to be both a manifestation, and guarantee, of economic strength and national well-being. The Shah has what can only be called a Gaullist view of Iranian 'gloire' and independence: Iran's armed forces are to reflect the country's standing in the world.[2]

Defence and the armed forces occupy the largest portion of the Shah's time. Not content with being the mere titular Commander-in-Chief, he is in active control, usually direct personal control, even down to monitoring the appointment of middle-ranking officers. They are *his* soldiers as much as Iran's. New recruits go through a thorough king-and-country propaganda course and the whole of the armed forces' credo has been modelled around the slogan 'God, Shah, Fatherland' (Khoda, Shah, Mihan). This is repeated every morning in barracks throughout the country. The Shah once confided to an interviewer: 'In this country, if the king is not the Commander-in-Chief of the armed forces, anything can happen.'[3] In a régime that cannot afford to trust its own people, this is a logical precaution.

Although Mohammed Reza Shah attended Tehran Military College, he does not have the military background of his father. Yet he has a self-confessed fascination for military affairs.[4] He enjoys the gadgetry of modern warfare and always impresses his visitors with his knowledge of weaponry.[5] His keen military interest has meant that throughout his reign defence expenditure has never been below 23 per cent of the general budget. During the fifties the proportion was much higher, and frequently topped 35 per cent.[6]

External Threats

All Iranians are afraid of foreign attack. The Shah's sense of insecurity differs only in degree from that of the rest of his fellow countrymen. No matter what the régime in Iran, there are seven prime factors in determining a defence policy for the 1980s:

(1) the location of Iran in an area of major international strategic interest that provides over 70 per cent of non-Communist crude oil exports;

(2) the sharing of a 2,000 kilometre border with the Soviet Union which both historically and recently has sought a pliant pro-Soviet Iran;

(3) the state of belligerence between the Arab countries and Israel that has led to four wars since 1947, each more lethal than the last;

(4) the potentially precarious nature of Pakistan's relations with India that has witnessed three wars since 1947;

(5) the uncertain alignment of landlocked Afghanistan on the Iranian eastern flank;

(6) the recent phenomenon of centralised authority in Iran that has still left regional autonomy a potentially divisive issue. Since 1946 there have been challenges to central authority, abetted from outside, through autonomy movements in Azerbaijan, Baluchistan and Kurdistan, while the oil-rich southern province of Khuzestan with its large Arabic-speaking population is still regarded by some Arab states as Arabestan (Syrian and Iraqi maps mark it as such);

(7) the need for stability in the Gulf to secure the free flow of Iran's vital oil exports, which involves balancing the emergent power of conservative Saudi Arabia with the radicalism of the Baathists in Iraq.

The Shah's insecurity and ambition were profoundly influenced by the withdrawal of British forces from the Gulf, and the ending, on 1 December 1971, of the treaties of protection that bound Britain to defend the Trucial Sheikhdoms. British forces, stationed in Bahrain and Sharjah, propped up the conservative rule of the Gulf Sheikhdoms and provided an effective insulation against the spread of any radical ideology. The British presence was also the central guarantee of the protection of shipping, especially oil tankers, in the waters of the Gulf. Britain had both naval frigates and minelayers as well as reconnaissance and strike aircraft.[7]

While this British presence was a useful stabiliser it nevertheless excluded Iran from playing a regional role of real significance. Equally important, British and Iranian interests did not always coincide. Britain, for instance, was pledged to support the independence and sovereignty of Bahrain to which Iran laid historic claim. The British military presence on the island helped to thwart this Iranian claim. The finding by a special United Nations mission in May 1970 that the majority of Bahrainis favoured independence was a bitter blow to Iranian pride.[8]

In 1968 the British decision to phase out its military role in the Gulf gave Iran the chance of becoming a serious regional power – if not *the* regional power. The changing strategic position of oil made this all the more important. By the late sixties the Iranian economy was largely dependent upon oil revenues. Unlike the other major regional oil producers, Iraq and Saudi Arabia, Iran had (and still has) no capacity for a strategic switch of crude exports via overland pipelines.[9] Iranian oil has to travel in tankers which must pass through the Straits of Hormuz, only 47 kilometres wide at their narrowest point. This is Iran's jugular vein, and with the departure of the British the Shah was determined that no one should press on it.

The Shah made this apparent with almost indecent haste. On the very eve of British withdrawal, Iranian special forces occupied three small islands near the Straits of Hormuz – Abu Musa and the Greater and Lesser Tunbs, belonging respectively to Sharjah and Ras al-Khaimah. A charade of historic claim, strategic necessity and regional stability was used to justify the move but in fact the Shah was merely demonstrating Iranian power in the Gulf, to say nothing of mollifying domestic opinion over the 'loss' of Bahrain.[10] The seizure contributed directly to the assassination of the Ruler of Sharjah (for acquiescing in the Iranian action) and resulted in considerable unrest in Ras al-Khaimah.[11] It also put Iran's larger Arab neighbours on the defensive, worrying over Iranian expansionism. However, in this act of military adventurism Iran established itself as the new policeman of the Gulf. The British government was well aware of Iranian intentions and did not disapprove of the principle. On the contrary, increased Iranian strength was part of the scenario. More importantly, the Shah enjoyed American backing for a larger regional role. Apprehensive lest British withdrawal create a power vacuum, the US encouraged the Shah's regional ambitions as the most effective check to Soviet influence in the area.

American Support

American grant aid for military purchases had been a key factor in assisting the Shah's build-up of his armed forces since the mid-1950s. However, with increased oil revenues the Shah sought to phase out this dependent relationship. The Shah's American military adviser at the time linked this decision to the holding of the Persepolis ceremonies commemorating 2,500 years of monarchy:

> in the fall of '71 they had their great party that could be best visualised as a debutante ball — a coming out party — when he [the Shah] announced to the world 'we are a developed country: we are going to stand on our own feet.' He specifically asked that we terminate all grant aid.[12]

Increased financial independence and the termination of US grant aid had an important consequence. Not only could the Shah now choose a wider and more sophisticated variety of equipment, but also the American arms salesmen did not have to worry about arranging credits with the Pentagon before beginning their sales pitch. Many ignored the Pentagon and came direct to Tehran so that the Pentagon had little idea of what was being co-ordinated.[13]

By 1972 the Shah was greedy for a whole range of sophisticated military technology. In May 1972, just prior to a visit to Tehran by President Nixon, Secretary of Defense James Schlesinger drew attention to two issues that became highly relevant four years later: the security risk of selling advanced equipment and the dangers inherent in providing equipment that required extensive technical back-up from US personnel. Schlesinger told President Nixon in writing it was unwise to sell Iran laser-guided bombs and advised against 'making a firm commitment to the Shah to sell the F—14 or the F—15 and advised against an increase in uniformed US technical personnel in Iran in order to maintain a low profile'.[24] This advice was ignored by Nixon with important long-term consequences. In retrospect the Nixon visit to Tehran was crucial in the Iranian arms build-up. Without the commitments given then, it is highly unlikely that the Shah would have been able to go for such a rapid and sophisticated weapons procurement programme. In subsequent testimony on the visit, the then chief of the US military mission in Tehran, Major-General Ellis Williamson, said, 'After the President's visit I became concerned because it was obvious that Iran expected to get from the US everything it wanted short of nuclear weapons.'[15]

On a number of important strategic points American and Iranian interests coincided. The strengthening of the Iranian military establishment tied in with the Kissinger-Nixon strategy of global containment of the Soviet Union, which included the historic opening up of relations between Washington and Peking. To counter the Soviet presence in the Indian Ocean the Shah was encouraged to extend his role of Gulf policeman into the Indian Ocean. This was the purpose of the naval and air base to be built at Chah Bahar, less than 100 kilometres from the Pakistan border. In the original plans for the base, submarine silos capable of housing and servicing American nuclear submarines were even included.[16]

To assist Iran in its new regional role the Shah was encouraged to purchase a $850 million electronic surveillance system supplied by Rockwell International. This enabled Iran to monitor and eavesdrop on the communications traffic of its neighbours — including the highly sensitive southern part of the Soviet Union that contained rocket-testing and armaments development facilities.[17]

With such facilities extensively manned by expatriate personnel, it is hard to believe that the United States was only concerned with Iran's own defence needs. Though never explicitly stated, Nixon was quite happy to allow Iranian funds and Iranian cover to extend US containment of the Soviet Union and monitor hostile Arab régimes in the area. For instance, allowing Iran to acquire the F–14 (Grumman 'Tomcat') fitted with the Phoenix missile added an entirely new dimension to the region's armed forces. Not only could this aircraft counter the high-flying Soviet MIG–25 reconnaissance plane but it could also master the MIG–23 fighter: a switch from passive defence to a more assertive stance *vis-à-vis* the Soviet Union.[18]

The final factor affecting the Nixon decision was the pressure from the American arms sales lobby. Iran was seen as a major new opportunity to sustain production lines as the Vietnam War weapon sales boom began to taper off. When the salesmen began to sound out the Shah and his senior military advisers, they found a willing audience. Moreover the way was smoothed by Iranian officials who realised the opportunities open to them from large contracts. A Pentagon study on bribery in Iranian arms contracts released in 1977 concluded that 'the past conduct of US corporations seeking multi-million dollar contracts indicates that the stakes are so high and the temptation so great that they will continue in the future to pay agents funds which can be shared by Iranian officials.'[19]

Since Iran was so clearly in the market to buy, it was a classic case of 'if we don't sell, someone else will.' This increased both the pressure on the Pentagon and White House to approve sales and, at the other end, the incentives to Iranian officials to ensure that contracts were awarded. 'The American promoters were bribing key people in an enormous way and spending millions on bribes with top level people,' a British arms salesman commented.[20] The pressure was such that on occasions major decisions were taken without proper forethought on either side. In evidence to the Senate Committee on Multi-national Corporations, Senator Church said: 'We have strong evidence that the F–14 was strongly pushed onto the Iranian Government long before our own Government made any decision that it should be made available for foreign sale.'[21] At stake was a $28 million commission on a $2.2 billion contract.

If the Shah had any doubts about the scale of procurement and Iran's ability to absorb it, these were dispelled by three events – the Arab-Israeli war in October 1973, the quadrupling of oil prices, and the explosion of a nuclear device by India. The Arab-Israeli war made clear the massively high rates of attrition in a modern war; the new oil money enabled the Shah to purchase the new weaponry; while the Indian nuclear explosion was a sharp reminder of the big gap that still separated Iran from military powers with advanced technology.[22]

Defence spending therefore accelerated sharply in 1974, giving the deceptive impression to the outside world that this was exclusively the result of the oil price rise (see Table 7). In fact this was only one of a series of catalytic elements. Rather than seek to control or co-ordinate the flow of arms to Iran, the US government was happy to let events follow their own course. There was no review of American arms sales to Iran until 1976, by which time the Iranian armed forces were slowly beginning to sort themselves out.[23] From 1974 to the end of 1976 there was incredible confusion, so much so that the US Department of Defense was obliged to send its own representative to Tehran in September 1975 to sort out 'the chaos and problems that had emerged in program management and implementation'.[24] Not the least of Iran's problems was that it had been foisted with equipment that the salesmen had not fully explained.[25] Although Iran now possessed a splendid modern arsenal it did not know how to use it. The Shah and his advisers consistently overestimated the technical capacity of the armed forces.

Table 7: Defence Expenditure (million dollars)

	1974/5	1975/6	1976/7	1977/8*
1. Supply, production and renovation	3,500	5,192	4,834	4,829
2. Personnel	812	1,095	1,877	1,858
3. Maintenance and operations	493	613	764	504
4. Special operations	653	636	658	681
5. Other	43	64	64	9
Total	5,501	7,600	8,197	7,881
% General Budget	24.2	29.2	27.6	24.4
% Increase	+189	+38	+7.7	−2.8

Notes
a. The exchange rate has been calculated on the following basis —
   $1 = Rs67.50 for 1974/5; S1 = RS69.40 for 1975/6 and 1976/7;
   $1 = Rs71.20 for 1977/8.
b. These figures are taken from the General Budget allocation under the heading 'Defence'.
c. These figures do not include allocations for Defence Industries (the Military Industries Organisation which receives a separate annual allocation equivalent to $106 million in 1976/7.
d. Additional military expenditure is contained in a separate heading in the General Budget 'Government constructions and establishments'. A small amount is directly itemised as for military construction ($33 million in 1976/7); but the bulk is contained in an item 'construction of other buildings of state'. This is believed to refer to military bases, housing and general infrastructure almost exclusively. In the three years through to 1976/7 the allocations amounted to $3.2 billion.

*   Projected.
Source: Plan and Budget Organisation.

Credibility and Effectiveness

A comprehensive defence strategy for Iran involves a complex series of measures because the country is so large, its centres of population so spread out and poorly linked, and because it borders so many countries with differing social systems at differing stages of development all with widely varied terrain. Iran has 5,170 kilometres of land frontier with five different states, and 2,510 kilometres of coast covering three wholly different waters — the Caspian, the Gulf and the Indian Ocean/ Sea of Oman. Iranian territorial waters are contiguous with nine states.[26]

The problem is comparable to the strategic defence of NATO but without the experience, technological backing or cohesiveness of an alliance.

Iran is part of the CENTO alliance, which includes its regional neighbours Pakistan and Turkey plus Britain and the US. The Shah, however, puts no great faith in its permanence or, more importantly, its efficacy. Unlike its predecessor the Baghdad Pact, CENTO has managed to survive so long largely because it is so innocuous. The Shah believes that the most effective policy is one based on the Gaullist principle of *tous azimuts:* everyone is potentially hostile.[27]

Such a philosophy has to be balanced with Iran's own financial and human resources. Iran cannot for instance seek parity with all its neighbours, especially the Soviet Union. Yet the Shah has sought as far as possible to do this. As a result his critics argue that he has overarmed Iran as a purely regional power but left it far too weak, especially without a nuclear option, to match up to the Soviet Union. Commenting on this, Shahram Chubin of the Iranian Institute for International Political and Economic Studies says:

> Iran's strategy is to create a trip-wire which would first deter and then delay an aggressor while diplomacy and friendly states come to its assistance. The Shah has likened the armed forces in this respect to a 'lock on the door'.[28]

The experience of the 1973 Arab-Israeli war and the thrust of more recent Soviet defence strategy highlight the lightning strike as the most effective option. This allows the aggressor to present international opinion with a *fait accompli* before friendly states can be mobilised. In this regard the massive Iranian arms build-up may be mere provocation to the Soviets and quite incapable of deterring them. This is where the American attitude is crucial to Iranian credibility. The Shah has not depended exclusively upon America for arms supplies, but over the years America has been the leading supplier.[29] In the four-year period up to the end of 1976 American arms sales had reached $10 billion.[30] The official justification for such a heavy flow of weaponry to Iran was the inherent threat posed by the Soviet Union – either through direct aggression or through indirect Soviet pressure.[31] Yet the specific nature of this threat has always been blurred in official American and Iranian comment. Is it a lightning thrust from the Caspian down to the oilfields of Khuzestan? Is it a similar thrust down through Meshed to the southern part of the Gulf to threaten Western oil supplies? Is it complete Soviet domination of Afghanistan? Or is it subversion that would lead to the establishment of a pro-Soviet and anti-American régime in Iran? This last scenario scares the Shah and the US most and is thought the most likely. It is also the hardest to combat.

It is this fear of Soviet subversion that has made it difficult for the Shah to entertain anything but correct relations with the Soviet Union. He has bought Soviet military equipment; but has never convincingly sought to play the Soviet Union off against the US. The Shah is too deeply committed to the West to be able to do this.[32]

Soviet actions towards Iran since the beginning of the Cold War have on occasions been both aggressive and subversive. However since the late sixties when Iran began to bolster its armed forces and move closer towards the US, it has been difficult to separate cause and effect. For instance Soviet arming of Iraq and the subsequent Treaty of Friendship in April 1972 could be interpreted as a response to American armament of Iran and the involvement of Israel, with Iranian approval, in the Kurdish rebellion. Soviet countenancing in the early seventies of urban guerrilla training in Eastern Europe and Cuba for Iranian dissidents, and the beaming of hostile radio broadcasts to Iran from Bulgaria, could be interpreted again as a response to Iran's more clear-cut anti-Soviet stance.[33] One theory, canvassed by Iranian intelligence, was that the assassination of three Americans installing the electronic eavesdropping system which enabled indirect increased American surveillance of the southern Soviet Union represented Soviet disapproval of this project.[34]

Although the Shah may have provoked the Soviets, this still does not alter his or the American perception of the Soviet threat. Prior to the Nixon administration, American governments had been committed to the survival of Mohammed Reza Shah as a strong pro-Western monarch. A bilateral treaty was signed in 1959 stipulating joint consultations in the event of aggression by a Communist or Communist-inspired country. US officials now say this was a fairly standard treaty for an important US ally of the time, and play down commitments of military support. It nevertheless indicated the nature of American policy: Iran was to be an American sphere of influence.[35]

Under the Nixon administration the US became committed, or rather entangled, in a way it was not before. By permitting the Iranian purchase of sophisticated equipment in unprecedented quantities, the US committed itself to make this hardware operational. This meant an exposed profile in the form of extensive military and civilian technical and advisory personnel in Iran to compensate for the serious shortage of skilled manpower. By 1976 it was reckoned that the majority of the 24,000 Americans in Iran were defence and defence-related. This number was expected to reach between 50,000 and 60,000 by 1980, largely as a result of purchases of arms from the US.[36] Such is Iranian dependence on expatriate personnel that it will be unable to fight on a day-to-day basis without American support through to the late 1980s.[37] Although this bore out Schlesinger's forebodings back in 1972, in strictly Iranian terms this American military presence provides a deterrent of a kind it never previously possessed. The prospect of American personnel being involved, even indirectly, in combat has given the US a strong incentive to ensure that such a situation never occurs. America must ensure that Iran is seen to be strong against potential aggression or in facing up to diplomatic pressure. For instance, in early January 1975, Iran and Iraq were on the verge of a major escalation of border fighting during the Kurdish rebellion. Iran pulled back in part because of American assessments that she would receive a bloody nose. This would have weakened Iran's image and the image of the US in relation to Iran.[38]

The credibility of the Iranian military is therefore only achieved at the expense of Iranian independence. Moreover, in the view of American defence experts the dependence is likely to grow if the equipment becomes more sophisticated. In relation to the F–14 Iran is like a Texan auto dealer dependent upon Detroit.[39]

Attempts to limit this heavy dependence have been initiated by licensing arrangements for local manufacture and assembly. But when the country's main motor company, Irannational, starts assembling cars in 1967 and ten years later can only manufacture the unsophisticated 55 per cent of the parts, the difficulties in obtaining anything but notional independence are apparent. Independence is further undermined by the distance that separates Iran from its major suppliers. This makes Iran vulnerable in a war where questions of overflying rights and availability of spares and transport capacity are key issues. The experience of Israel in 1973, whose fighting performance would almost certainly have been different without the massive US airlift, has not been lost on the Shah. Iran since 1973 has set out to acquire the most comprehensive airlift capacity in the Middle East, in addition to a heavy stockpiling of spares.[40] This however is a costly solution.

Although the Shah's military build-up could not easily sustain a conventional war, its main function is as a foreign policy option. Increased military potential has provided increased foreign policy flexibility and credibility, especially when combined with oil wealth diplomacy. In this sphere it has not mattered that Iran's military effectiveness is an unknown quantity. Increased military strength and oil wealth have been used to good effect in bolstering Pakistan, assuring the neutrality of Afghanistan and in improving relations with more powerful Arab states like Egypt and Syria. It has also enabled Iran to maintain its independent approach to Israel.[41] During the 1973 war, Iranian naval vessels escorted Israeli tankers down the Gulf at the same time as Iranian transporters helped to airlift Saudi troops to Syria and permitted limited Soviet military overflights of Iranian territory *en route* for Iraq and Syria.[42] Since the 1975 Sinai disengagement agreement between Egypt and Israel, Iran has been providing 90 per cent of Israel's oil needs.[43] Increased regional strength has also enabled Iran to lessen dependence upon the politically hazardous Iranian-Israeli-South African axis which dated back to the Nasser era.

Testing the Military Machine in Oman

The most obvious demonstration of Iran's regional strength has been its intervention in Oman to assist Sultan Qaboos in suppressing the rebellion in Dhofar. The Shah was invited to despatch troops to Oman by Sultan Qaboos in 1972. The prime motive for accepting the request was not the publicised danger of a radical régime across the waters of the Gulf but to demonstrate unequivocally that Iran was to be *the* regional power. A secondary motive was the need to provide practical training for the military.

In some respects this was the most remarkable aspect of the intervention. The Shah was able to utilise the excuse of a Communist-supported liberation movement undermining a neighbouring friendly Arab régime as a means of giving Iranian troops their first real taste of counter-insurgency operations. As one Arab commentator pointed out, 'Had Dhofar not existed, Iran would have invented it.'[44] Apart from Oman, the Iranian experience of battle conditions or counter-insurgency has been limited. Iranian tanks and artillery were used in sporadic border clashes with Iraq up until the March 1975 treaty of friendship between the two countries; and Iranian artillery units plus logistical back-up operated inside Iraqi Kurdistan in support of the Kurdish rebels in the latter stages of the rebellion. Iranian helicopter units have also taken part in cross-border co-operation with Pakistan to combat Baluch separatism. But such experience does not really test the military machine.

The function of the Iranian troops in Oman was to increase the size of the Sultan's Armed Forces (SAF) and to provide logistical support, particularly making good the Omani shortfall in helicopter capacity.

In 1971 SAF strength was under 10,000 men, including expatriate
officers and NCOs and seconded British personnel. Although the total
strength of the Dhofari guerrillas was never more than 2,000, with
perhaps 1,000 inside Oman at any one time, SAF strength was inadequate even for a holding operation. The advent of Iranian forces
allowed the SAF to release troops for duty outside Dhofar province
and to go on the offensive inside Dhofar. This was the essential value
and importance of Iranian forces. At the height of the fighting, from
September 1974 to March 1975, there were some 4,500 Iranians in
two battalion strength; roughly a quarter of all the forces deployed in
Dhofar.

The Iranians can be credited with two achievements. An Iranian
battle group in December 1973 opened up a 50 kilometre stretch of
road linking the Dhofari coastal capital of Salalah with the inland air
base of Thumrait. The following December, Iranian forces established
a defensive line from the coastal village of Rakhyut inland across the
principal guerrilla infiltration trails. This line, the 'Damavand line',
effectively isolated those rebel groups inside Dhofar from their rein-
forcements infiltrating across the border from South Yemen. However,
too much should not be read into these actions. More than anything
else they were the inevitable consequence of SAF's numerical superiority, increased skill in the SAF command and large-scale desertions
from the guerrilla side rallying to Sultan Qaboos. In the opinion of the
British military involved in the fighting, the Iranian forces displayed
several important weaknesses. Because the Iranian troops were mainly
composed from élite units of the Special Forces these weaknesses concern Iran's best-trained soldiers. The first shortcoming was the rigid
nature of the Iranian command structure and the seemingly inseparable
gulf between officers and men, which rendered the communication of
all but the simplest of orders a complex and unwieldy operation. In
guerrilla operations textbook plans rarely materialise and successful
action depends upon initiative. When the whole command structure
mitigates against initiative by junior officers and NCOs, this is a serious
disadvantage.

A second shortcoming concerned the ethos and training of the
Iranian troops. They were organised on the American principle of
lavish back-up and PX-type facilities — fresh food, dairy products and
water were flown in each day from Shiraz. This tended to reduce combat morale. Third, the Iranian forces suffered seriously from the Shah's
determination to use Dhofar as a training exercise. To gain the maximum advantage, troops were rotated on a three-month basis. This dis-

couraged the development of proper experience since units were withdrawn too soon. The rota system also led to unnecessarily high casualties from basic failures such as inability to read map references, or
helicopter landings on silhouetted ridges or the laying of mines without charts. (At one stage a senior British officer was obliged to go to
Tehran and bring back the Iranian responsible for a minefield since he
had left no charts.)

The Iranians never released their casualty figures — not even to the
SAF general command. SAF officers reckoned that the Iranian casualty
rate was about three times that of SAF. From January 1971 to the end
of December 1976 (eight months after the formal cease-fire) SAF
losses totalled 188 killed and 574 wounded. Thus, even on a three to
one ratio on these figures Iranian casualties were not excessive. However, this was a small war, tucked away in a remote corner of the
Arabian Peninsular, with casualty levels that raised no questions in
Tehran and which presented the Shah more than a fair chance of being
on the winning side. The Iranian presence was essential to the war
effort but the Iranian performance gave no indication of the effectiveness of the Shah's military machine. If anything, it exposed the inherent weakness of a bureaucratic command structure that stifled initiative. Some argue that had the Iranians been alone they would have
been as muscle-bound as the Americans in Vietnam and would probably have fared little better than Nasser's ill-fated venture into the
Yemen.

Despite these negative elements the Shah could claim to be satisfied with the impact on the region of Iranian intervention. Governments like Saudi Arabia and Iraq expressed varying degrees of unease
over the intervention. But the Shah was able to ride this out. He was
able also to withdraw the bulk of Iranian troops in January 1977 with
comparatively little fuss.[45]

Political Role

In political terms the possession of a large, bureaucratic and unwieldy
military establishment is not necessarily a disadvantage. Indeed the
Shah regards this as an advantage and has encouraged such a structure.
It is a function of the dual role of the military in Iran. Since they
are also the ultimate guarantors of the throne, a small but cohesive
military would present a greater threat to the régime. A large military
establishment enables the Shah to fragment individual power bases,
making it much more difficult to dissident elements to mount a cohesive opposition.

The constant concern with loyalty has led the Shah into keeping the three services well apart. They are rarely linked except through the person of the Shah. Loyalty has been more rewarded than brilliance, and royal relatives are placed in strategic posts. The Shah's brother-in-law, General Mohammed Khatemi, commanded the Air Force until his death in a hang glider accident in 1975.[46] Khatami was the man who was expected to rally the loyalty of the armed forces in the event of the Shah's death: and his own death has left the position vacant. An important figure in the Navy, earmarked for future prominence, is Captain Prince Shafik, a son of Princess Ashraf.[47]

In his dealings with the military, the Shah tends to treat separately with commanders, and the command structures are so arranged that it is difficult for groups to gather without the notice of security agents. The army's crack units, and the best armed, are the Imperial Guard, whose task is to protect the monarch. The Imperial Guard were among the first units to learn to use the Chieftain tank. Troop and aircraft dispositions reinforce the impression that the Shah's defence policy is intimately linked with his own protection. For instance, there is an unnecessarily high concentration of armour in and around Tehran which can only be explained in this way (although a secondary factor is more mundane — officers prefer to be near the capital). The same applies to aircraft. The heavy concentration of aircraft at Mehrababd airport creates serious problems for civil traffic using this, the capital's only international airport.

By virtue of their role as defenders of the throne — not of the realm — the officer corps has become a privileged class. Their pay and fringe benefits put NATO to shame, including the provision of villas, domestic personnel, low taxes on luxury goods and holiday compounds. Senior ranks are pensioned off on full pay and are frequently drafted into the boards of state companies and institutions.

The military are governed by their own rules and regulations and are kept apart from the rest of society. No one below the rank of colonel can visit a foreigner, especially a military attaché, without permission. This is rarely forthcoming. Even generals rarely show up at diplomatic receptions.[48] This separation is reinforced by a tendency for the officers to marry within the military establishment, which is formed mostly from the ranks of middle-class families of modest origins. Unlike the Turkish armed forces, where poor but ambitious youths join as a means of self-advancement, the social structure of the Iranian officer class is less varied — especially since the purges in the late 1950s following the overthrow of Mossadegh. The style and pace of the military build-up has also created opportunity for monumental corruption.

In February 1976 the head of the Navy, Rear Admiral Ramzi Abbas Ata'i, was found guilty with ten other officers on unspecified charges of embezzlement and fined $3.7 million. This is believed to have been the amount Ata'i, a man of modest means, had seized from his various bank accounts.[49] The Shah was forced to act in this instance because of the demoralising effect corruption was known to have produced within the Navy. Among the things Ata'i is alleged to have permitted was the use of Iranian vessels to transport duty-free goods, including cars, from Dubai to Iran.[50] Corruption has also extended down to extensive draft evasion. In June 1977 a military tribunal sentenced a group of officers and NCOs who had been operating 62 draft evasion networks.[51] Such activities may not detract from the loyalty of the armed forces to the Shah; but they certainly do not contribute to operational efficiency.

Finally it should be stressed that the military, as seen in the previous chapter, are deeply involved in the Shah's system of parallel government. They provide many of the key personnel for SAVAK and the Shah's own Imperial Inspectorate and are responsible for a wide area of 'justice'. They are also involved in more benevolent activities like the supervision of the literacy corps. The literacy corps is a system of using high school and university graduates eligible for national service to carry out this service as teachers in rural areas. This is the central element in the campaign to eradicate rural poverty and illiteracy.

Value for Money

Iran spends four times as much *per capita* on defence as Turkey, yet the numerical strength of its armed forces is over 30 per cent less.[52] Turkey is a NATO member and comes under the NATO umbrella, so the comparison between these two countries with similar-sized populations can be misleading. Yet the comparison does serve to pose the question of whether Iran is getting value for money.

Since 1973 the military build-up has been at the expense of the civilian sector in three main areas — the allocation of funds, competition for scarce human and material resources, and access to technology. Of these by far the most significant has been the expansion of the numerical strength of the armed forces on the scarce manpower market. Between 1972 and 1976 the Iranian armed forces expanded from 191,000 to 300,000. This was an annual increase of 11 per cent, only surpassed in the region by Syria, whose numerical strength expanded directly as a result of the 1973 Arab-Israeli war.[53] In the case of

Iran this was not merely an increase of foot-soldiers but a response to the demands of the new sophisticated equipment.

This expansion of uniformed personnel was paralleled by an increase in the number of civilian personnel in desk jobs and technical roles, and more importantly construction workers for new bases, housing, etc. The military became the biggest single client for skilled and semi-skilled labour. It also became the prime importer of foreign skilled and technical personnel. Almost half the foreign personnel employed in Iran by 1977 were estimated to be defence or defence-related.[54] There appears to have been no attempt to co-ordinate the manpower needs of the military sector with those of the civilian in the Plan Organisation. This created tremendous competition for scarce manpower and invariably the military won out.

The fact that a sizeable part of the new military investment was capital-intense made little difference in the short term because it merely exacerbated competition for such skills as computer programmers or mechanics. For instance, supporting the operation of 80 F–14s requires 6,500 personnel, of which 2,650 will need special skills.[55] For the more advanced F–16 fighter, of which Iran wants to buy 300, 218 technicians will be needed for each 18 aircraft.[56]

These shortages are expected to get worse between now and the early 1980s as Iran takes delivery of the bulk of the sophisticated equipment first considered for purchase in 1973-5. The Iranian Air Force (IIAF) will probably have to increase its personnel by 50 per cent by 1981 to operate all the systems. In 1976 there was a shortfall of 7,000 from a technical manpower requirement of 20,000. Even by 1981 Iran could be short of some 10,000 technical personnel just for the IIAF, which is considered the most prestigious of the service arms.[57]

The price of obtaining such personnel is very high. Either the military offers wages and conditions that better the civilian sector – competition that itself boosts wage costs – or skills are imported. This makes the software element in Iran's defence purchases extremely expensive. Including training, technical maintenance, language schooling plus spare parts, testing, etc., software has devoured 50 per cent of the defence expenditure since 1973.[58] The priority accorded the military has also affected the introduction of technology to the civilian sector. The Shah's emphasis on indigenous armaments production has turned the defence industries into the most technically advanced of the economy outside oil and petrochemicals. In this respect Iran is attempting to cope not with low or intermediate technology but is making a quantum leap direct to the most advanced technology, with only the slimmest base. For instance, Iran is seeking to establish an advanced electronics industry in Shiraz which will be able to assemble and manufacture sophisticated weapons systems. Agreement has already been reached with the British Aircraft Corporation for partial manufacture of the Rapier missile system; while agreement in principle has been reached upon co-production of the TOW anti-tank missile and the Maverick missile.[59] Despite scaling down the original project, Iran is pressing ahead with a major ordinance factory complex at Isfahan producing certain types of guns (Bofors) and advanced automatic weapons (in association with the Czech company Omnipol) plus standard artillery munitions. The War Ministry also intends to incorporate a degree of local manufacture into the Chieftain tank and tank transporters via co-operation with British Leyland and Rolls Royce.[60] More revealing of Iran's military technology ambitions is a highly secret facility, at Pachin, south-east of Tehran, geared to the testing and production of advanced warheads and rocket motors. Some 80 West German chemists, explosive experts and rocket engineers are employed in the complex. Suggestions that Iran is seeking to develop an indigenous medium-range missile capacity are impossible to confirm — or that the Pachin research is linked to the work of German rocket scientists operating in Zaire. However, it is known that the Shah wants to have a missile that will balance the Soviet-made Scud possessed by neighbouring Iraq.[61] There is also a strong belief that the Shah's determination to build up nuclear technology in Iran is linked to an eventual hope of possessing nuclear weapons. The Shah has sounded out the French on their view of Iran sharing in the nuclear reprocessing facilities pledged to Pakistan and had apparently been given an understanding by former Pakistani Premier Bhutto that Pakistan would consider favourably such an arrangement if the French approved.[62] The Iranian Navy meanwhile, since early 1977, has been toying with the idea of acquiring nuclear submarines.[63] The desire for independence through broad-based indigenous production is wholly understandable. Yet so long as the economy remains relatively backward there are considerable dangers in this approach. By going straight for advanced systems, Iran risks obtaining a once-and-for-all transfer of technology from which it is much harder to generate a large spin-off. The technology is merely grafted and stands in isolation. Iran is also vulnerable to the transferring country deciding what technology is supplied. The risks of Iran ending up producing the non-essential items, with only the appearance of production capacity, are high.

Moreover the real cost of local production has only been measured against the notional concept of independence. A naval dockyard at Bandar Abbas became operational in late 1977, giving the Iranian Navy the ability to refit and repair its own frigates and destroyers. But a complete refit would take three years, against 18 months in Britain, and cost twice as much.[64] This is the cost of independence. The sophistication of the sytems ordered frequently made it difficult – and will continue to make it difficult – to monitor overcharging. Between December 1973 and September 1974 the Shah ordered six Spruance class destroyers at a price per vessel of $234 million. By February 1976 the price had risen to $338 million each, and the order had to be cut to four.[65]

This was for an item which at best was of marginal value to Iran.[66] The destroyer, one of the most advanced vessels in the US Navy's inventory, which it was itself finding difficult to handle, was designed for an ocean-going role: in Iran's case policing the Indian Ocean. Although it fitted the strategic plan of the Chah Bahar base, no one gave thought to manning. Training of personnel was meant to have started in July 1975 with 16 people per week. By March 1976 only 23 had begun training.[67] This was because it proved impossible to find the personnel to train. The Spruance purchase, like so many other items, was predicated on Iran's ability to buy and took no account of the human element.

However, the most puzzling and the most damaging element in the Shah's defence philosophy was his premium on speed. The dangers of trying to build up the military in a hurry were self-evident. Yet he insisted on this course, delivering himself into the hands of the seller. The pace of delivery contained a large built-in wastage, and hindered efficient use. For instance, pilots who had no sooner finished training on the Phanton F–4 aircraft were drafted on to the more advanced F–14 programme – sacrificing barely complete mastery of one aircraft for incomplete mastery of another.[68]

Because of the taboo surrounding military purchases or performance, this tremendous wastage has not been properly challenged. Nor has there been any debate over whether Iran would be better served by opting for more readily attainable objectives in the civilian sector. The most candid comment was contained in a paper prepared by the Iranian Institute for International Political and Economic Studies.

The flood of weapons, for example tanks (or helicopters), is likely to result in remarkable waste in two respects. First, in stretching the capacity of existing trained crews and decreasing their efficiency, and/or in the inability to maintain and operate these vehicles leading to warehousing, deterioration, or falling into disrepair. It may indeed be the Government's assumption underlying the large numbers of weapons ordered, that many will be used up, or crashed in trial and error and that this type of attrition is a natural corollary of the rapid attainment of skills.[69]

Notes

1. Mohammed Reza Shah in interview with *Newsweek,* 14 October 1974.
2. The Shah has declared that defence and national indpendence are two 'super-principles'. See *Kayhan International,* 25 October 1976.
3. Mohammed Reza Shah in interview with *Newsweek,* 1 March 1976.
4. Mohammed Reza Shah Pahlavi, *Mission for My Country* (London, Hutchinson, 1974 edition), p. 64.
5. Comment to the author by Sir Ron Ellis, chief of defence sales, Ministry of Defence (UK).
6. Julian Bharier, *Economic Development in Iran: 1900-1970* (London, Oxford University Press, 1971), p. 67.
7. *British Defence White Paper* (London, HMSO), 20 February 1969.
8. *Arab Report and Record,* 1970, p. 263.
9. The US group, Bechtel, carried out a study for the Iranian government in 1969 on the routing of a pipe through to the Turkish coast at Iskanderum; but this project was excluded as being too costly. Also the Shah distrusts being dependent upon a pipe that crosses another country.
10. John Duke Anthony, *Arab States of the Lower Gulf* (Washington, The Middle East Institute, 1975), pp. 26-8.
11. Ibid., pp. 200-2.
12. Committee on Multi-national Corporations, Committee on Foreign Relations, US Senate, September 1976.
13. Ibid. See comments by Senator Church.
14. Ibid.
15. Ibid.
16. Based on information supplied to the author by senior executives involved in the Chah Bahar project, and expatriate defence officials in Tehran. US use of Chah Bahar was in reply to the Soviet build-up of Berbera, Somalia. When the project was reviewed in 1976 a combination of new US strategic considerations, plus altered American sensitivities over their profile in Iran, helped scrap the idea of nuclear submarine pens.
17. The project was known as Ibex. Also it was hinted that the potential closure of US facilities in Turkey had created stand-by radar and monitoring in Iran. See *Financial Times,* 23 November 1976; also *Guardian,* 2 January 1977.
18. Shahram Chubin, 'Implications of the military build-up in non-industrial states: the case for Iran', special paper prepared for circulation by the Institute for International Political and Economic Studies, Tehran, 1976, p. 13.
19. *Financial Times,* 2 December 1977.
20. *Financial Times,* 17 December 1977. This comment was made during court hearings of an arms bribery case in the UK.
21. Committee on Multi-nationals.

22. Mohammed Reza Shah, interview with BBC. Text *Kayhan International,* 18 December 1976.

23. The first attempt at serious review was the preparation of the report 'US military sales to Iran' (op. cit.) for the US Senate.

24. 'US military sales to Iran'. Staff report to the Subcommittee on Foreign Assistance of the Committee on Foreign Relations, US Senate, July 1976, ix.

25. Ibid. 'The services did not inform the Iranians of the full extent of the training, logistics and maintenance implications of the systems they were trying to sell.'

26. *Iran Almanac. Echo of Iran,* Tehran, 1977, p. 67.

27. Abbas Amirie (ed.), *The Persian Gulf and Indian Ocean in International Politics: a symposium* (Tehran, Institute for International Political and Economic Studies, 1975), p. 268.

28. Chubin, 'Implications', p. 6. Interestingly the US administration as far back as 1962 felt the Shah was over-arming. President Kennedy's adviser, Theodore Sorensen, said the US regarded the Iranian army as too large for border incidents and internal security but of little use in a war situation. See *Kennedy* (New York, Harper and Row, 1965), p. 268.

29. Britain is supplying Iran's main battle tanks: 792 Chieftains in a first batch whose delivery was completed in 1977 and 1,297 in a second batch delivered in three phases. The latter will have larger engines.

30. 'US military sales to Iran', p. 58. Total orders in 1973-6 amounted to $9.85 billion. This compared with orders totalling $11.62 billion from 1950 through to 1976. The rate of delivery does not match up to orders. For instance in 1974, orders were $3.92 billion and deliveries were $509 million.

31. *Financial Times,* 9 August 1976. This justification was stressed in Tehran by US Secretary of State Dr Henry Kissinger in the wake of the publication of the US Senate report, 'US military sales to Iran'.

32. The most recent Soviet purchase was $550 million worth of equipment, which included tank transporters, APCs and SAM–7 missiles, following a visit to Moscow by Vice-War Minister General Toufanian in October 1976. The bulk of the Iranian armed forces' transport is Soviet-supplied – on a barter basis against Iranian gas.

33. These radio broadcasts were halted in early 1977 following secret negotiations that involved the return to the Soviet Union of an ex-fighter pilot who defected to Iran in a light aircraft on 23 September 1976. The Soviets were understood to have threatened to escalate hostile propaganda if the pilot was not returned. The pilot's return was an unpopular move in Iran, not least because it showed the Shah bending to Soviet pressure.

34. This theory has not been disproved. In this connection see *Guardian,* 2 January 1977.

35. Mohammed Reza Shah in an interview with *Newsweek,* 14 November 1977. The Shah interprets the treaty as a positive US obligation to provide assistance.

36. 'US military sales to Iran', viii.

37. Ibid., p. 50. 'Informed US personnel believe that it is unlikely that Iran could engage in major combat operations during the next five to ten years with its current and prospective inventory i.e. purchase to date, of sophisticated weapons (as distinct from some less sophisticated ground equipment) without sustained US support.'

38. Based upon information supplied to the author by a US defence official. In the Kurdish conflict Iran also deployed the British Rapier missile which was responsible for shooting down an Iraqi TU–16. British advisers were said to have been close by during this incident.

39. 'US military sales to Iran', p. 51. The report points out that in the event of a change of regime, the US would be able to cripple the Iranian military establishment.

40. The IIAF has purchased twelve Boeing 747 jumbo jets converted for military use. The Shah sought to purchase the Galaxy giant transporter but the production lines could not be reopened.

41. The Israeli presence in Iran was at its height during the Kurdish rebellion. Israeli military assistance to Iran has been small but important. In the early stages of Iran's acquisition of the F–4, these aircraft were serviced in Israel (also some in Spain). Some equipment from the US was transhipped via Israel to Iran. The size of the Israeli presence can be gauged from the Israeli school in Tehran, which has 300 pupils. There is a large Israeli mission which has no formal diplomatic status but full diplomatic privileges.

42. Amirie, *The Persian Gulf and Indian Ocean*, p. 277.

43. Ths oil is primarily supplied by the international oil companies and not NIOC. Mexico provides the remaining 10 per cent of Israel's needs.

44. *The Persian Gulf and Indian Ocean*. See comments by Riad el-Rayyes, p. 307.

45. These observations are the result of two visits to Dhofar in March and November 1976. There are no Iranian sources for this information, but it is based upon discussions with SAF officers, official SAF military briefs – in particular Military Press Brief, Dhofar, November 1976 – and an interview with Sultan Qaboos in November 1976.

46. *Kayhan International*, 14 September 1975.

47. Prince Shafik obtained the Sword of Honour at Dartmouth Naval College (UK), the highest award open to a cadet.

48. Based on information supplied to the author by foreign defence attachés in Tehran.

49. *Kayhan International*, 24 February 1976.

50. Based on information supplied to the author by an expatriate familiar with the case.

51. *Kayhan International*, 11 June 1977. Draft evasion is widespread and in some parts of the country can be accomplished with under-table payments of no more than $100.

52. International Institute for Strategic Studies (IISS), *The Military Balance, 1976-77* (London, IISS, 1976).

53. Ibid.

54. Based on information supplied to the author by the main embassies in Tehran. Also see 'US military sales to Iran', p. 33.

55. 'US military sales to Iran', p. 28.

56. *New York Times*, 2 November 1977.

57. 'US military sales to Iran', p. 25.

58. Chubin, 'Implications', p. 19.

59. To find technicians with the necessary qualifications to assemble just part of the Rapier missiles BAC expects to have to look for 14-year-olds in the schools who will be then placed on special technical training. This is considered the sole guarantee of having the right kind of apprenticeship with no technical backing.

60. Tank tracks are already being made at a plant in Dorud.

61. Little is known of this facility other than that German personnel are supplied by the West German company Von Braun. The more sensitive parts of the tracked Rapier missile will be assembled here.

62. Based upon information supplied to the author by an expatriate familiar with Iran's nuclear programme.

63. A contract to survey Iranian waters was awarded in October 1977. See

The Times, 14 October 1977.

64. This £60 million facility was built by Laing in co-operation with Millbank Technical Services. British seconded naval personnel will help maintain the dockyard.

65. *International Herald Tribune,* 6 February 1976. Also General Toufanian told the author in August 1976 that the unit cost of the Chieftain tank had risen from £295,000 to £350,000 and then stood at £450,000.

66. 'US military sales to Iran', xii.

67. Ibid., p. 22.

68. Ibid., p. 29.

69. Chubin, 'Implications', pp. 24-5.

11 PROBLEMS OF CULTURE

So I like to think that in our thousands of years of continuous civilisation, we Persians have gained certain insights and exhibited certain characteristics that the world needs.[1]

A Tehran policeman has as little control over the traffic as a parent over a child who knows there are no effective sanctions. Every driver knows that the traffic policeman holds no real authority and therefore can be ignored or, if necessary, bribed. So the rules are broken and there is chaos on the roads. Iranians are openly proud of this anarchy, seeing in it the embodiment of individualism to which part of their culture pays such deference.[2] Yet individualism under Mohammed Reza Shah has been permitted only so long as it does not challenge the system of power. Within these limits it is tolerated, even deliberately encouraged, as a release from repression.

In urbanised Iran, these two worlds of repressed individualism and enforced conformity live in constant friction. The ancient culture adjusting to the impact of new and alien influences imposes an acute psychological strain on many Iranians. The Iranian identity is rooted in an illustrious past and a profound pride in things Persian; yet the future taking shape round them is being made of ideas, habits and technologies imported wholesale from outside that undermine or render obsolete traditional values. This tends to arouse a latent chauvinism and at times xenophobia, which is exacerbated by the Pahlavi dynasty's emphasis on looking to the past as reference for the future greatness of Iran. There could have been no more conscious revival of the past than the Persepolis ceremonies in October 1971 celebrating 2,500 years of monarchy. The political motive was transparent: to consign to oblivion the less glorious dynasties so that the Pahlavis could stand out in relief alongside the great names of the past. But the ceremonies also played on deep-felt sensitivities about the uniqueness of Iranian institutions and Iranian culture, of which monarchy had been the central continuous thread. This consciously evoked sense of Iranian uniqueness has been a natural shield behind which even opponents of the Shah have sought to hide at a time of rapid cultural change.

The Iranians' sense of their uniqueness derives from a somewhat romanticised view of their history, but centres round the suppleness with which they have been able to survive different waves of conquest and absorb cultural influences without having their own identity submerged.[3] The most striking instance of cultural absorption was the Arab invasion and the introduction of Islam. The propagandised view and the one accepted instinctively by Iranians is that put forward by the Shah in his memoirs:

> The Arabs, like previous invaders, found the Persian spirit unconquerable. The Zoroastrian religion died out, except among small remnants which still exist but otherwise the Persian culture triumphed for, as Arab scholars like al-Masudi and Ibn-Khaldun have recognised, it was so clearly the higher that there is no wonder Persian administrators, scholars and artisans continued to be employed.[4]

The fact that Persians adopted Arabic script and that the language henceforth relied extensively on Arabic loan words has been largely ignored to uphold the strength of indigenous culture.

Despite this rose-tinted view of cultural absorption, the Arab invasion none the less showed how the Iranians were capable of giving their own contrary twist to things. Rather than adopt the full credo of Islam propounded by the Arab invaders, they opted for a new branch, Shiism, which regarded Mohammed's son-in-law, Ali, as the first true Immam, and rejected the three caliphs recognised by the orthodox Sunni Moslems as the Prophet's proper heirs. Further, through a mixture of legend and casuistry they managed to relate by marriage Ali's son, Hussein, to an Iranian monarch — so incorporating Shiism into nationalism. Although Iran is not the exclusive domain of the Shiia faith, the Iranians attach enormous importance to the distinguishing features of Shiism that separate it — and therefore them — from the main body of Islam. For instance, an Arab ambassador new in Tehran recalled trying to find common ground with a senior Iranian official by pointing to their shared faith in Islam. 'Ah, but we are Shiia!' was the immediate response.[5] The significance of the Shiia faith is also reflected in the choice of Ali and Hussein as the boys' names still most widely used in Iran.

The sense of uniqueness also stems from a justifiable pride in the richness of past Iranian civilisations of which there are still tangible signs, like the ruins of Persepolis, the mosques of Isfahan, or the sophistication of Iranian poetry at a time when Europe was first emerging from the Dark Ages. Official propaganda has consistently played up this sense of uniqueness; and by and large, because it flatters the Iranian ego, such propaganda is bought wholesale. The Shah himself has employed the fact of the monarchy's 2,500 years of existence as a sort of stamp of moral rectitude for his opinions — especially in defending Iran against its foreign critics.

Emphasis on this uniqueness has tended to develop in direct proportion to the stress brought to bear on Iranian culture as it absorbs more and more from the West. This is a natural development for a proud people, but it complicates Iran's relations with both its surrounding neighbours and its Western allies: with its immediate neighbours from a sense of superiority and essential difference (despite being quite similar), and with the West through a sense of not wanting to look inferior, or wanting to imitate yet remain Iranian. These difficulties apply at both the formal diplomatic level and at a personal level. They account for a good deal of touchiness that provokes all sorts of irritants and problems. At its least complex, this takes the form of hyperbole and boastfulness. This can be seen in the Shah's boast of making Iran the world's fifth industrial nation by 1990. The advertising of Iran Air is another example. Although carried out by a foreign agency it nevertheless projects Iran the way Iranians wish it to be seen.[6] Wish fulfilment and the possible are merged into one.

At a more complex level this pride develops into an impatience with learning from foreigners, and a refusal to admit mistakes. This has seriously hindered the implementation of many development projects, especially since the 1973 oil price rise which itself further inflated the Iranian ego. Impatient to learn and convinced they know best, Iranians frequently ignore detail and berate their foreign instructors. Foreigners familiar with Iran and the Arab states of the Gulf confirm unanimously that the Arabs are easier to train and quicker to learn — one suspects this is because they are not burdened with the same weight of cultural baggage.

The greatest hindrance to the assimilation of new technology can be a refusal to admit ignorance. The shame of ignorance is very strong, but among Iranians the shame of being seen to be ignorant is even stronger. An expatriate manager of a large manufacturing complex found a machine-operator one day standing idly by his lathe. The lathe was not working, he explained. The manager subsequently discovered that the man had turned off the machine accidentally and was afraid to admit he had forgotten how to restart it.[7] The fear of loss of face through seeming ignorant is very marked throughout Iran. The authorities are always loath to admit mistakes. For instance, the reorganisation of agribusiness in Khuzestan has been held back primarily because it has been unacceptable to admit mistakes have been made. Reorganisation

would require the declaration of bankruptcy of a least two of the
ventures, but such a move would lead to too big a loss of face.[8] The
corollary to this is refusing to accept blame: a woman recounting the
death of her husband in a car accident explained he overtook a truck
on the brow of a hill and an oncoming car refused to get out of the
way! Another comic instance was a report filed at the tank depot in
Shiraz by a soldier who claimed his Chieftain tank had been damaged
when the compound wall 'leaped at the tank'.[9] When Iranian self-
esteem is more seriously threatened, there is resort to chauvinism, and,
in extremes, xenophobia. The gradual erosion of the close-knit family
ties in urban areas, the advent of permissiveness among the younger
generation, the infiltration of pornography and the spread of Western
pop music have all put Iranian culture on the defensive. The Shah in a
national call for cultural order when opening Parliament in October
1975 declared:

> The determination of our nation that in this new era, it [Iran's
> cultural spirit] should obliterate all signs of weakness, decline,
> corrupt disorder, reflects the intellectual meaning that the positive
> and immortal Iranian culture should be cleansed of all pollution
> which might have crept into it through foreign elements.[10]

Blaming the foreigner is a time-honoured ploy and not the exclusive
preserve of Iran; but the suspicion and mistrust of the foreigner that
exists in Iran has been exploited to good effect by the authorities. In
the summer of 1977 when the major cities were seriously affected by
lengthy power cuts, the blame was put on the foreign contractor for
failing in his obligations. In fact the reason was much more complex,
resulting from pressure to install extra generating capacity without
proper planning.[11]

This chauvinism has been exacerbated by a realisation that the
foreigner with his much-needed skills and technology is exploiting the
country. It is not like the past when Europeans came to Iran, albeit
with the intention of exploitation, but with the time and leisure to
appreciate the country and get to know its people. The new breed of
foreigner in Iran is altogether more mercenary, less interested in understanding the country and more happy to live in isolation from Iranians.
This can generate serious friction — most noticeable in Isfahan where a
large group of American defence employees have found themselves in
brawls directly attributable to their being obtrusive foreigners.[12]

But some of the reactions to Iran's accelerated contact with the

Western world have been purely xenophobic. This has been provoked in part by a pained sense of inadequacy at Iranian culture being by-passed, especially in the language of higher education as a means of expression. Alarmed at the spread of foreign children's names, the publisher of one of Iran's leading newspaper groups, Farhad Massoudi, wrote in an article entitled 'Culture – the driving force behind Iranians': 'Should a parent become so estranged with his own national culture as desire to give his child a foreign name, the Government has every right to move in.'[13] Yet there is a more basic xenophobia which is less easy to understand. For instance, when a foreigner tried to settle a traffic accident dispute by using his secretary and driver, both were told by senior police officers that, as Iranians, they should be ashamed of trying to help a foreigner.[14] This is not an isolated instance. A sort of mutual solidarity pact has grown up among Iranians when they feel threatened by foreigners.

Stirring up xenophobia is a strong political weapon which so far Mohammed Reza Shah has sought to avoid.[15] For a while it was success-fully exploited by Mossadegh during the initial oil nationalisation period – arguably this was the element that unified the country behind him when he first made the move. More recently, xenophobia has been used by the more extreme and reactionary religious figures as a means of opposing the Shah. It has also been an undercurrent in some of the urban guerrilla ideology, especially those members recruited from fanatically religious families.

The Search for Security

The stress placed upon Iran's historic cultural identity underlines the tremendous sense of insecurity that runs right through the Iranian psyche. Attempts have been made elsewhere to explain some of the causes for this all-pervading sense of insecurity – invasions and occupa-tions by outside powers, poverty and a harsh climate and centuries of arbitrary and repressive rule. Yet remarkably, during a period of unpre-cedented social and economic progress, this sense of insecurity is still much in evidence.[16] The chief symptom is a mistrust: mistrust both of people and events. One of the stories attributed to the famous Mulla Nasrudin catches this feeling very aptly – 'Take up this sack and carry it to my house', said Nasrudin to a porter in the market. 'May I be your sacrifice, Effendi. Where is your house?' The Mulla looked at the porter aghast. 'You are a disreputable ruffian, and probably a burglar. Do you think I could ever tell you where my house is?'[17]

No matter how favourable a situation might be, there is a general refusal to believe that it can last. Life is seen as inherently arbitrary and cruel. Those that succeed have been selected by God to do so — the Shah himself subscribes strongly to this view.[18] This fatalistic view of life is confirmed by religion rather than caused by it, although others would argue it was the other way round. With life so uncertain, the sole obligations owed are those to oneself and immediate family. The family is still regarded as the only effective bulwark against the hostile outside world. Support for the government is regarded as wise, only so far as this support can be easily removed. To survive and prosper you need a combination of luck, connections, sharp wits and few principles that risk being compromised by deviousness. With deviousness Iranians have made a virtue of necessity. The wily Isfahani, Hajji Baba — the fictional Iranian character depicted by the early Victorian diplomat, James Morier — showed this was a key to survival. So too did the quixotic Bahram Kirmani who was one of the portraits in Christopher Sykes' *Four Studies in Loyalty*.[19]

In practical terms this sense of insecurity means that few Iranians believe that the present fortuitous wealth from oil can last. It generates an innate cynicism.[20] There is little faith in public pronouncements and vague future goals. For instance, the Shah's vision of the great civilisation may appeal to the Iranian ego, but Iranians are so sceptical that few rate it credible. Moreover, because oil is a wasting asset, this adds to the sense of impermanence to wealth generated by it. The accrual of oil wealth has had little impact in dispelling national and personal insecurity.

The way in which this oil wealth has been spent also reflects this sense of insecurity and impermanence. Many a developing country with Iran's history of economic vicissitudes — especially the disastrous consequences of being unable to sell oil during the oil nationalisation by Mossadegh — would have chosen to act with more thrift. But there was no attempt at thrift. Why? Ostentation, itself a product of insecurity, has always accompanied new and quickly earned wealth. But ostentation alone cannot explain the almost frenetic spending that occurred in the two years after 1973. It seems that the sense of impermanence of oil wealth created an attitude of 'Now we've got it, we had better spend it; because we don't know how long it will last.' Where national wealth is generated primarily from one source, which itself owes little to local initiative, there is less reverence for its accumulation. So money earned in this way becomes easier to spend. Also Iranians do not suffer from the same moral restraints over spending money that those in the bourgeois capitalist economies do. The Puritan capitalist ethic is wholly alien to Iran — and the Middle East as a whole for that matter. A bigger house or a bigger car earns more respect; and money spent with the sole object of impressing other is not considered ill spent. Envy and greed are encouraged, but not restraint. This accounts in large measure for the importance attached to lavish entertainment. Transferred on to a national scale, the same psychology can be found in the Shah's arms build-up, the unnecessarily large foreign assistance programme in the wake of 1973, and the purchases of Iranian shares in blue-chip Western companies.

In Iran's case, too, attitudes towards expenditure are affected by a residual bazaar mentality. The technocrat element within the administration is little more than one generation deep, and the mentality of the decision-makers is still strongly influenced by the bazaar. The Iranian bazaars have produced generations of astute tradesmen, but in a modern developing economy their philosophy of quick profits, quick returns is a handicap. Long-term planning and long-term investment are new phenomena, products of a still unfamiliar concept of long-term security.

Judgements about the use of private wealth can also be misleading if viewed solely against the experience of bourgeois capitalist economies. Iran aspires to a market economy yet capital is accumulated more through influence, political favour and monopoly than by hard work, initiative and competition. So too the ultimate purpose of private capital is not pleasure or reward for hard work. It is to ensure political influence for an individual and members of his family. This is the sole guarantee of long-term financial, and personal, security. Therefore the safest investment is the one that secures access to the most influence and political favour. So long as the Iranian system of power ignores institutions and relies upon relationships between individuals, this situation will persist.

Because there is such a premium on acquiring influence, corruption flourishes. When real power is in the hands of only one person, the best proven means of acquiring influence in the administration is through the purse. Moreover, because influence and political favour are the most valuable commodities, there is no moral stigma attached to paying to obtain them or for receiving payment in return for giving them. Corruption is therefore built into the system; and oil wealth has simply stimulated the practice, not discouraged it. (There is an Iranian proverb to the effect that if you give a man an egg he will then want the chicken.) Foreigners have always been dismayed by Iranian corruption. The Victorian traveller Arnold speaks of the 'universal corruption of government'.[21] The Shah has at regular intervals half-heartedly sought to stamp it out; but measures will work only when the system changes.

Just as corruption flourishes in this environment, so does flattery. The Iranians have learned over the centuries that flattery is one of the tools of survival. Perhaps with the exception of Kim il-Sung of North Korea, no other world leader tolerates — or encourages — flattery so much as Mohammed Reza Shah. The local press on his birthday and other auspicious occasions carry full-page advertisements from institutions and companies extolling his virtues in the most sycophantic prose. Anxious to please, foreign companies are among the most obsequious. Where else but Iran could one find an advertisement bannered across a full page from a group of Italian companies that declared their executives

> and personnel assigned anywhere in the world, and those hosted by the generous Imperial Iranian nation with its trait of plurimillenary civilisation, and traditions of hospitality, feel proud and rejoice in having the honour of witnessing the Fiftieth Anniversary of the illustrious Pahlavi Dynasty, as well as the dynamic progress, the tangible achievements and the gigantic strides of the great Iranian people, under the illuminated guidance of the indefatigable farseeing Shahanshah Aryamehr Mohammed Reza Pahlavi.[22]

One effect of the rapid generation of new wealth has been to permit not merely the ruling élite but also the burgeoning middle class an alternate means of security. With day-to-day financial security in Iran assured by high incomes, there has been a tremendous movement of excess capital outside the country — in far greater quantities than the conditions of apparent security and rates of return in Iran should justify. This excess capital has gone mainly into the purchase of property and bank deposits in Western Europe and America but sometimes the investment has been in more ambitious ventures like manufacturing.[23] The scale has been such that since late 1975 about $100 million worth of private capital has been leaving the country each month.[24] The official view is that this is part of a two-way process, and a sign of Iran's emergence from being a developing economy.[25] But all the indications are that this is a demonstration of the Iranian sense of insecurity. Refusing to believe in the durability of the boom or prosperity, the bourgeoisie have sought to insulate themselves against any future changes of fortune by securing a second life for themselves outside Iran.

This permanent quest for security, and the consequent need to feel reassured and to be seen coping successfully with life has made dealings among Iranians, and between Iranians and foreigners, an extraordinarily complex affair. It is no accident that commercial and diplomatic negotiations drag on interminably; for negotiations begin with the suspicion of the simplest of statements and the most straightforward actions. Nothing is taken at face value. A mundane example was the publication of a photograph of a bank in the *Financial Times*. A senior bank official was convinced this was a deliberate choice designed to highlight certain recent activities of the bank which had been under scrutiny, when in fact the motive was the bank's design. The man refused to believe it.[26]

New Influences

Religion is still the biggest single binding cultural influence, and acts as the most common point of reference for all classes of Iranians. A firm belief in God remains the ultimate refuge from the arbitrariness of life, and among the poorer and uneducated a pilgrimage to one of the Shiia shrines remains an important goal and a strong duty. Meshed receives some 3.5 million Iranian pilgrims a year.[27]

Despite its continued strength religion is being placed in an increasingly ambivalent position. For nationalistic reasons religion is encouraged; yet the authorities seek to suppress the influence of attitudes engendered by Islam when they conflict with modernisation. The authorities are also permanently on the watch lest religion be exploited for political ends opposed to the government. Religion is encouraged in that state funds are used to build mosques, and even Pahlavi funds have been used to help restore the shrines of Meshed. It also suits the Shah to encourage the Shiia cult of paying homage to saints and martyrs as a means of deifying the Pahlavi dynasty's founder Reza Shah (the large mausoleum at Rey is ample evidence of this). Strict observance of Shiia holy days is part of the national calendar, particularly Muharram, which contains the Shiia's holiest day Ashura, celebrating the martyrdom of the Immam Hussein.[28] The clergy retain a strong hold over society, especially its poorer and less educated members, which constitute over two-thirds of the population. Religious fanaticism persists in cities like Qom.

This situation tends to cause a good deal of confusion and misunderstanding when the government decides to by-pass religion and religious ethics. For instance, the civil status of Iranian women on paper is among the most advanced of any developing nation. But in practice it is still among the more backward. Reza Shah abolished the veil in 1936; but still today the vast majority of Iranian women are symbolically veiled outside the house in that they continue to wear the *chadoor* — a loose length of cloth covering the head and stretching to the ground that is held in place either by the hands or the teeth. Women may wish to exercise their rights and act more freely but are prevented from doing so by their families, husbands or the force of social convention. For instance, a physiotherapy lecturer discovered the women students refusing to learn massage techniques until the mullah approved.[29]

Official initiative has been less important in eroding the hold of religion than the accelerated pace of economic development and the accompanying social changes. Aspirations to possess new and better housing, modern domestic appliances, cars and status clothes have had a major impact in the large cities since the early 1970s. The pressures created by these changes on traditional and highly conservative backgrounds have been considerable. Iran's urban youth has borne the chief brunt of this. In a study on suicide in Tehran, it was noted that the most prevalent instances of attempted suicide were among the 16-20 age group coming from very strict and fanatical families.[30] Non-Islamic youths from Armenian, Jewish or Zoroastrian backgrounds have managed to cope with change more effectively; perhaps because as minority groups they have to be outward-going to survive.[31]

As a sign of these pressures — and as a reaction to the insecurity seen to surround the lives of their parents — students at the universities try to enter professions that combine financial reward with security and social respectability. There is a special mystique about studying medicine. In 1977 over 15 per cent of the 300,000 students applying for entry to Tehran University wanted to do medicine as their first choice. This meant that upwards of 45,000 students were competing for a mere 300 places in the faculty.[32] Perhaps it is no coincidence that a qualified doctor is one of the persons who has the least difficulty in finding a job outside his own country.

While traditional values are under attack, little of cultural worth is being substituted. The aim is that Iran import whatever is culturally valid from abroad (in practice Western Europe and America) and the inherent Iranian genius will mould this into a new and regenerated national culture. Unfortunately ideas and habits brought in from abroad which are considered politically embarrassing or inconvenient, are immediately branded as foreign: polluting Iranian culture. Culture, in fact, is just another tool of the political system in Iran, and survives only where it is allied to the system. Despite an appearance of liberalism and cultural dynamism in international arts festivals and the like, modern Iran is culturally bankrupt. Culture at this level is a plaything of the élite, in particular those surrounding Empress Farah, and exists in a complete vacuum. The annual Shiraz arts festival and the Tehran film festival are primarily designed to associate international culture with Iran; but the domestic impact of these festivals can be found in the long queues for cinema festival tickets and half-empty cinemas with unused seats reserved for the well connected. The interaction of politics and culture is well reflected in a provincial theatre where the auditorium is dominated by a royal box liable to be used once a year. Yet for security reasons the seats are so recessed that the audience cannot see the stage properly.[33]

Moreover the Iranian's cultural superiority complex makes it virtually impossible to look for inspiration within the region or among their neighbours. The natural assumption is that Iranian culture should link up with Western culture. So when Iranians travel they go to Europe or America. Travel, an important means of education, is carefully controlled. Apart from security screening there is a punitive exit tax, equivalent to $280 per person, which affects precisely those who could benefit most — students and lower-income groups. It also means that when people have only one opportunity to travel, they want to travel outside the region.

Since 1973 enormous sums have been spent providing modern Iran with a tailor-made national culture. Iranian *objets d'art*, paintings and antiquities have been bought in international auctions, museums opened, a collection of Western painting begun, a series of nation-wide cultural complexes designed, education expanded and historical monuments restored.[34] Though well intentioned, the over-all effect is that of a wealthy businessman filling a newly built house with things chosen by someone else, yet which he seeks to identify with. The correct objects and institutions are there, but often poorly utilised or appreciated for the wrong reasons. Yet none of this bears any real relation to the country's own cultural vigour. The two most readily identifiable indexes of a nation's cultural vigour — the state of the universities and the strength of the publishing industry — speak for themselves.

Despite a sharp increase in the number of people able to read and write, the number of titles published is in decline. Between 1970 and 1976 the number of new titles and reprints published annually dropped by almost 30 per cent. In 1976 only 3,200 titles were published, of which 1,580 were new (accounted for 36 per cent by literary books and 18 per cent by religious subjects).[35] The level of titles published is infinitely lower than nations of similar size like Turkey or Egypt.[36] The circulation is also revealing. No more than 13 per cent of all non-school books have a sale of over 3,000. The best-selling non-school book is *How to care for your car*, with sales of 15,000.[37]

The publishing business has been seriously hit by the major increases in production costs which have occurred since 1970. In turn sales have been affected by higher cover prices. But commercial considerations are intimately linked to political ones. Fewer and fewer publishers want to stay in a business where one 'error' in a book could lead to heavy fines or closing down of production. Further, the time-consuming nature of censorship and its attendant restrictions have taken their toll of the industry. Parallel with this, authors in protest at their lack of freedom have refused to allow publication of their works for fear that they be seen as condoning the régime and their being adopted as a cultural mascot. Writers and artists are subject to intimidation or repression, including inability to have their works published, if they appear remotely critical. Since 1976 the Writers Association of Iran has been seeking in vain to register and acquire legal status so that it may hold meetings.[38] Tougher measures have also been applied to some of the country's best-known artists and intellectuals. For instance Iran's best historian, former Ambassador to India Fereidoun Ademeyat, and Gholam Hussein Saedi, responsible for the prize-winning film 'The Cow', are among the more internationally recognised who have served prison terms.[39]

The plight of the universities is in many ways more serious.[40] The universities represent the pool of talent and ideas for the future. If Iran is to cope with modernisation and absorb successfully all the highly sophisticated technology it is importing, the universities and other institutes of higher education have to produce students of good calibre. The Shah certainly appreciates this. But the quality of the universities has been sacrificed to preserve the stability of the régime. Rather than allow the universities to be free and independent, they have been kept under tight political control for fear they might develop as centres of political opposition. In consequence, the quality of staff and the calibre of the graduated students has gradually declined. The situation was summed up in a pained open telegram sent by a dissident lawyer to the Prime Minister, Jamshid Amouzegar, in October 1977, shortly after he took office.

You are certainly aware that for the last twenty years as a result of

successive governments abusing individual freedoms, our universities — the nation's most valuable educational resource — have
ceased to be places of learning. Instead they have been transformed
into military fortresses with the setting up of iron barricades, the
disposition of armed security guards and inadmissible interference
by the security forces. This can only incite anger and disgust among
young free thinking people ... Not surprisingly the universities of
Tehran and the provinces have been in a state of closure or semi-
closure most of the time.[41]

The emasculation of the universities' vitality and the damaging effects
of frequent disruptions throughout the academic year because of strikes
or forced closure have been major handicaps to the development of
quality education. More insidious, but equally damaging, has been the
pressure on universities to churn out an ever-growing number of graduates to fill the skilled manpower shortage. Tehran, the oldest and
largest university, is attempting to resist further expansion from 18,000
to 25,000; but such is the pressure that the volume will almost certainly have to be increased, with yet a further dilution of quality.[42]
Lower down the scale, the educational system needs 40,000 new
teachers a year but can produce only half this amount. The shortfall
is being made up largely by expanding the existing student-teacher
ratio so that it now stands at 100 to 1.[43]

Where possible a parent will try to ensure that a child attends a non-
state school (an option mainly for those in Tehran) and all the
foreign schools in Tehran are heavily over-subscribed. The wealthier
seek schooling abroad; some on political grounds that syllabuses are
propagandised to favour the régime, most out of simple considerations
of quality and greater opportunity. The same goes for university
education abroad, although here government loans and grants are available — against guarantees of subsequent government service for a
specified period of time. About 60,000 Iranians are studying abroad in
universities or technical colleges, mostly in Europe and America. Of
these a small proportion each year refuse to return home, the catalyst
being the prospect of military service. For those who opt to go back,
the return can prove a traumatic experience with an eventual cynical
trade-off: reduced freedom for greater material gains. Poking fun at
themselves, Iranian intellectuals tell the story of an Iranian dog that
crosses over into Afghanistan where he is met by a host of hungry,
scrofulous dogs. After lengthy formal greetings and many compliments
on the elegance of his fine coat, the Iranian dog begins to boast about

how well he is fed and housed, the magnificence of the hospitality in Iran. Puzzled, the Afghani dogs ask why he has come across the frontier? When he has finally finished boasting, the Irani dog turns and says, 'I wanted to come across here to have a good bark.'

None of this is conducive to a flourishing national culture or the development of new ideas. It merely makes for a more troubled national psychology and exacerbates the negative responses of chauvinism, cynicism and suspicion.

Notes

1. Mohammed Reza Shah Pahlavi, *Mission for My Country* (London, Hutchinson, 1974 edition), p. 31.

2. Ibid., p. 29. 'I won't dispute with those who claim to see Persian individualism reflected in the wild and free tactics of Tehran's famed taxi drivers.'

3. See Roger Stevens, *The Land of the Great Sophy* (London, Methuen, 1971 edition), p. 34. 'There is perhaps some peculiar suppleness, some inherent flexibility in the Iranian character.'

4. Mohammed Reza Shah Pahlavi, *Mission*, p. 23.

5. Recounted to the author by the ambassador concerned. Iranians play down as far as possible their historic links with the Arab world.

6. See *Financial Times*, 5 May 1976. The campaign is geared to make the public believe Iran is in the top league of nations.

7. Recounted to the author by the manager.

8. A concensus view of foreign experts connected with agribusiness in Khuzestan.

9. Recounted to the author by a British official involved.

10. *Tehran Journal*, 25 October 1975.

11. One of the most unusual instances of blaming foreigners was a court action against a Swedish company, Sentab, for responsibility for the collapse of Tehran International Airport roof in December 1974 (causing the death of 17 persons). Sentab built the building in 1947 and the collapse was caused by subsequent unauthorised covering of the roof and heavy snow.

12. Recounted to the author by US defence employees in Isfahan.

13. *Tehran Journal*, 25 October 1975.

14. *Tehran Journal*, 13 June 1977.

15. SAVAK exploits xenophobia to damage intellectuals. For instance, in September 1977, to discredit intellectuals calling for greater freedom, SAVAK-sponsored leaflets were circulated from 'The Committee Against Worshippers of Foreign Elements', saying they had been corrupted by foreign culture.

16. For an exhaustive analysis of Iranian feelings of insecurity, see Marvin Zonis, *The Political Elite of Iran* (Princeton, N.J., Princeton University Press, 1971), pp. 199-298.

17. Idries Shah, *The Exploits of the Incomparable Mulla Nasrudin* (London, Picador Edition, 1973), p. 87.

18. Mohammed Reza Shah, *Mission,* pp. 54-8. See also his interview with Oriana Fallaci, *Interview with History* (Boston, Houghton Mifflin, 1976), pp. 267-8.

19. James Morier, *The Adventures of Hajji Baba of Ispahan* (London, Oxford University Press, 1939). When this book was first published the Iranians refused

to believe its author was an Englishman. It remains one of the most witty and perceptive views of the Iranian character. See also Christopher Sykes, *Four Studies in Loyalty* (London, Collins, 1946), pp. 40-79.

20. Zonis, *The Political Elite,* pp. 251-9. Zonis regards Iranian cynicism as highly damaging to political development. 'Beset by personal insecurities, mistrustful of themselves and their fellows, and cynical about the motives of all persons and the outcome of all programmes, the elite respond by coping with the system, not by attempting to alter it in fundamental ways . . . while conducive to stability, the consensus is maintained only at great costs to the processes of political development in Iran' (p. 329).

21. Arthur Arnold, *Through Persia by Caravan* (London, Tinsley Brothers, 1877), Vol. I, p. 207.

22. *Kayhan International,* 5 August 1976.

23. Unlike the Gulf Arabs and Saudis, the Iranians have been more discreet about their investments. One Swiss investment specialist dealing with Iranian clients estimated to the author that these clients had between 15 and 35 per cent of their total assets outside Iran. Each client's external portfolio was over $1 million. The most publicised manufacturing interest purchased by an Iranian has been Philco Italiana. See *Financial Times,* 18 January 1977.

24. Based on conversations with Bank Markazi and checking with the experience of individual banks. From 10 April to 10 May 1977 one small bank processed $34.5 million of special dollar transfers and almost £15 million of sterling transfers. The capital outflow was increased following the switch to payment of foreign contractors in rials at the end of 1976. There is no distinction in the Bank Markazi books between this and private Iranian outflows.

25. Comment to the author by Hushang Ansari, Finance Minister, 4 May 1977.

26. The photograph was of the Iranians' Bank.

27. *Iran Almanac,* 1977, p. 394. This compares with only 39,296 going to Mecca for the Hajj in 1976. The Hajj is made prohibitively expensive for prospective pilgrims, costing about $1,700 per person for a month.

28. The government has sought to prevent ritual beatings with chains and thongs at Muharram but the practice continues.

29. Recounted to the author by the lecturer concerned, who taught at Tehran University.

30. *Kayhan International,* 29 December 1976.

31. There are some 250,000 Armenians, 80,000 Jews and 30,000 Zoroastrians in Iran.

32. Based on author's interview with Dr Mofidi, Assistant Vice-Chancellor of Tehran University, on 16 July 1977. Students have ten faculty choices. Failure to get first or second preference leads to drop-outs who try to take entry again. The drop-out rate is 10 to 12 per cent.

33. Recounted to the author by consultants charged with restructuring the theatre.

34. For comment on the purchases of Iranian dealers and the Queen's Office, see the weekly column by Souren Malikian in the *International Herald Tribune.* Since 1973 Iranians have been bidding against each other, paying inflated prices. By 1976 state funds for art purchases abroad had begun to be cut drastically.

35. *Iran Almanac. Echo of Iran,* Tehran, 1977, pp. 141-2.

36. Ibid.

37. *Kayhan International,* 22 November 1976.

38. *Guardian,* 26 October 1977. The main objection recently was that the writers refused to become members of the single political party, Rastakhiz.

39. These were among 40 artists and intellectuals who sent a three-page letter in June 1977 to the Prime Minister, Amir Abbas Hoveida, calling for greater

freedom.

40. In 1976 Iran possessed 21 universities and 206 colleges of higher education, with a total student population of 154,000 (110,000 male; 44,000 female).

41. This telegram, of which the author has a copy, was also sent to the national press but was not published. The sender was Dr Mostafa Bagher-Kermani

42. Information supplied by Dr Mofidi, Assistant Vice-Chancellor, Tehran University.

43. *Kayhan International,* 21 October 1976.

12 CONCLUSION

Has Iran been able to maximise the opportunity created by the incredible wealth that accrued from the 1973 oil price rises? Even discounting normal errors of judgement, the answer can only be no. The grand vision of Iran on the threshold of the ranks of the world's industrialised nations has faded. In the space of three years a more mundane reality has emerged — a nation rich in financial resources but still poorly endowed with trained manpower and adequate infrastructure, grappling with the problems of development, heavily reliant upon foreign technology and unable to switch away from dependence upon oil to a self-sustaining economy.

To pretend that Iran could maximise this opportunity was an illusion in the first place. Money seemed the panacea for Iran's problems of development, when in fact it merely disguised them. More importantly, Iran's system of government is incapable of handling a dynamic development process. Mohammed Reza Shah's system of government, fashioned from the traumatic Mossadegh experience in 1953, is geared to the politics of his own survival. He has deliberately fragmented and weakened the authority of all individuals and institutions that might challenge him. His own power has been buttressed by repression and a refined system of rewards. Only in the sense that he has kept his throne and consolidated his authority has the Shah's system of government proved effective.

This same system is wholly inadequate to cope with the increasingly complex administration of modern Iran, which requires the delegation of authority and the willingness of officials to accept the responsibility of such authority. The Shah's system cannot afford to risk delegation. To a greater or lesser degree this could be said of all authoritarian régimes. However, no authoritarian régime had previously been faced with the kind of challenge that the quadrupling of oil revenues presented to Iran. The Shah's decision to go for accelerated growth and double planned expenditure placed a tremendous burden on the administration. The challenge would have swamped most governments but the Iranian administration was especially unsuited. Conditioned by the fear of sanctions and the hope of financial reward, and mistrustful through deliberately created mutual antagonism and job duplication, officials inevitably opted for the line of least resistance. The easiest orders to execute were the negative ones – the 'don't dos'. This was why the anti-profiteering campaign and price control in August 1975 were pursued with such zeal. Policies that required initiative were inherently dangerous to execute. To step out of line risked losing a job; yet to be too successful was equally risky – success and popularity tended to detract from the authority of the Shah or to undermine the positions of interest groups that supported the Shah. At the time of Land Reform in 1962, the Agriculture Minister, Hassan Arsanjani, lost his job because he, not the Shah, was actively trying to make Land Reform work and was getting the credit among the farmers. In February 1976 Commerce Minister Fereidoun Mahdavi was sacked because he upset vested interests when he tried to initiate a thorough reform of distribution, an essential prerequisite for better control of prices.

The bureaucratic stupor and mediocrity that such a system encouraged were evident again in the creation of a single-party system. The creation of the single Rastakhiz Party seemed a genuine attempt to provide a new form of national dialogue, albeit well controlled. Yet the party's effectiveness was doomed from the start because success would have made it an alternate power base to the Shah. Those involved in trying to make it work knew that it could disappear as suddenly as it was conjured up – its life being dependent upon its usefulness to the Shah. Inevitably the party was dragged into the limbo of the state apparatus with no clear function or purpose.

Another instance of the conflicting interests of the Shah's own power and the interests of State has been decentralisation. Every Minister, and the Shah himself, has talked of the need to decentralise. It is the only way to deal with the complex problems of governing Iran with its widely dispersed centres of population and distinct regional characteristics. Yet the Shah is unwilling to risk loosening the reins of central authority. Instead he creates overlapping responsibilities and parallel agencies to assist him exert more central control. Senior officials live in fear of incurring the Shah's displeasure. The measures to dampen the over-heated economy in late 1975 were held up by almost nine months because Ministers were afraid of losing face and admitting the chaos that had overtaken the march towards the Great Civilisation. The Ports and Shipping Organisation, under pressure to reduce the appalling log-jam that had developed in the ports, told the Shah in late 1975 that the situation had improved. This improvement had been achieved by the simple expedient of redirecting a large number of ships waiting to unload at the main port of Khorramshahr to the neighbouring ports of Bushire and Bandar Shahpour. Similar legerdemain was taking place throughout the administration to conceal realities and protect comfortable jobs.

As leader, mentor and father-figure, the Shah believes that his own survival guarantees the stability of Iran. Yet he is unwilling or unable to distinguish between his own interests and those of the state. Because he believes he embodies the state, his decisions are justified before God and the crowded galleries of posterity. Undeniably he has provided stability. But is a repressed stability which has to be carefully watched, nursed and controlled lest his power be challenged. Such stability can never be properly harnessed to the good of the nation so long as the Shah is obsessed by the possibility of events getting beyond his control. Stability has become an end in itself, not the launching pad for economic and social development. A striking instance of this has been his attitude towards education. There has been reasonable success in fighting illiteracy. Quite rightly the Shah regards the elimination of illiteracy, together with the elimination of rural poverty, as a key step towards modernism. Yet he will not permit academic freedom in higher education. University education, arguably the most important resource for the nation's future, has been deliberately sacrificed to his own security. Learning is tolerated only so long as it does not question the régime. Equally, the cultural regeneration of Iran is given a high priority; but it only tolerates writers, artists and film-makers who accept to act as servants of state.

At a more general level the Shah has refused to countenance debate on key issues affecting the life of the nation, like defence, internal security, the freedom of expression or the priorities of the country's development needs. Partly, it seems, this has derived from a belief that as Leader (Farmandeh) he should always lead decision-making; if not, his stature as Farmandeh is compromised in the eyes of the nation. But he also realises that once debate is initiated it becomes more difficult to impose limits. This was why it was almost inevitable that the flowering of protest inside Iran, in the wake of President Carter's espousal of human rights in 1977, was only briefly tolerated then quickly snuffed.

In the end the Shah's vision of the future of Iran has always been made subservient to political expediency. Astute in his perception of internal developments, he has sought to anticipate any pressure that might embarrass him. Often this has produced policies based on sketchy study or only concerned with political effect. Land Reform in 1962 was not really intended to improve agricultural production. It was a political manoeuvre designed to bring the rural masses into the political

spectrum and to curb the influence of the large landlords. Land Reform
was a temporary palliative to the discontented rural peasantry, but
only at the cost of parcelling up the bulk of agricultural land into uneconomic holdings, without any significant redistribution of wealth.
If anything, the landlords — through the sale of divested land — consolidated their wealth by moving into the purchase of more remunera-
tive urban real estate. Today agriculture still suffers from the consequences of Land Reform as the authorities try to consolidate the uneconomic parcels of land that it created. The instruction in July 1975
that large manufacturing companies should divest over a three-year
period 49 per cent of equity to the employees had a similar effect. If
such a move had been motivated by economic considerations, the
scheme would have been geared to promote industrial productivity.
Instead, it was intended to appease the industrial work-force that was
beginning to feel restive at not receiving a fair share of the nation's
new wealth. The scheme was hurried through with scant preparation.
As a result, the initial list of 320 eligible companies was quietly dropped within 18 months and the three-year completion date gradually
ignored. The scheme was essentially a disguised subsidy to a limited
number of persons in the industrial sector (plus some in agriculture)
who were already comparatively privileged. The mass of the labour
force was outside the scope of the scheme since they were employed
in companies too small to qualify for inclusion. It was not an exercise
in industrial democracy: merely a limited transfer of resources, traded
against tranquillity on the shop-floor, where organised labour remained
illegal. The effect on industrial management was almost completely
unforeseen. At first dismayed by what was seen as direct government
interference, the industrialists then realised that this was a chance to
obtain liquidity for assets which normally would be difficult to sell.
This cash, instead of being reinvested, generally found its way abroad.
An equally unflattering view could be taken of the Shah's adoption of
the ambitious targets in the revised Fifth Plan. In 1973 the economy
was already stretched by substantial oil revenues that had fuelled high
growth. It needed soundly based manageable growth with the focus
first on such essentials as building up the infrastructure of ports and
roads and ensuring a proper supply of trained manpower. This would
have meant a politically unacceptable delay of three or four years,
during which the Iranians would have seen little of their enhanced
status, preached aloud by their leader and the international community
alike. The Shah also, one suspects, wanted to concertina the timespan
in which he could create a society where all classes had a sufficiently

strong stake in the *status quo* to allow an orderly transfer of power to his son and heir.

In the event, the pressures to spend this new wealth immediately proved too great. This was an unprecedented opportunity to consolidate the Shah's position, because for the first time he possessed the financial means to satisfy the aspirations of all segments of society — or so it seemed. By opting for super-growth, the Shah made the error of overestimating Iran's financial resources and underestimating the country's ability to absorb surplus revenues.

Surplus oil revenue was a phenomenon of unexpectedly short duration. At the time of the revision of the Fifth Plan, it seemed that oil revenue would eliminate the need for foreign borrowing until around 1978. But foreign borrowing began in 1975. Revenues were eroded by a mixture of imported and home-generated inflation, by higher wages and production costs, by shortages and bottlenecks, by expensive subsidies and generous foreign assistance, by general inefficiency and elaborate graft. Added to which there was the incalculable extra cost of trying to do too much too quickly without proper preparation.

The waste was incredible, surpassed only by Gulf states like Abu Dhabi or Saudi Arabia. It was waste Iran could ill afford with a 35 million population growing at almost 3 per cent a year. Her oil is running down and will not last much beyond the turn of the century. Already production has reached a ceiling and by 1984/5 will have fallen to around 6.2 million barrels per day. Meanwhile, with increasing domestic consumption, the quantity available for export will by then be below 5 million barrels per day unless major new discoveries are made, which, on current evidence, is unlikely. Much, of course, depends upon world energy demand, which could boost the value of Iran's huge gas reserves and sustain oil prices against the cost of development.

Because foreign exchange seemed the main constraint on growth prior to 1973, the removal of this constraint disguised the real problems. Moreover, the hectic growth between 1973 and 1976 tended to exacerbate these problems, making their ultimate solution more complex. Development costs were aleady high before 1973 because of the nature of the climate, the country's size and the lack of infrastructure. Development costs now threaten to destroy the beginnings of the industrial base the Shah is trying to create. This is the key to a self-sustaining economy that can survive independent of oil. Iranian industrial products even now have priced themselves out of all but the barter market except where they can benefit from low-cost energy like steel or petrochemicals.

Second, the country has been burdened with very heavy servicing and maintenance costs through the wholesale importation of advanced equipment. Local industry cannot provide the back-up for advanced technology because Iran has only the slimmest technological base to build upon. In this respect the military and nuclear sectors have been earmarked for priority, instead of opting for more readily attainable intermediate technology objectives in the civilian sector. Unless there is a change, defence and nuclear energy will be absorbing over a quarter of all foreign exchange earnings for the foreseeable future.

Third, the generation of wealth from oil revenues has concealed continuing rural backwardness. Rural incomes have risen, but the rise is deceptive since the benefits have been largely eroded by higher living costs. Increased rural income has not narrowed the disparity between the urban and rural communities. If anything, the expenditure pattern of the revised Fifth Plan reinforced this disparity and accelerated the rural exodus. The government has preferred to hide behind a smokescreen of Land Reform, distribution of Crown Lands and literacy drives. Agriculture has been sacrificed to industry. At the same time food consumption has been stimulated by heavy subsidies without a corresponding increase in agircultural production. Foodstuffs impose an increasing burden on foreign exchange. Neglect of the rural areas has a direct effect on industry. Since the majority of the population still live in the countryside, there can be no expanding market for industrial goods unless rural incomes begin to compare with those of the towns.

Finally, it will take time to disabuse Iranians of the idea that the state cannot afford to take care of everything. In 1974 the Shah fostered the concept of a welfare state with the government ready to pick up the tab on everything from education to low-cost energy. The relaxation of budgetary discipline and minimal resort to taxes encouraged this belief. The reality was — as the Shah conceded in October 1976 — that people had to work harder and pay more taxes to ensure Iran's future viability.

For the Shah the increase in development costs and the evaporation of surplus income means he is no longer able to appease all sections of the community with financial rewards. With a much smaller cake he has to try and satisfy the aspirations of the rural peasantry, the industrial urban work-force, the burgeoning middle class and the factious élite who help sustain him in power. He has created a situation where, to placate one group, he risks alienating another. His only defence is the loyalty of the armed forces and the efficacy of the security services.

To cast the Shah as the villain is in one sense misleading. There is nothing to suggest that another leader or group of leaders in Iran would have done better or behaved much differently under the circumstances. It would be surprising if the same basic motivations did not apply; namely preservation of personal power, a concern with prestige, a chauvinistic pride in seeking Iranian solutions, and a general impatience with detail. The Shah's critics decry his authoritarianism, but there is scarcely a liberal tradition in Iranian history. A liberal reformist movement at the turn of the century succeeded in establishing a constitution for a Western-style democracy; but since then Iran has suffered authoritarian monarchy. Even Mossadegh in his brief experience of power dismissed Parliament and displayed a penchant for authoritarian rule.

This is not to say that Iranians do not want a more liberal régime or a new system of government. The 3,000 plus political prisoners languishing in jail, the urban guerillas, the human rights campaigns and dissident clergy are witness to this. Yet of those who wish change, the majority merely want observance of the Constitution — not an end to the Shah — which would probably entail no more than a greater distribution of power among the élite. Those out to change society now have to cope with a formidable array of vested interests, not least the clergy. Revolutionary change could not be brought about without the backing of the religious community. Provoking the clergy has, and almost certainly will, cause bloodshed and riots. The serious country-wide anti-Shah riots in May 1978 were religious-inspired and it was no accident that the worst clashes between the security forces and demonstrators were in the religious city of Qom. It is also worth noting that the arrest of Ayatollah Khomeini was the catalyst for the 1963 riots and officially inspired attacks on him, now living in exile in Iraq, were a contributory factor to the 1978 riots. Religious dissent, of all forms of protest, has consistently proved the hardest to handle.

Traditionally the pressures for change have been strongly affected by external factors. The British encouraged the constitutional reform movement at the turn of the century. The British too appointed Reza Khan as effective commander of the country's armed forces, fully aware that he would challenge the weak Qajar rule. It was British and Soviet pressure that forced Reza Shah to abdicate during the Second World War. Mossadegh pursued his nationalism policy in the mistaken belief that the US supported such a move; and it was American and British assistance that ensured the downfall of Mossadegh and the restoration of Mohammed Reza Shah.

More recently, challenges to the Shah's absolute power have coincided with genuine or perceived American pressure for greater liberalism. Dr Ali Amini, the last Premier to exercise a degree of independence, was appointed against the Shah's will on the prompting of the Kennedy administration in 1960. Again in 1977, the Shah felt obliged to respond to President Carter's policy on human rights by carrying out some cosmetic legal reforms and permitting a degree of domestic criticism. In both instances, the Shah yielded the minimum necessary and then slammed the door shut at the first available opportunity. He was able to do this because in the last resort no American administration has found it in its interests to see the authority of a pro-Western monarchy weakened in an oil-producing state. American support has been — and still is — a critical factor sustaining the Shah. The Carter switch from the Nixon era emphasis on Iran and Israel to a stronger interest in a special relationship with Saudi Arabia has affected American perception of Iran. Although the increased importance of Saudi Arabia has been to some extent at Iran's expense, the American commitment to, and involvement in, a powerful pro-Western Iran is strong. Iranian dependence upon the US, especially in the defence field, is such as to make it difficult for any régime to shake free without the risk of seriously weakening itself.

APPENDIX: PAHLAVI FOUNDATION: KNOWN ASSETS IN DECEMBER 1977

A. Banks/Investment Companies

1. *Bank Omran* (100%). Capital Rs5bn ($70m). Total assets Rs75bn. Investments Rs1.4bn. Dividend Rs30 m. Commercial bank.
2. Bank Iranshahr (30%). Capital Rs3bn ($42m). Total assets Rs38bn. Commercial bank.
3. Development and Industrial Bank of Iran (1.3%). Capital Rs3bn ($42m). Share valued by PF at $700,000. Development bank.
4. *Bank Etebarat* (2%). Held 400 of original 20,000 shares. Capital Rs1.5bn ($21m). Commerical bank.
5. *Irano-British Bank* (1%). Held 200 of original 20,000 shares. Widely believed to have purchased much larger stake subsequently. Capital Rs1bn ($14m). Commercial bank.
6. Industrial Guarantee Fund (?%). Capital $11m. Industrial finance for small companies.
7. Omran Trinwall (30% held by Bank Omran). Capital Rs12m ($170,000). Investment in Iran and overseas.
8. Iranshahr Finance (21% held through stake in Bank Iranshahr). Capital Rs70m ($980,000). Commodities and securites trading.
9. First National Wisconsin Milwaukee, USA (5%). Held by Bank Omran.
10. Hispan-Iran (11%). Capital $150,000. Spanish-Iranian service and investment group.

B. Insurance

1. *Bimeh Melli* (80%). This stake is now believed greater. Capital Rs150m ($2m). Total premiums approximately Rs800m.

C. Property

Hotels (all 100%)

1. Tehran area: *Darband; Hilton; Evin; Vanak.*
2. Caspian area: *Babolsar New Hotel + motel; Chalus Old and New Hotels; Hyatt; Ramsar Old and New Hotels.*
3. Other: *Khorramshahr Hotel; Shiraz Hotel; Meshed Hotel; Booali*

214

*Hotel, Hamadan; Obali Hotel; Shahi Hotel; Abali Amul
Hotel; Sakhtsar New Motel; Gachsar Old and New Hotel.*

Tourist Complexes/Leisure

1. Namak-Abroud complex near Chalus (100%).
2. *Villas at Ramsar* (1) and *Babolsar* (1) (100%).
3. Casinos: *Ramsar Casino and Club*; Hyatt; Kish Island (100%).
4. Kish Island Development Board (20% held through Bank Omran): 3 hotels, casino and 1,000 villas when complete.
5. *Mehrabad Airport*, Tehran: restaurant (25%).

Residential/Commercial

1. Sherkat Shahr Aram (0.4%). Satellite town development project.
2. Bungalow project near Niavaran, Tehran (219 units) (100%).
3. Vanak Tower Block (three block multi-storey residential and shopping project), Tehran (100%).
4. Farahzad Development Project (30% held by Bank Omran). Construction of 25,000 upper-income units.
5. Levittshahr (?%). Involvement in $500m new town via Bank Omran.

International

1. Pahlavi Foundation Building, Fifth Avenue/52nd St., New York (100%). Book value 1975 $14.5m.
2. Canal Street Project, New Orleans (?%). Bank Omran in neighbourhood development scheme, believed on 50/50 basis with local interests.

D. Industrial Holdings

Building Materials

1. *Tehran Cement* (25%). Capital Rs1.15bn ($16m). Cement.
2. *Fars and Khuzestan Cement* (?%, believed substantial). Capital Rs3.5bn ($49m). Cement.
3. *Iranit* (30%). Capital Rs? Cement imports, asbestos, cast-iron fittings.
4. Panasuz. Stake held though Fars and Khuzestan Cement (95%). Production of asbestos material.
5. Montex (35%). Capital Rs12m ($170,000). Liquidated June 1977. Steel structures.
6. Sangvareh Mining (40%). Capital Rs? Provision of building

materials from quarries.

Automotive Industry

1. GM Iran (10%). Capital Rs1.5bn ($21m). Assembly of saloon cars and trucks.
2. *B.F. Goodrich Iran* (9.5%). Stake believed to have expanded to around 45% as a result of divestiture of 58% share of US parent company. Capital Rs917m ($13m). Tyre manufacture.
3. Hepco (10% held by Bank Omran). The Foundation is believed to hold an undisclosed 45% stake. Capital Rs? Joint venture with IDRO for road-making equipment.

Miscellaneous

1. National Cash Register Iran (38%). Capital Rs? Office accounting machinery.
2. Sedco (5%). Capital Rs? Drilling operations.
3. *Iran Skin & Leather Company* (100%). Capital Rs? Tanneries.
4. Khorrasan Skin and Lather Company (100%). Capital Rs? Tanneries.
5. *Daru Pakhsh Pharmaceuticals* (? %). Jointly owned by Foundation and the Imperial Organisation of Social Service (IOSS). Capital Rs? Largest pharmaceutical producer in Iran.
6. Union Carbide (Puerto Rico) (20%). Capital Rs? Batteries.

E. Printing/Publishing

1. *Bunghah Tarjomeh va Nashr Ketab* (book distribution and Translation Company (100%). Capital Rs? Translation of foreign classics, Persian reprints.
2. The 25th Shahrivar Printing House (? %). Stake held through involvement in the IOSS. Capital Rs? Printing of all school textbooks used in Iran.
3. Danesh Now Printing and Publishing Company (? %). Capital Rs100m ($1.4m). Books for the young.

F. Agribusiness

1. *Ahwaz Sugar Beet Factory* (16%). Capital Rs? Sugar mill and refinery.
2. *Kermanshah Sugar Factory* (0.4%). Capital Rs607m ($8.5m). Sugar-beet processing.
3. *Hamedan Sugar Factory* (1%). Capital Rs? Sugar mill and refinery.

4. *Kooar Shiraz Sugar Factory* (1.7%). Capital Rs? Sugar mill and refinery.
5. *Farinan Sugar Factory* (? %). Capital Rs? Sugar mill and refinery.
6. *Ghahestan Birjand Sugar Factory* (? %). Capital Rs? Sugar mill and refinery.
7. Ziaran Meat Production (20%). Capital Rs400m ($5.6m). Meat production and processing operational 1978.
8. Iran Shellcott (10%). Capital Rs500m ($7m). Agribusiness in Khuzestan. In process of being restructured.
9. International Agribusiness Company of Iran (2%). Capital Rs441m ($6.2m). Agribusiness in Khuzestan.
10. Agricultural and Industrial Company of Khuzestan (10%). Capital Rs700m ($9.8m). Agribusiness in Khuzestan.

Notes

1. This list is not complete. Some of these holdings may have increased or been reduced. Very few of the companies are publicly quoted. All information is based on either access to the original list of assets; or companies that have admitted having shares in the Foundation. The companies in italics constitute the original known assets.
2. Not included is the National Iranian Tanker Company sold to NIOC in 1970 or the land/assets of some 73 nurseries and orphanages.
3. Income from Crown Lands handed to the Foundation is not included but mainly comprises loans repaid to Bank Omran.

INDEX

Abadan Refinery 35, 119-20
Abdul Azim, Shrine of Shah 23
Agha Mohammed Khan 23
Agricultural Development Bank
    159
agriculture:
    ILO mission (1972) 115
        10 point programme of 116
    national state of 38-43:
        climatic limitations 38
        geographic limitations 38-9
        land available 39
        Qanat system 39
        opium poppy 39-40
        tribal livestock 40
        land reforms *see* land reform
    'pole' system (1976) 42-3
Ahmad, Sultan Shah (deposed 1925)
    54
Ahmad Khayami 47-8
Ahmad Qavam (Prime Minister)
    62, 63
Ahmed Zaki Yamani, Sheikh 16, 100
Ahwaz City and sugar factories at 27,
    107, 121, 161, 216
aircraft purchases 171-3, 183, 185
air force base 27
Alam, Assadollah 139, 158
Alborz Mountains 25, 32
Amini, Dr Ali 69, 70, 131
Amir Hushang Davalou 67
Amouzegar, Jamshid 132, 135, 136,
    201-2
Anglo-Iranian Oil Company (1933)
    34-5, 38, 65, 66
Anglo-Persian Oil Company 34:
    after 1933 *see* Anglo-Iranian Oil
        Company
    after 1957 *see* National Iranian
        Oil Company
Ansari, Cyrus 114
Ansari, Hushang 78, 83, 114, 132,
    135-6
Arab-Israeli War (1973) effects of
    173, 175, 178
arabs of Iran 27, 191
Arak, machine tool complex at 44,
    120

Aramco 37
Arbitration Councils 137-8
architecture 22
armed services *see* aircraft; Chah
    Bahar naval base; defence; mili-
    tary tribunals; security services
army base 27
Arnold, Arthur 22, 28, 196-7
Aryamehr, the Shah's Royal Title
    61
Aryamehr Steel Complex 27, 49, 107
Ashraf, Princess (Shah's twin sister)
    57, 65, 139-40, 164, 181
Ashraf Pahlavi Foundation 157
assassination attempts on Shah 57,
    129
Ata'i, Rear-Adm. Ramzi Abbas 111-
    12, 182
Atomic Energy Authority 133
author, background to study of
    11-12
authority, use and abuse of 129-49:
    background 129-30
    Prime Minister 130-2
    Cabinet 132-4
    Ministries 132-4
    Rastakhiz Party *see* Rastakhiz
        Party
    judiciary 136-8
    Imperial Court 130, 138-40
    unconstitutional aspects 140-2
    security services 142-9
    see also money, control through:
        SAVAK
automotive industry *see* General
    Motors (Iran); GKN; Irannational
Azerbaijan, USSR of 62-3

Bahai sect, 97
Bahktiar, General, 70
Bakhtiari faction, 40, 147
balance of payments, comparative
    tables of 99
    figures for 1977 154
Baluchi peoples 27
Bandar Abbas Port 87, 88, 89
Bandar Shahpour project 108, 207
Bank Etebarat 160

banking interests, international 33, 158
Bank Iranshahr 160
Bank Markazi *see* Central Bank
Bank Omran 158-63
banks, names and addresses of 214
Behbanian, Mohammed Jafer 159
Behshahr Industrial Group 48
Beitz, Berthold 114
Bharier, Julian 11, 43
Bimeh Melli Insurance Co. 160, 214
birth rate 116
black market in food 116-17
BP, Iran acquires shares in 115
Britain, Iran invests in 112-13
British foreign policy 32, 57, 66, 67, 169-70, 212
Brown and Root (US firm) 111-12
Burmah Oil 33
Bushehri, Medhi 140
business ventures into big 47-9: some addresses of 215-17
Butler, William 146

Cabinet 130, 132
cable links, international 32-3
calendar, change in 61
Canard Enchaîné, Le 154-5
capital-intensive solutions 119-22
casinos, 161
caviar industry 32
Cementation, British firm of 109
cement production project 106-7, 160
censorship 145
CENTO Alliance 175
Central Bank (Bank Markazi) 83, 86, 93, 106, 154
Chah Bahar naval base 102, 111-12, 172, 185
chain stores 48
charity foundations 155-7
Chaban-Delmas, M. 18
Chubin, Shahram 175
Churchill (Sir) Winston L.S. 34
CIA 65-6
cinemas 25
civil service:
    salaries 163
    tribunals 137
Communism, Shah's views on 62-4: *see also* Tudeh Party
companies, huge increase in registra-

tion of new (1974) 83
concessionary rights, 1870s on 33
conclusions of this study 206-13
Concorde 105
Consortium Oil Company 35-6 *later* Oil Service Company of Iran *q.v.*
constitution 56, 129
consumer price index 91
contractors, government withholds payment to 98
co-operatives, agricultural 41
coronation 1967, 61
corruption 57, 141, 182, 196-7
Cossack Brigade 53-4
Costains (British firm) 111-12
Court:
    Imperial 130, 138-40
    Ministry 138-9
credit controls:
    relaxation of 85-6
    used up 87
cultural problems 190-203:
    search for security 194-8
    new influences 198-203
Curzon, Lord 34
Cyrus the Great, King of Persia 53

dam constructions 39, 117-18
Darband Hotel, Tehran 161
D'Arcy, William 33
defence:
    expenditure tables on 174
    influence of military forces 168-86:
        external threats 169-70
        American support 171-4
        credibility and effectiveness 174-8
        activities in Oman 178-80
        political role 180-2
        value for money 182-6
    policy 133-4, 153
Denmark, Iran invests in 112
deserts, Iranian 38-9
Development Bank (DIBI) 160
development plans go haywire, *see* development prospects *under* Iran; successes and failures
Dez Dam 117-18
Dhofar offensive 178-9
DIBI (Development Bank) 160
disabled, financial assistance for 156

Doha, OPEC's 1976 meeting at
98-101
double cropping system, 38

*Economic Development in Iran:
1900-1970*, (Bharier) 11
economy:
disaster to, 1974-76 *see* development prospects *under* Iran
duality of 28
national *see* oil and the national
economy
see also agriculture; industry, slow
diversification towards;
business, ventures into big;
money, control through
education:
free for all instituted 18, 81
payment for overseas 156, 162,
200
university 201-2, 208
see also University of Tehran
Education Corps 28
electricity, *see* power supplies
Elghanian, Habib 96, 97
Emami, Jafar Sharif 156, 158, 162
Empress, controlling influences of
139
see also Farah Diba
Energy Ministry, emasculated power
of 133, 140
ENI, negotiations with 115
Eqbal, Dr Manouchehr 153, 159
espionage 143
Evin Hotel, Tehran 161
'Exile Courts' 147
exports 40

family planning 116
famine (1925) 28-9
Farah Diba, 3rd wife of Shah 61, 139
created Queen and Empress 1967,
140, 200
Farah Pahlavi Foundation 157
Fardust, General Hussein 141
Farman Farmayan family 47
Fatima, Princess 67
Fawzia, Princess of Egypt (Shah's
1st wife) 57
fertilizers 49
Fiat Cars 49
Fifth Plan (1973-8) 38, 77, 142:
abandoned 18
major revision of 77-80

table of 81
see also development prospects
under Iran
finance, bazaar mentality over 196
see also economy; money, control
through; oil wealth, limits to;
per capita income; wages
Finance Ministry 78, 93, 137
financial centre, Tehran to be a world
111
Financial Times 11-12, 198
First Plan 37
food, subsidies planned 81, 117:
1974 imports of 116
foreign attack, Iran's fear of 169
foreign exchange matters 79, 98,
113, 154, 210
foreign investment programme,
Iran's 112-15, 153, 161-2
foreign labour, importation of 90,
119
foundations, charitable 155-7
Fourth Plan (1968-72— 37-8, 45, 79,
105-6
France:
1971 snub by and then ingratiates
18
Iran invests in 112-13

Gajareh, meeting at 77-9
gas, *see* liquid petroleum gas
GDP comparisons (1959 and 1972)
45
General Motors (Iran) 95, 121, 160,
216
Geological Institute 49
Ghahestan Sugar Corporation 163
GKN (British firm) 110
Golestan Palace, 26
Goodrich, B.F. (US firm of) 95,
162-3, 216
Government *see* authority
Governorates 130, 134, 147

Habib Sabet 48, 96, 97
Hammer, Arnold 114
Hassan, Arsanjani 70, 207
Hejira Years (Calendar) 61
Hepco road-mending project 120-1,
216
Hilton Hotel, Tehran 161
holy days 198
hospital programme 109-10, 119-20
hotels:

industry 161
names of 214-15
housing reorganisation plans 81, 89,
    105-6
Hoveida, Amir Abbas 77-9, 131-2,
    136, 139, 142
Hudson Institute 16
Hushang-Arbabi, Abdolqassem 137
Hussein Fatemi 66

illiteracy *see* literacy
ILO 27, 115
IMF:
    Iran puts cash at disposal of 112
    1974 visit of team from 80-1, 85
Imperial Aviation Club 152
Imperial Bank 33
Imperial Commission (on waste) set
    up 103, 142
Imperial Country Club, Tehran 152
Imperial Court 130, 138-40
Imperial Horse Society 152
Imperial Inspectorate *see* SAVAK
Imperial Organisation for Social
    Service (IOSS) 156, 157
imports:
    Iran heavily dependent on 40
    huge increase in (1973-74) 83
    ports jammed 87-8
        see also ports
    of foreign labour 90, 119
    of livestock 117
industrialisation policy:
    mentioned 18
    centre of, at Tabriz 27
    slow diversification of 43-7
        principal products 44
        steel plants 44-5, 49
        Russian aid 44
        petrochemicals 44-5
        factory construction problems
            45
        fatal delays, reasons for 46-7
industry, Pahlavi Foundation's assets
    in 160-1
inflation, 1974 prospects of roaring
    85
International Commission of Jurists
    1976 report of, 146
international matters *see under*
    foreign
IOSS 156, 157
Iran:
    boom comes to 15-20

development prospects, 1974 on
    77-91:
    problems facing 5th planners
        77-80:
    main objectives 80-3
    ten points of progress set out
        81-3
    new receipts and expenditure
        targets, table of 82
boom accelerates 83-6:
    revenue, comparative table of
        84
    carelessness and slackness take
        over 84-5
    inflation is born 85, 91
    IMF advice disregarded 85
    credit control relaxed 85-6
out of control 86-91:
    ports, expenditure on and
        muddle at 87-8
    Ministry muddles over permits
        87
    truck drivers disappear 88
    costs of delays incurred 88
    land costs begin to rocket 88-9
    spiral of wages and rents 89
    sudden absence of labour 90
    Consumer Price Index effects
        91
OPEC 1973 oil price rise effects
    15-20
name changed from Persia (1934)
    55
occupation forces in war (1941)
    24, 44, 57, 67
political orientation of 17
summary of its problems today
    (1978) 208-13
wealth of *see* oil wealth, limits to
    see also successes and failures
        of projects
Iran Air 159, 160, 192
Iranian National Insurance Company
    157-8
Irannational (Motor Cars) 47-8, 110,
    161, 177
Iran Novin (political party) 131-2
Irano-British Bank 160
Iran Shellcot 161
Ironside, Major-Gen. (*later* Fd.-
    Marshall) Lord (Edmund) 54
irrigation 39
Isfahan City 23, 27, 193
    see also Aryamehr Steel Complex

Islam, introduction of 191
 see also religion

Jews, anti-profiteering laws and 97
J-2 143
judiciary 136-8, 147

Kayhan International (newspaper)
 19-20, 61, 102
Karaj Steel Plant 44
Kerman, land costs in 88
Khademi, Lieut.-Gen. 159
Khatemi, Gen. Mohammed 67, 181
Khomeini, The Ayatollah 69
Khorramshahr Port 87, 97, 207
Khuzestan Farming Experiment 117-
 18
Khuzestan oilfields 36-7, 107, 161
Kish Island, new resort at 159-60,
 215
Kissinger, Dr Henry 172
Kouroush Stores 48
Krupp, Iran negotiates with 113-14,
 163
Kurds and rebellion 27, 62, 176-7

labour:
 shortage of local, leads to imported
  90, 119
 lack of, destroys projects' chances
  108-9, 119
 deserts agriculture for the towns
  118
 SAVAK control over 145
land:
 tremendous increase in price of
  88-9, 120
 reform schemes (1960 on) 40-3,
  94-5, 207, 208-9
Langeh, Bandar 147
legal system *see* judiciary
 see also SAVAK
legislature *see* Majles
Liquid Petroleum Gas 44, 107
Literacy Corps 29
literacy rate 18, 29, 200, 208
literature 200-1
livestock, importation of 117

Mahabad, Kurdish Republic of 62
Mahdavi, Fereidoun 97, 207
Mahvi, Abdol Hassan 153
mail interceptions in the 148
Majidi, Abdol Majid 78, 80, 100,

 142
Majles (Parliament) 129-30, 135, 142
manpower *see* labour
Marble Palace, Tehran 26
marxism, allegations of 148
Massoudi, Farhad 194
Mattei, Enrico 36
medical services 25, 109-10, 119-20
Medicorp, US 109-10
Melli Industrial Group 48
Military College, Tehran 168
military intelligence 143
military matters *see* Defence
military tribunals 136-7, 143-4
Mina, Dr Parviz 154
Ministers, limited powers of 132-3
missile systems 184
Mohammed Khatemi 67
Mohammed Reza Pahlavi, Shah:
 *for details of personal life and
 reign see under Pahlavi dynasty*
 mentioned 11
 announces 1973 oil price rise 15
 policy following that 16-18
 financial plan runs into trouble
  19-20
 turns to industry rather than agriculture 43, 44
 then switches back to agriculture
  50
 trials of strength with Mossadegh
  61, 64-7
 regards 1962 as turning point in
  fortunes 61
 effects of wartime experiences
  62
 Soviet influences and Azerbaijan
  62-3
 states views on communism 63,
  71-2
 flees the country and returns,
  1953 65
 consolidation tactics as Supreme
  Ruler 66-71
 American financial aid 68
 Qom riots put down 69
 institutes one-party system 1975,
  72
 presides over Ramsar Conference
  77-9
 its disastrous results 86-91
 admits error of going too fast 93
 is not strong enough to confront
  Bazaar merchants 97

underestimates Saudi Arabia 100
barters for arms against crude oil 101
publicly admits country's problems 102-3
sets up Imperial Commission to investigate wastage 103
decides on overseas investment 112
becomes absolutist 129-30
views on governmental system 130
his method of testing public opinion 136
mode of absolutist rule 129-49
control over SAVAK 140, 143-9
control over NIOC 153-5
personal wealth 155-60
armed forces, his interest in, and is Commander-in-Chief 168
call for a new cultural order 193
thrives on flattery 197
present-day problems summarised 208-13
Moinian, Nasratollah 138, 142
monarchy *see* Mohammed Reza Pahlavi; Pahlavi dynasty; Qajar dynasty; Reza, Shah Pahlavi
money control through, 152-65:
    background 152-3
    NIOC's role 153-5
    Pahlavi Foundation 155-65:
        asset extent 157-60
        conservative approach 160-3
        uses of income 163-5
money supply:
    rocketing 85-7
    controls imposed 93
Morrison Knudson (a consultancy firm) 43
Mossadegh, Mohammed 35, 61, 64-7, 146, 212
motor industry *see* General Motors (Iran); GKN: Irannational

Nasrudin, The Mulla 194
Nassiri, Gen. Nematollah 67, 144, 150
National Front Party 68-9, 146, 147
National Insurance Company 157-8, 217
National Investment Company of iran 94
National Iranian Oil Company (NIOC)

(1957):
    mentioned 16, 36
    as Anglo-Persian and Anglo-Iranian Oil Companies 34-5
    takes full control, 1973 36
    shortfall in production 37
    offers discounts 98
    switches plans to one of its own 108
    Shah virtually in control of 133, 153-5
    role in monetary matters 153-153-5, 164
National Iranian Tanker Company 158
Nationalisation of Oil Industry 35, 65
National Plans *see under* First, etc.
Navy, forces and arms in 185
    see also Chah Bahar naval base
needy, financial aid for 156
newspapers *see* Press
Niavaran Palace 26
NIOC *see* National Iranian Oil Company
Nixon, President Richard M. 171-2

Occidental, negotiations with firm of 114
oil:
    and the national economy 32-5-:
        historical background 32-4
        D'Arcy's concessions 33
        first discovery (1908) 33
        first production (1912) 34
        revenue (1911-30) 34
        effects of World War II 34
        nationalisation 1951, 35
        1954 agreement 35
        NIOC formed, 1957 36
        Tehran Agreements, 1971 36
        Iran takes over full control, 1973 36-7
    development project for 107-8
    1973 OPEC price rise in 15-16
    wealth from, limits to 93-103:
        money curbs 93
        profiteering outlawed 94, 96, 97
        political gestures 94-7
            Share Divestiture Scheme 94-5
            National Investment Company of Iran, floating of 94

business fears 95-6
arrest of prominent businessmen 96
price controls, disruptive effect
of 96
ports, controls seriously restrict
use of 97
oil as a variable 97-101
fall in revenue from 1975 97-8
climatic effects on sales 97
contractors' bills unmet 98
discounts used to improve
trade 98
foreign exchange problems 98
more sales drops (1977)
99-100
1977-78 budget rewritten
99-100
full circle 101-3:
arms bartering 101
PBO speaks up 101
projects begin to be abandoned 102
public kept in ignorance 101
Shah decides to admit problems and calls for hard
work from nation 103
anti-waste campaign 103
Oil Service Company of Iran (OSCO)
36-7, 49
Oman, Iranian intervention in 178
Omran Trinwall 163
one-party system (1975) 72
OPEC 15-17, 36, 97-8, 100
opium poppy 39-40

Pahlavi dynasty 19, 53-72:
from Cyrus to the Qajars 53
Reza Khan, Shah 53-7:
born (1878) 53
joins Cossack Brigade (1892)
53-4
becomes commander 54
marches on Tehran 54
gives ultimatum to Shah
Ahmad 54
who is deposed 54
Reza replaces Ahmad 54
is crowned (1926) 54
changes Persia to Iran 55
son marries Princess Fawzia of
Egypt 55
ruthlessness as Shah 55-6
his achievements 56

abdicates (1941) 57
goes into exile 57
dies (1944) 57
Mohammed Reza, Shah 57-61:
born (1919) 57
twin of Princess Ashraf 57
Crown Prince (1926) 57
ill health in childhood 57
character 57
assassination attempts on him
57-8
education at home and abroad
58
authoritarian outlook 58, 60
marries Princess Fawzia 55
difference in public and private manner 60
marries Farah Diba as 3rd wife
61
who gives him son and heir 61
coronation (1967) 61
takes title of Aryamehr 61
Golden Jubilee (1976) 60-1
alters calendar arrangements
61
see also Persepolis Festival
*for political and governmental
activities see* Mohammed Reza
Pahlavi, Shah
Pahlavi Estates Office 155
Pahlavi Foundation (Charity) 155-7:
assets of 157-60
conservative approach of 160-3
uses of income 163-5
Pakravan, General 70
Pan Am, Iran negotiates with 113
Parliament *see* Majles
peasants:
life-style of 28
land reform and 41-2, 122
per capita incomes 18, 83, 118
Persepolis Festival (1973) 18, 60,
111, 171
Persia becomes Iran (1934) 55
Persian Gulf Ports, revenue of 32
petrochemicals 44-5, 108
Peykans (cars) 48, 91
philanthropy, Shah's 155-7
Plan and Budget Organization (PBO):
mentioned 77, 142
changes made (1974) 77-8
disastrous results of 86-91
criticises Shah's policy 101
NIOC budget and 153-4

Plans, national *see* First, etc.
'pole' system for farming land 42-3
Police 133, 147, 156, 190
Political Elite of Iran, The (Zonis),
    11, 55 *but see also* Zonis, Marvin
politics:
    internal *see* authority, use and
        abuse of Iran's world-orienta-
        ted aspirations 17
population of Tehran 22, 24
ports:
    development plan for 87
    mounting delays at 87-8, 120,
        207
    price control's effects on 96-7
    capacity inadequate 108
post, unauthorised opening of the
    148
power *see* authority
power supplies 118, 120-1, 193
Press 25, 130, 135, 136, 147, 194
    see also Kayhan International
price war 95-7, 134
Prime Minister, office of 130, 131
printing industry 25, 200-1, 216
priorities, no thought given to 105
public health, development plans for
    81
public transport system in Tehran 22-
    22-3, 190
publishing 200-1, 216

Qaboos, Sultan of Oman 178-9
Qajar dynasty 23, 33, 53, 54-5
Qanats 39
Qashgai peoples 40
Qazvin 62, 122, 161
Qom City 147:
    riots at 69
Queen Pahlavi Foundation 157

railways 23, 24, 33, 102
    Trans-Iranian Railway 43
rainfall in Iran 28, 38
Ramsar, 1974 Conference
    at 19, 77-9
Rasht, land costs in 88-9
Rastakhiz (newspaper) 135
Rastakhiz Party 72, 96, 130, 134-6,
    146-7, 207
referendum 1963, 71
religion 191, 195, 198-9
rents, soaring costs of 89
Reporter, Sir Shapoor 67-8, 153

Republic, Reza Shah considers a
    54
Reuter's News Agency 33
revenue, phenomenal rise in 16
Rezaieh, City of 62
Reza Khan Shah Pahlavi (d. 1944)
    23, 24, 47, 50, 64, 153, 212
    for personal life see under Pahlavi
        dynasty
Reza Pahlavi, Prince, son of ruling
    Shah (b. to Farah Diba, 1960) 61
roads, effect of inadequacy of 108,
    120-1
    see also Hepco road-mending
        project
Roosevelt, Kermit 66
rural society 27-30, 40, 122
Russian policy 32, 44, 57, 62-3,
    67, 175-6, 212

Saadabad Palace 26
Sabet, Habib 48, 96, 97
Samii, Mehdi 159
SAVAK 67-71, 90, 103, 130:
    activities of 140-9
    80% stake in Kish Island resort
        159-60
Schlesinger, James 171
schools *see* education
Second Plan (1955-62) 35, 37
security services 142-9
    widows' pensions of, 156
Sedim (a French firm) 109
sewerage system of tehran 22
Shafik, Captain Prince 181
Shah of Iran *see* Mohammed Reza
    Pahlavi, Shah; Pahlavi dynasty
    and Reza Khan, Shah Pahlavi
Shahestan Pahlavi Commercial Centre,
    Tehran 26, 60
Shahnaz Youth Clubs 157
Shahram, Prince 164
Shahyad Monument, Tehran, signi-
    ficance of name 60
sharecropping system 40
Share Divestiture Scheme 94
Shiism (Shiia religion) 191, 198
Shiraz, City of 23, 27
    Arts Festival at 200
Shuster, Morgan 152
Sixth Plan (scheduled 1978) 18-19,
    103
social insurance, development plans
    for 81, 156, 164

society, nature of dual 27-30
Soraya Esfandiari, Princess (Shah's 2nd wife(70
Soviets *see* Russian policy
Special Bureau, Shah's 130, 138-9
steel, projects for 107-8
steel plants:
  Isfahan 44, 49
  Karaj 44
Strait of Hormuz, strategic importance of 170
study:
  outline of this 11-12
  conclusions arrived at in 206-13
successes and failures of projects 105-22:
  housing 105-6
  cement 106-7
  steel and oil 107-8
  infrastructure 108-9
  manpower shortages 108-9
  real and marginal need 109-12
  investment abroad 112-15
  Concorde aircraft 105
  delays and time-lags 107-8
  roads, inadequacy of 108
  port capacity inadequate 108
  hospital programme 109-10
  motor industry 110
  Tehran plan as centre of world finance 111
  armed forces projects 111-12
  Chah Bahar naval base 111-12
  investments overseas 112-15:
    funds made over to IMF 112
    to Britain and France 112-13
    company negotiations 113
    Krupp arrangements 113-14
    refinery ventures 114-15
  agriculture 115-18:
    ILO dealings 115-16
    accent on family planning to overcome food shortages 116
    food imports lead to black market 116-17
    subsidies 117
    Khuzestan Farming Experiment 117-18
    labour migrates to the towns 118
  capital-intensive solutions 119-22:
    industry 119
    labour problems 119-20
    spiralling costs 120

power, insufficiency of electric 120-1
Iran prices itself out of export market 121-2
effects on rural community 122
Sugar, Pahlavi Foundations' interests in 161, 163:
  factories 216-17

Tabriz, City of 23, 24, 27, 62, 88
Taheri, Amir 102
Taleghani, Ayatollah Mahmoud 144
Tate and Lyle (British firm of) 141-2
Tehran, city of:
  present-day problems 22-3
  area 23, 26
  untypical of Iran itself 23
  growth of 23-5:
    population 24
    industrial 24-5
    land costs following 25, 88
  design 25-7
  film festival of 200
  hotels in 161, 214-15
  Imperial Country Club at 152
Tehran Agreements 1971, 36, 37, 79
Tehran Cement Company 160
Tehran Military College 168
Tehran, plan to make it world centre of finance 111
Tehran Poultry Farm 122
Tehran University *see* University of Tehran
telegraphic links, international 32-3
telephone system 22
textiles, importance of 44
Third Plan (1963-67) 38, 45
torture, allegations of 146, 148
tourist centres 215
tractor assembly 49
traffic problems of Tehran 22-3, 190
tribalism 24, 27-30, 40
tribunals 136-7
Tudeh Party 66, 146
Turkoman people 40

underemployment, plans to reduce 108-9
unemployment, plans to reduce 108-9
United Arab Emirates 169-70
University of Tehran 25, 55, 57-8, 58-9, 69, 146, 201, 202

Urban development 22-30
urbanisation, sudden tendency
     towards 24, 29
urban society 27-30
USA:
     moves to take over oilfields
          (1972) 17
     moves of Mossadegh 66-7
     support for Iran's military forces
          171-4, 176-7
USSR *see* Russian policy

Vahidi, Iraj 140
Vanak Hotel, Tehran 161
Vienna, OPEC meeting at (1975)
     97-100
Vosokh family 47

wages, 30% rises in 89-90, 120, 121
Wahabzadeh, Mohammed 96
Walker, Peter 111
wastage, campaign against 103, 210
water, serious lack of 38, 39, 117-18
wealth *see* economy: money, control
     through; Oil wealth, limits to;
     per capita income; Wages
'White Revolution' 71-2, 134
Williamson, Major-Gen. Ellis 171
World Bank, Iran invests in 112
World War II, effects of 34, 57
     see also occupation *under* Iran

xenophobia 104

Yamani, Sheikh Ahmed Zaki 16,
     100

Zagros Mountains 32
Zahedi, General 70
Ziyaee, Taher 159
Zonis, Marvin 11, 55, 129, 155, 163